Confessions of a
Serial Biographer

Confessions of a Serial Biographer

CARL ROLLYSON

McFarland & Company, Inc., Publishers
Jefferson, North Carolina

LIBRARY OF CONGRESS CATALOGUING-IN-PUBLICATION DATA

Names: Rollyson, Carl E. (Carl Edmund), author.
Title: Confessions of a serial biographer / Carl Rollyson.
Description: Jefferson, North Carolina : McFarland & Company, Inc.,
    Publishers, 2016 | Includes index.
Identifiers: LCCN 2016007843 | ISBN 9781476663258
    (softcover : acid free paper) ∞
Subjects: LCSH: Rollyson, Carl E. (Carl Edmund). | Biographers—
    United States—Biography.
Classification: LCC CT275.R7713 A3 2016 | DDC 920.073—dc21
LC record available at http://lccn.loc.gov/2016007843

BRITISH LIBRARY CATALOGUING DATA ARE AVAILABLE

ISBN (print) 978-1-4766-6325-8
ISBN (ebook) 978-1-4766-2541-6

Front cover image of computer at night © 2016 m-gucci/iStock

Printed in the United States of America

McFarland & Company, Inc., Publishers
  Box 611, Jefferson, North Carolina 28640
    www.mcfarlandpub.com

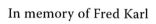

In memory of Fred Karl

Acknowledgments

Portions of this book have appeared, in different form, in *Biography and Source Studies*, *History Now*, the *Dictionary of Literary Biography*, *The Writer*, *The Advocate*, *The New York Sun*, and *University Bookman*. Much of what I wrote in those publications has been recast, but I am grateful for the opportunity I was given to test out my ideas. Thanks as well to Carol DeBoer-Langworthy for suggesting I write "Missed Connections." I also want to honor the memory of Fred Karl, a fine biographer and editor who inspired much of the writing in this book.

Table of Contents

Preface

I am not the first biographer to write a memoir about his work. But after reading the reminiscences of my colleagues, I am still looking for the kind of insider look this book offers. I show not only how I became interested in my subjects, but I also reveal the mechanics of the trade, so to speak—how I put together book proposals for publishers, conducted interviews and archival research, and sometimes had to joust with editors as much as with my subjects and their literary estates. A reader of biography will discover how biographies get made. A scholar will appreciate discussions of methodology and strategy. I show what it is like for a professional biographer who moves from subject to subject. A librarian jocularly wrote to me asking about my "next victim." Those hostile to biography rank professional biographers just above serial murderers. And while I don't share their horror at my work, I do believe that serial biographers develop a hardened attitude toward the lives of others. I don't mean such biographers lacks empathy. Quite the contrary, without empathy biography is impossible. But I am of the Samuel Johnson school of biography that adheres first to the truth as the biographer sees it, and not first to the feelings of others.

What I seek to show is that biographies are not lives, but books about lives. An obvious distinction, you might say. And yet the subjects of biography, those close to those subjects, critics of the genre, and other readers, treat the published biography as if it were the life itself instead of recognizing that biographies are always provisional. However great a place a certain biography may hold in the esteem or the opprobrium of others, that biography will be augmented, qualified, and even contradicted, if not superseded, by others on the same subject. Biography is cumulative and incremental, and never definitive—no matter what publishers or critics claim when they find a biography they like. And to understand just how flawed but also indispensable biographies become, one has to have an

1

understanding of process, of how the biographer goes about his business. Other biographers, to be sure, have described this process, but usually they remain discreet—not wishing to offend their sources and supporters. In this book, I have eschewed that kind of caution, and I aim, as my introduction promises, to be resolutely indiscreet.

Introduction:
Resolutely Indiscreet

Anyone familiar with the treatment of biographers in fiction knows that they are often portrayed as—to use Henry James's term—"publishing scoundrels." Biographers belong among the criminal classes in fiction at least, although in reality very few of us have served jail terms. But just as there is a code of honor among thieves, so is there one among biographers. Of course, we may differ on our interpretations of how that code should be applied, so let me begin with first principles: I concur with Samuel Johnson, the father of modern biography: Biographers owe their loyalty to the truth, not to respecting the feelings of others, or to any standard of behavior that interferes with the discovery of that truth. Inevitably, then, the biographer runs afoul of those who want to maintain certain proprieties.

The two greatest biographers, James Boswell and James Anthony Froude, made biography an art by remaining resolutely indiscreet. They lapse from their own high standards of truth only when they capitulate to societal norms that are forever at war with honest biography. What a blessing to biography it would have been, for example, if Froude had openly discussed Carlyle's impotence, rather than revealing it in a posthumous memoir. Even the frank Boswell shied away from retailing certain stories that supervened his august subject's dignity.

The free-for-all nature of biography disturbs those who are mainly concerned with invasion of privacy, and they have a point, of course. But it is only a point to the piratical biographer who knows that even with his best efforts he will fall short of plundering all the treasures of his subject's life. In the end, privacy can be invaded but not commandeered. Always, there are aspects of a subject's life that elude the biographer's inquiry. And that is why biographers should share as openly as possible the plunder they do amass. Ultimately, what seems like a selfish and conniving enterprise is actually an act of generosity and fellowship that the critics of biography have yet to appreciate.

Biography, as we know it, began with Plutarch. He wrote about character more often than he wrote about events. He reported not just what his subjects did, but how society discussed these men and women. Thus we learn that Pericles had a son who liked to gossip about what his illustrious father said at the dinner table. Plutarch's point? Pericles (no less than the biographer's readers) had a private life—a private life that biography had to probe, since this genre explored the whole man. Think of those extraordinary scenes in *Coriolanus* featuring the hero with his mother, when he gives up his plan to sack Rome in the face of her plea to save his natal home. Shakespeare couldn't resist turning those Plutarchian passages into a psychological drama.

But what of the biographer's psychological drama? It is an aspect that still has not been explored, despite the existence of many novels—beginning with Henry James's *The Aspern Papers*—that take on biographers as subjects. James and his cohort have revealed a good deal about the biographer's sensibility. But in most cases they lack the knowledge and the interest to revel in the nuts and bolts of the biographer's story, to investigate how a biographer pieces together, bit by bit, a work that simply would not exist without his effort. This is the mighty secret biographers have withheld from their readers. And this secret is what I propose to reveal.

Nothing like this book exists. Other biographers have written up their experiences, reminiscing about their successes, trials, and tribulations, their interviews and reviews, their modes of research, and about why they picked certain subjects. But take it from me: THOSE MEMOIRS DON'T TELL HALF OF WHAT GOES ON. Where is the book on biography that explains how book proposals are put together, and what happens when the literary community coalesces around its favored sons and daughters, shutting out the interloping biographer? As Andrew Wylie said when my wife and I were on the trail of Susan Sontag, "Who are these people? I've never heard of them." His query was disingenuous, since he had already answered our letter asking for an interview with his client. Even journalists and literary critics concerned with biography rarely inquire into how biographers choose their subjects—in part because biographers are unwilling to level with these investigators. Controversies engulfing a given biography may get fulsome coverage, but the terrain on which biographers actually operate remains largely unexplored. For example, in a profile of Sontag's publisher, Roger Straus, the *New Yorker* quotes what he told an editor at W. W. Norton, our publisher: "Kill the fucker!" But nothing is said about how it is that we managed to provoke such ire merely because we *dared* to write a biography of Straus's pet author without his imprimatur—and without the blessing of a literary establishment that is hostile to the very nature of biographical work. To avoid such consequences, biographers tend to camouflage their own outrage in the cloying, sycophantic acknowledgments they publish in their biographies. Because who knows? You just might need the sufferance of someone like Roger Straus for another project.

In a previous book, *A Higher Form of Cannibalism? Adventures in the Art and Politics of Biography*, I began to reveal the kind of bludgeoning biographers can expect if they roam outside the boundaries of accepted norms, but references there to my own experiences were fitful and fugitive. I am now igniting what was once a series of flashpoints in a series of chapters that are indeed adventures. Embarking on each new biography is like beginning the world anew, establishing—once again—a network of contacts and conspirators, and inciting the enmity of countless cronies and court whores who do their best to make the biographer seem unworthy of the approbation they have so acidulously sought from their literary sovereigns.

In *Footsteps*, renowned biographer Richard Holmes transforms biography into a romance about the biographer's quest to recreate his subject's world. In a series of memoirs, Michael Holroyd has fashioned a narrative that cunningly turns his biographical works into a *Bildungsroman*. In *Biographia Literaria*, Leon Edel extols biography as an elite enterprise that need not go slumming among the profiles of movie stars and criminals. Refusing to reveal some of the more degrading aspects of his work, celebrated biographer Richard Ellmann never could bring himself to actually write about what he had to do to pry material out of James Joyce's contemporaries—or about how his own publisher resisted the biographer's determination to publish the scatological Joyce.

It's time to rip the veneer off the works and days of biographers' lives. Biography deserves its Marlow, one who flinches not and is willing to see the horror as well as the hope in the biographer's heart. Thomas Carlyle once complained about mealy-mouthed biographers. I've done my best not to be one of them.

1

Richard Ellmann and the Advent of Ruthless Biography

> You've got to be a bit ruthless, I think, to write a biography.—
> Peter Cameron, *The City of Your Final Destination* (2002)
>
> ... be versatile, cunning, and ruthless in his pursuit—in
> other words, have all the attributes of a good spy.—Erika
> Ostrovsky, *Eye of Dawn: The Rise and Fall of Mata Hari*
> (1978)

The face of modern biography changed forever when Richard Ellmann published his biography of James Joyce in 1959. This widely acclaimed book and biographer set a new standard for biography of all kinds. For academics, Ellmann represented the epitome of the scholar/stylist, impeccable in his use of sources but also attentive to the story values of his art. Outside the academy, Ellmann's penetration of Joyce's private life extended a new license to explore the nexus between the subject's personal and public personae.

To this day, few critics seem to realize the revolution Ellmann effected in life writing. In the ante–Ellmann period, academics tended to produce fact-filled, well-documented tomes like Arthur Hobson Quinn's incredibly boring *Edgar Allan Poe: A Critical Biography* (1941). The biography as reference book approach continued, of course, in tomes like the Baker and Blotner biographies of, respectively, Hemingway and Faulkner. But après Ellmann, a new generation of academic fast-trackers appeared, spearheaded by professors like Jeffrey Meyers, who began to write clipped and candid biographical narratives. Compare, for example, Meyers's treatment of Hemingway's third wife, Martha Gellhorn, the product of Meyers's knockdown and drag-out interview with her, with Baker's genteel handling of Gellhorn after she had given him a good drubbing over the first draft he had sent her.

Ever the gentleman in print, Ellmann was every bit as tenacious as Meyers, but also far more circumspect. His papers at the University of Tulsa read like the portfolio of a great spy. Slowly, carefully, he insinuated himself into the lives of Harriet Shaw Weaver, Stanislaus Joyce, and many other Joyceans. Like a gifted espionage agent, he never tried to steal too much at one time. Instead, he kept coming back for more, always in the guise of an interviewer who had just one more question that would straighten matters out. Soon he had a network of Joyceans operating on his behalf—none more important than Weaver, who began by wondering who this Ellmann character was and ended by becoming his champion. Ellmann accomplished this feat surreptitiously. He never bragged and *never* revealed his modus operandi. Ellmann's Tulsa archive includes his letter begging off writing a piece about how he went about doing biography. He told his correspondent that he could not bear to explain it all.

To have explained all would have been to unmask Richard Ellmann, the biographer who quarreled with his publishers about printing Joyce's raunchy letters, for example. Ellmann was all for it; his publisher thought the letters demeaned Joyce. To Ellmann, everything was grist for the biographer's mill. Yet his reticence was so effective that he remains the patron saint of modern biography. Very few critics—Hugh Kenner is a notable exception—have taken Ellmann to task for his full-blown exposure of Joyce's life.

But what of Leon Edel? Surely he has been as much of a force as Ellmann in shaping modern biography. To be sure, Edel used psychology to probe the nuances of Henry James's sensibility in new ways, although Edel's work marked not a new beginning but a culmination of the psychobiographical techniques pioneered by Sigmund Freud himself and Marie Bonaparte. Edel brought to psychological biography an increasing sophistication and a literary sensibility, but he refused to emulate Ellmann's examination of his subject's sexuality.

Edel was rather old fashioned in his deference to James's heirs. Only when those James relatives died—and even then the process was gradual—did each new edition of Edel's biography (he did two revisions) reveal what he knew about James's intimate life. And Edel bridled at the idea that James's sexuality per se was within the biographer's purview. When asked about James's private life at a PEN meeting in the 1960s, Edel curtly cut off the questioner as if his integrity as a biographer had been impugned. I doubt whether many biographers today would adopt the kind of offended air Edel affected then.

If literary biography was never the same after Ellmann, other forms of biography were slower to change. Although scholarly interest in popular culture was in full swing by the end of the 1960s, when Ray Browne and others established the Popular Culture Association and a Popular Press imprint at Bowling Green State University, the gap between "serious" and sensational biography persisted. Here is the way Edel saw the chasm in 1979:

> We need not concern ourselves with "camp" biographies or daubs, the ephemeral figures of movie stars, dope addicts, Boston stranglers; they belong to certain kinds of life histories by journalists in our time. They belong in a wax works. They are documentary and often vividly mythic; they are more related to the photographic, the visual moment, the changing world of entertainment or crime, the great and flourishing field of interminable gossip disseminated by the media. This is quite distinct, as we know, from serious artistic biographical and pictorial quests to capture the depths and mysteries of singular greatness.

I especially like that parenthetical expression of utter confidence Edel employs, thereby including his audience (a gathering at the Library of Congress) in the righteousness of his observations. No doubt Edel distrusts the "interminable gossip disseminated by the media" because it fragments his cherished interest in "singular" greatness, dislocating what should be the biographer's concern with the permanent constituents of culture.

Might it not also be true, however, that this "interminable gossip" has always been with us, and that the media have simply forced us to confront how our grand sense of ourselves has perennially been ground down and dissolved by tittle-tattle, by what used to be called "table talk" in an earlier age? How many different photographs do we have of Norman Mailer? Suppose we had only five painted portraits of him, like the five Joshua Reynolds did of Dr. Johnson? Would Mailer's greatness seem more singular? Would Dr. Johnson's uniqueness suffer from various replications of his likeness in photographs?

Mailer's *Marilyn* (1973) was as much a breakthrough in popular culture biography as Ellmann's was in the literary kind. Edel seemed to sense as much because he felt compelled to comment uneasily: "And Norman Mailer, whatever his motivations, revealed a proper sense of biography when as a novelist he sought to capture a figure as elusive and delicate as Marilyn Monroe. Even if we judge his work a failure, we must praise his undertaking." Mailer treated Monroe as a historical figure with Napoleonic ambitions—the first biographer to do so. Just compare the books before and after Mailer; the stunning change in approach to Monroe is palpable.

No longer is she passive, a Hollywood victim, but a complex person whose life verged on tragedy, not pathology.

In the controversy over Mailer's appropriation of Monroe (culminating in a disastrous interview with Mike Wallace on *60 Minutes*), Mailer's contribution to biography was not even noted, let alone explored—a misfortune that I tried to rectify in a piece I wrote in 1978 about Mailer's *Marilyn* in the journal *Biography*. Realizing that much more needed to be explored about how her dedication to acting shaped her persona, I embarked on my own biography, only to find that as an academic I was in No Man's Land. There was not then a single biography of a film star published by an academic press, only biographies of directors written in the heyday of the auteur theory, when professors felt justified in treating filmmakers like literary authors.

In effect, I wrote a book that reified what Sidney Skolsky, a Hollywood columnist and Monroe confidant, asserted: Marilyn Monroe knew more about making a Marilyn Monroe movie than any of her directors or co-stars. An editor at Doubleday wanted to publish the book, but her editorial board rejected my manuscript because it "fell between two stools"; it was attempting to appeal to both a scholarly and popular audience, and Doubleday had no experience selling such a book. Well, no one did, and in the end I had to settle for a small press publication, although the book was resold and sold well here and in the UK.

It is a different world now, Leon Edel, one in which the University of Chicago Press has published a biography of Liberace, and literary biographers like Kenneth Lynn and Jeffrey Meyers have turned out biographies of Charlie Chaplin and Humphrey Bogart—not to mention Kenneth Silverman (a Pulitzer Prize winner for his Cotton Mather biography), who has published a powerful biography of Harry Houdini—not what used to be expected of English professors.

Seen from another perspective, ours is a world that has returned to the ethos of Samuel Johnson, who would have been perplexed by the modernist notion that it is undignified and irrelevant to dwell on the personal side of writers' lives. Here is Johnson's comment on writers' lives in his exculpatory biography of his friend, the rogue poet Richard Savage: "The heroes of literary as well as civil history have been very often no less remarkable for what they have suffered than for what they have achieved." This is the Johnson who also noted:

> There are many who think it an act of piety to hide the faults or failings of their friends, even when they can no longer suffer by their detection; we therefore see whole ranks of characters adorned with uniform panegyric, and not to be known from one another but by extrinsic and casual

circumstances. "Let me remember," says Hale, "when I find myself inclined to pity a criminal, that there is likewise a pity due to the country." If we owe regard to the memory of the dead, there is yet more respect to be paid to knowledge, to virtue, and to truth.

Which returns my argument to the epigraphs of this essay, the first from a novel by Peter Cameron, *The City of Your Final Destination* (2002), the second from biographer Erika Ostrovsky's *Eye of Dawn: The Rise and Fall of Mata Hari* (1978).

Despite his decorous 18th-century prose, Johnson is urging biographers to be ruthless. Somehow this kind of unblinking, unvarnished treatment of real people, especially literary figures, can still invite outrage from critics, while those same literary figures, skewering their family and friends in novel after novel, take refuge in high art. It is their privilege as novelists to cut real lives loose from their moorings in biography, even as biographers fret about libel laws and suits over invasion of privacy.

I'm not sure what Richard Ellmann would have made of the current climate, in which biographers regularly appear as villains in novels (a vindictive lot much tougher than James's remorseful biographer in *The Aspern Papers*). I do feel sure that Ellmann would not be pleased that I have blown his cover. And he might say I'm giving his Joyce biography too much credit for introducing a new level of candor and intensity to biography.

But think of it this way, St. Richard: You are the only biographer, I believe, who is actually revered by modern readers, and that is because you pretended to preserve the niceties while excavating what Joyce himself and certain of his friends would not have wanted to surface, let alone figure in what many regard as a definitive biography. You wanted it both ways: to be scholarly and popular, to reach an educated audience beyond the precincts of your peers. And you succeeded, which meant your aggressive methods—if not your demure prose—would be applied to more than literary subjects, because your literary audience also watched movies and listened to contemporary songs. You were a double agent straddling the divide between the reputable and disreputable aspect of your business, like Johnson tracking his scoundrel sidekick Richard Savage. Biographers everywhere should gratefully acknowledge the ruthlessness of your tradecraft.

2

Picking a Victim

A librarian wrote to me that she had not "picked a victim" yet, but she was giving serious thought to writing a biography. How did one go about it? she wanted to know. The biographer, after all, has enormous power, picking and choosing what aspects of a life to emphasize, what parts to leave out. Like a novel, a biography is a story in which characters are manipulated and moved about to suit a controlling sensibility. My attraction to the form derives from this urge to reconstitute a life within the covers of a book. But I don't blame anyone for feeling victimized by the biografiend. In miniature, a biography is rather like having to sit still for a photograph that you do not want taken of yourself. You're robbed in some way of your substance. And you are probably not consoled by the biografriend's insistence that he or she is an admirer and must have a picture.

I subscribe to a conflict of interest theory of biography. There is my interest in writing a book about, say, Susan Sontag. And then there is Susan Sontag's interest in herself. These interests are mutually exclusive. Susan Sontag is the subject of my book, whereas Susan Sontag is the subject of *her* life. Biographers often ignore this fundamental point or won't admit it—at least they won't own up to it when they are writing about writing biographies. If you've read biographers on biography, you know they sound like a very noble lot—especially his majesty, Leon Edel. You'd never guess he was a snoop just like the rest of us, trying to get the low-down on Henry James. Do you think Henry James would have given Leon Edel permission to write a biography about him?

Recently I came across a particularly foolish passage in Stephen Oates's biography of William Faulkner. He speaks of a dream in which the great novelist appeared to him, urging the biographer to undertake a book on his life. Anyone who knows anything about Faulkner will howl at this biographer's illusion that he was actually encouraged by his subject. Faulkner was an intensely private man and wrote a series of essays expressing his

12

anger over the way he felt his life had been violated by a prying press. If Oates really did have a dream about Faulkner, if he actually did have a vision of the writer approaching him, I guess he woke up too soon or somehow failed to notice the horsewhip in Faulkner's hand.

In a playful mood, I wrote my own parody of the biographer's belief he can summon his subject's cooperation. See "William Faulkner: A I Lay Dreaming," in *AfterWord: Conjuring the Literary Dead*, ed. Dale Salwak (Iowa City: University of Iowa Press, 2007), pp. 160–72. I like the feeling of working against my subject, of trying to find out things that he or she has tried to bury or to obfuscate. I have learned to be wary of my subjects. I find them enormously entertaining. I learn a great deal from them. But I don't trust them. Not because they're all liars, but because they want to have it their way.

It may sound as though I take a hostile attitude toward my subjects. No, I'm just skeptical, and I like to turn over their lives from many different angles to see what I can shake loose for my narrative. Without this sense of resistance, of friction, I wonder whether biography would be quite so appealing. As much as most kids growing up I liked digging for buried treasure, and when there was no buried treasure to be found, I buried some myself for later discovery. I think of my subjects the same way: they like hiding things, and they may even have a sneaking admiration for the one who finds them out. In his 1995 *Paris Review* interview, Ted Hughes confessed: "Maybe all poetry, insofar as it moves us and connects with us, is a revealing of something that the writer doesn't actually want to say but desperately needs to communicate, to be delivered of. Perhaps it's the need to keep it hidden that makes it poetic—makes it poetry. The writer daren't actually put into words, so it leaks out obliquely, smuggled through analogies ... we're actually saying something we desperately need to share. The real mystery is this strange need. Why can't we just hide it and shut up? Why do we have to blab? Why do human beings need to confess? Maybe if you don't have that secret confession, you don't have a poem—don't even have a story." I don't think Hughes's word apply only to poets. I know I have conducted more than one interview where the interviewee was not forthcoming until it was made clear that I had already done some digging and had turned up some pretty tantalizing items.

I think the biographer is ultimately his or her own authority. I borrow that phrase from R. G. Collingwood, who argues that any genuine work of history is more than the sum of its evidence; it depends, in fact, on the interpreting mind of the historian, who must bring together disparate materials and insights—rather like a detective—into a unified, organic whole. That whole is, essentially, a story, a narrative of meaning. Otherwise, Collingwood contends, there is only scissors-and-paste history, in which the historian slaps together fragments of evidence and testimony from his sources or authorities. This quilt of fact and speculation might make a rather gaudy design, but it would not be a work of history.

The biographer does much the same thing. I assemble the following data: a letter from Walter Jackson Bate (at one time chair of Harvard's English department), a journal kept by Ken Stuart (a student in Lillian Hellman's Harvard writing class), interviews with Hellman's students, interviews with other faculty members who knew Hellman during her Harvard stay, an interview with her physician, and a few newspaper articles. This is the raw material for Chapter 17 of my Hellman biography. If you had all these materials in front of you, they would not add up to Chapter 17. First of all, I don't use all of the evidence. Some of it is redundant; some of it is fascinating and yet there is too much of it to fit into my narrative, which is already burdened with significant detail. Readers can stand for only so much material on this phase of Hellman's career. To relate all of it would seriously damage the shape of my book; it would place too much emphasis on this period of Hellman's life.

These are esthetic considerations. I want to write a good book and know I have to be selective. Just as important, however, are the selections made in previous chapters, where I have emphasized Hellman's contentiousness, her pride in her work, her attraction to young people, her generosity, and her tendency to be high-handed. All of these qualities I find in the evidence for Chapter 17—although as individual bits of evidence these sources contradict each other. Bate, for example, was offended by a demanding and insensitive bitch, while Ken Stuart was charmed by her shrewd and patient handling of young writers, including himself. In the writing of the chapter, I hope these seeming contradictions are resolved—that is, that they are understandable given the different contexts Hellman found herself in. She never treated students as she did Bate. He was supposed to be the red carpet man, the one who should have fawned over her. With Ken Stuart, it was just the opposite: Hellman knew she was there to give him something. Nowhere in Chapter 17 do I make this comparison between Hellman's treatment of Bate and Stuart, but I believe it is there in the narrative configuration, and that it can be found by following the whole story of the biography.

While writing my Hellman biography, I had a sense of her struggling for possession of the book. Undoubtedly, she did not want me to write it my way. Not just because I would find out things—like her Communist

Party membership—but because, like a dramatist, I was setting her up in scenes that were not of her own making, questioning her memoirs and producing an alternative version of her life.

Biographers worry when they are cut off from some of the evidence. When I began my research on Hellman, I did not know that she had restricted her archive. Richard Wilbur announced that piece of shocking news during an interview. "I hope the unavailability of the Texas material does not pose too great a problem for you," he remarked in his characteristically understated way. "What?" I gulped. "Oh, I hear that Lillian restricted everything for the use of her authorized biographer," Wilbur casually noted. "Oh yes," I said, with as much of a knowing air as I could assume. I had a good sweat over this setback. I remember announcing it to a colleague in the street, which I think was my way of admitting the worst and taking it as a challenge. Somehow I forced myself to feel good that Lillian Hellman was going to make things hard for me. I wanted to write about her so badly it may not have made a difference if I had gotten the word about Texas earlier. Still, I am grateful for having begun in ignorance of this fundamental fact.

I knew I had to replace the Texas archive with other sources. I reasoned that through a long career Hellman would have left papers, letters, and various traces all over the country—especially in New York and Hollywood—and I was not wrong. Not only was I able to locate much that was in Texas in the Academy of Motion Picture Arts and Sciences, the University of Southern California Library, Boston University Library, the Wisconsin Center for Film and Theatre Research, and in the hands of her friends all over the country, I found new material—hundreds of letters, a screenplay Hellman never acknowledged, her husband's diary, and many other items that were not in the Texas archive. I also consulted half a dozen excellent dissertations written during the years the Texas archive was open, and this doctoral work proved invaluable in reconstructing my understanding of Hellman's working papers.

For me, the most important thing is the overwhelming desire to write about a particular figure. That usually means I already have—even if I can't articulate it yet—a vision of my subject. I have already decided I'm right for the biography. Everything else, then, will have to fall in line, no matter what obstacles I encounter. To prospective biographers I recommend that you know yourself first, that you know why you want to write about so-and-so. When you have convinced yourself—or as I like to say, deluded yourself—that you are the best person for the job, then it is time to take on all the other troubles you will surely face. I'm reminded of

Brenda Maddox, who has written a splendid biography of Nora Joyce. She went to Richard Ellmann, generally acknowledged to be *the* Joyce biographer. "A biography of Nora?" Ellmann asked incredulously. "What for?" There was no new material worth writing about. Besides, hadn't he, *the* Richard Ellmann, done the definitive biography of James Joyce? There was nothing left to be done. And Maddox, the Joyce scholar apparently observed, was only a journalist. Thank God Brenda Maddox went ahead—discovering, by the way, much new material and changing the way James and Nora Joyce are viewed.

I hope to tell a good story. Because it is a story, I have to deal with everything—not just my subject's public face. I want the gossip, the intimacies, everything that I can find out that made that person what she or he is. Writing biography is a shameless profession, an exercise in bad taste, a rude inquiry. Most biographers prefer not to say so. We are journalists and sometimes scholars who try very hard to be accurate. But is it any wonder that the biographer's choice gets expressed as the picking of a victim?

Chapter 3

Becoming a Biographer: Marilyn Monroe Made Me Do It

I developed my interest in Marilyn Monroe while reading the works of Norman Mailer. Before his *Marilyn* (1973), she was viewed as a rather pathetic figure—a victim of Hollywood, a vulgar popular culture figure, just a generally messed up human being. Of course, there were exceptions to this view. Diana Trilling wrote a sensitive piece about Monroe's artistry, and other writers and artists who met Monroe were impressed with her wit. Two biographers, Maurice Zolotow and Fred Guiles, took her seriously, but still treated her mainly as a woman who all too often succumbed to the pressures of her career and rarely seemed in control of what was happening to her. Embedded in their narratives, however, was another Monroe, one far more proactive, canny—even cunning—that was overwhelmed by tales of how many takes it took for her to say, "It's me, Sugar," in *Some Like It Hot*.

Enter Norman Mailer, genuinely interested in Monroe but also weighted down with the urgent need to produce a big picture book and sensational copy that would yield significant royalties to be applied to his prodigious alimony payments. Reading Norman Mailer then was like encountering the fog of war. Feminists were on his case for his baroque depictions of a sex goddess and his penchant for working up burgeoning conspiracies about her connections with the Kennedys and the plots to murder her. After an appalling performance on *60 Minutes*—edited to make Mailer look as crass as possible—few reviewers took his book seriously.

What a pity. To date, Mailer has been the only American writer ever to explore the problems of biography seriously as a genre while actually writing one. He even quotes Virginia Woolf on the subject—although, in fact, he filches the quotation from Zolotow's book. Both Zolotow and

Guiles accused Mailer of plagiarism—not a charge either could sustain, but he did rely heavily on their work. Such reliance was, in fact, his strength. He drew on their evidence to demonstrate that much of Monroe's unhappiness had to do with thwarted aspirations. He did not deny her self-destructive impulses so much as show how they were like contraindicated drugs that interfered with her artistic genius.

When Mailer's book appeared, it had so many strikes against it that no one seemed to notice that for all its failings, his work marked a fundamental shift in perceptions of Monroe, a shift that could be summed up in one word: Napoleonic—his term for her overweening ambition. For the first time, really, he displayed that side of her for everyone to see—that is, everyone who was not busy clucking over his opportunism and sexism.

In 1978, I published an article about his biography of her in a new journal, *Biography*, explaining that with his work our understanding of Marilyn Monroe had turned a corner. A year later, a small press offered me a contract to produce a bio-bibliography of Monroe. Only then did I seriously consider what I could contribute to the already voluminous literature about her. I spent the summer of 1980 re-reading Guiles, Zolotow, Mailer, and many other books and articles. I realized two things: (1) I was getting bored reading and summarizing what others had written about her, which is what I was supposed to be doing in a bio-bibliography, and (2) her three best biographers knew next to nothing about acting and had missed what should be the focus of Monroe biography. In my view, her biographer needed to address two questions: (1) Why did she turn to acting as a way of finding an identity and fulfilling herself? and (2) To what extent—on the screen—did she actually achieve her goal? Previous biographers had no vocabulary to describe her acting, and thus were at a loss when it came to discussing the nexus between her life and her art.

Not having written a biography before, I sought out both Guiles and Zolotow for inspiration and guidance. Both of them welcomed my focus on Monroe's acting and seemed delighted that a young academic (I was then an assistant professor of humanities at Wayne State University in Detroit) took them seriously. Zolotow became a friend and advisor. Guiles greeted me from a hospital bed, having just suffered a heart attack. He supplied me with a recording of his interview with Lee Strasberg discussing Monroe's work at the Actors Studio. Mailer wished me well, but pleaded overwork and the claims of friends wishing his help and endorsement. In a memorable letter, he referred to their supplications as part of his "guilt impost pile."

I wanted to meet people who knew Marilyn Monroe, but where to start. Fortunately, many years earlier, while working in summer stock in Cape May, New Jersey, I met Bruce Minnix, director of the soap opera *Search for Tomorrow*. Later, we did some television work together in Detroit. He told me that he knew two of Monroe's friends. He put me in touch with Ralph Roberts, Marilyn's masseur and confidant, and Steffi Sidney, the daughter of Hollywood columnist Sidney Skolsky, who helped Monroe invent some of the more dramatic stories about her life. They, in turned, connected me with others, like Rupert Allan, Marilyn's most important publicist.

But I had no idea how to organize my research, let alone write a biography. Graduate school had been no help in that regard. As a literary scholar, I just studied and wrote about books. I had no experience interviewing people. I just did it as on the job training. I had to learn how to write narrative. The breakthrough moment came when Susan Strasberg read part of an early draft. I had interviewed her about her memories of Monroe and Actors Studio, and we got along very well—in part, I think, because she could see I was going to write about Marilyn as an actress in a way no one else had done before. I sent her an early draft of the book, and she said: "When you tell the story of her life and her acting you establish your voice. But then there is also this other stuff that sounds like a treatise. Who are you trying to impress—your colleagues?" That's when I threw out about two-thirds of the book and rewrote it as a narrative. As soon as I had my story, the organization of research fell into place.

Do you know what it was like for a neophyte biographer like me in the early 1980s? You don't unless you understand what academia was like then. It was all right to write a book about a Hollywood or foreign film director. After all, this was the heyday of the auteur theory, when certain directors were treated like authors. But to write about a movie star? Find a biography of a movie star published by a university press before the year 1986. I dare you. My female colleagues looked askance at my work, although most were polite enough not to come right out and say my subject was unworthy. I say most, because at a popular culture conference in the mid–1980s a prominent feminist scholar told me that next time I should pick a "strong woman to write about."

It is not an exaggeration to say that in the mid–1980s I was in the wilderness. In Detroit, I would pick up the phone and call editors in New York, pitching my book. I got polite responses but no takers. Now I'm astonished that those editors even deigned to talk to me. In frustration, I turned to Matthew Bruccoli, a professor at the University of South Carolina who had all sorts of contacts in publishing. A friend had recommended him. The brusque Broccoli suffered my importuning telephone call for several minutes before finally coughing up a name: Shaye Areheart. She was an editor at Doubleday he thought would be receptive to my approach to Monroe. She was, but she could not get the publisher's editorial board to buy my book. "It fell between two stools," I was told. It was written in an engaging style, but it was also "serious" and "scholarly." The question of how to market that kind of book puzzled them.

Eventually, through Shaye, I found an agent who convinced me no trade house would publish my book. But if I convinced UMI Research Press, publisher of my revised dissertation on William Faulkner, to take the book and limit their rights to a three-year deal for the hardcover, I could launch my biography. Then she could get deals for paperback and foreign publication. And that is what happened. Souvenir Press published the hardcover in England, then Hodder & Stoughton came out with a paperback, followed by Da Capo Press with the American softcover, and finally University Press of Mississippi with a revised and updated edition— proving not only that a market existed for my book, but that readers were eager to see more facets of Marilyn Monroe than had been on display in the earlier biographies. I asked readers to consider what Marilyn had been confronted with: the prospect that she was going to portray basically the same character, the so-called "dumb blonde," in picture after picture. If she took herself seriously, then she had to find a way to make each of her characters live within the very narrow range the sex symbol occupied. By describing Monroe's incredible repertoire of gestures—from *Bus Stop* to *The Misfits*—I showed that she was, indeed, a consummate professional and more: She was a great artist. When Gloria Steinem read my book, she concurred, writing this blurb for it: "More than anything else in her life, Marilyn Monroe wanted to be taken seriously as an actress. Rollyson has done just that in *Marilyn Monroe: A Life of the Actress*, the first and only book that is entirely an analysis and appreciation of her work. It will be important to both film historians and to Marilyn's fans—it would have made Marilyn feel honored and worthwhile."

Steinem also contributed an important feminist analysis of Monroe to a book published the same year as mine. Steinem wondered whether Marilyn might have been heartened by the second wave, which would have put her plight into a historical context and made her protest against male chauvinist movie making all that more powerful. Perhaps—although another recent biographer, Lois Banner, who is sympathetic to this argument, also wonders if Monroe, as a male-identified actress, would have been able to make the transition to a new era. On balance, I side with Steinem because of what I know about Marilyn Monroe: She never stopped reading and learning and arguing. Hers was not a closed mind.

At the same time as I was writing my interpretative Monroe biography, I encountered Anthony Summers, then very involved in researching the star's life, especially her connection with the Kennedys. He called me at the urging of one of our mutual friends, Steffi Sidney, who was impressed with the extent of Summers's research. I exchanged information and ideas with Summers and agreed with his assessment that we were writing very different kinds of books. When his book *Goddess* appeared in 1985, it was highly praised and roundly denounced. In over six hundred interviews, he had amassed an astounding record of testimony that some deemed gossip and others suggestive evidence that considerably widened and deepened our understanding of the incredible range of Monroe's connections. It is not too much to say that Summers's work made the endeavor to comprehend Marilyn Monroe into a Napoleonic campaign that attracted other ambitious biographers. Without Summers's spade work, I don't see how the noteworthy biographies of the 1990s by Donald Spoto and by Barbara Leaming would have been published.

I doubt that I would have realized the deficiencies of earlier biographies if I had not been a trained actor, one who at a very early age turned to acting for many of the same reasons that Monroe was attracted to the art. In brief, acting allows you to be someone even before you know who you are or what you want to become. And as an actor, you can't just say you are so and so; that so and so has to arise from a complex arrangement of gestures, postures, and mannerisms that are developed both in the privacy of a rehearsal room and in front of fellow actors, audiences, crews, and directors. Monroe began to form a self in the absence of a "mirror," a parent who could acknowledge and validate her. Her mother was mentally ill, and Monroe was never sure about the identity of her father, so she turned to acting as a kind of compensation—as I did after my father died when I was thirteen.

Because of my own voracious reading and commitment to acting I also understood why Monroe assembled a library of works on psychology and physiology, keeping copies of Mabel Elsworth Todd's *The Thinking Body* as well as an edition of Freud's letters on her bedside table. But what interested me as a younger man in the 1980s was Monroe's battle with concentration. When she remained focused, she created an extraordinary range of performances, from the introvert in *Bus Stop* to the extrovert in *The Prince and the Showgirl*. Watch just those two films, and you will see why I think she is a great actress. Each performance is a *de novo* creation of a vocabulary of gesture and movement that is inimitable. In her major roles, Marilyn Monroe did not repeat herself.

What broke Monroe's concentration, I thought, was related to her traumatic childhood and to the factory-like process of motion picture making, the rigid schedule of Hollywood productions that she detested. In this regard, my conclusions were not much different from those of other biographers. What I failed to realize then is that it was not her background or her working conditions that did her in. I decided to revise and update my Monroe biography after two collections of primary source materials yielded new insight into my subject that I could work into and enrich the narrative I had written twenty years earlier.

Fragments: Poems, Intimate Notes, Letters of Marilyn Monroe (2010) and *MM—Personal: From the Private Archive of Marilyn Monroe* (2011) have received considerable attention, but no published review—so far as I know—seems to understand what a momentous change in Monroe's biography these books constitute. I mean a change in writing about her life. For one thing, I never expected to see these books about her discussed in *The New York Review of Books*, but they are.

Fragments and *MM—Personal* reveal her acute self-consciousness, her Virginia Woolf–like obsession with watching herself and scrutinizing her relations with others. She did not keep diaries as faithfully as Woolf did, and she did not have Woolf's literary gifts, but Monroe had a sensibility like Woolf's that ultimately pursued itself to the point of extinction. In short, it was not the traumatic childhood, not the movies, not the failed marriages—not her even her disappointed hopes—that led to her demise, but rather her unrelenting focus on herself. (This self-consciousness appeared very early, at least as early as her first marriage, which is to say years before she became a star, or even had an acting career.)

I can best illustrate my point by analyzing a six-page typewritten, undated personal note, probably written in 1943, less than a year after Marilyn married James Dougherty, her first husband, on June 19, 1942, just over two weeks after she turned sixteen (then the age of consent in California). I had no access to this letter when I wrote my biography. I relied on other biographical accounts, Monroe's own published statements, and photographs that present a fresh, healthy, and apparently untroubled and unsophisticated young woman. When I first read the personal note in *Fragments*, I thought the editors had misdated it. Monroe writes part of it in the past tense, employing a ruminative tone that is startling coming from a teenager.

Before commenting on what Monroe says, though, I need to ask: Is this a personal note? That is just the title her editors supply. Was Monroe writing for herself? The piece does not read like a scrap of a diary or journal. It is retrospective, as if the marriage were over—which in a way it was, even though the couple would not divorce until September 13, 1946. Whatever you call it, this piece of writing is suffused with an intense disenchantment bearing no relationship to the cheerful, dependent creature Dougherty described in his memoir about his marriage to Monroe. Judging by her "personal note," the man never sounded the depths of the young woman he married. He was nearly six years older, but she was the mature one—or should I say the perceptive one? Dougherty always professed amazement that his Norma Jeane had metamorphosed into Marilyn Monroe. "I never knew Marilyn Monroe," he liked to say. He did not realize, however, that he never knew Norma Jeane either.

Monroe begins her self-analysis by calling herself an "advanced child," more comfortable during her adolescence (an in-between age) with younger children or adults than with her peers. Dougherty—a little sophisticated, with a love of classical music—seemed a mature match for her. In retrospect, however, she speculated that she may simply have made him into a sort of dream man, a projection of her own desire to feel secure. He was one of the few men she did not see as sexually repulsive, one who could fulfill her fleeting notions of romantic adventure. And she wanted to please her elders (chiefly her guardians, Ana Lower and Grace McKee) who thought the marriage a good idea. The marriage also served, she thought, as an escape from the problems of adolescence.

Norma Jeane's understanding of mixed motivations and the complex of factors that governed her early marriage is, as the editors of *Fragments* observe, impressive. It is fascinating to see how she describes a "nervous tension" derived from her playful fantasies of becoming a model. I thought immediately of how quickly and decisively she left Dougherty behind when photographer David Conover showed up at the airplane factory where Marilyn worked, telling her she was a "natural." I had written in my 1986 biography that then and there Norma Jeane settled on a career, but I had no idea of how ready she already was for the appearance of someone like Conover. I had presumed her decision was spontaneous and took her by surprise. But it is apparent now that his entrance into her biography provided not only an opportunity, but was also a release for her pent-up energy.

She describes herself in the first year of marriage as an "intense introvert" with very little connection to others, except for a very few people who had some understanding of her desire to withdraw. She mentions reading as one of her solitary pleasures. Although some of her syntax is hard to follow, the overall impression she conveys is that of a profoundly alienated young woman easily depressed by even "slightly foreboding" circumstances.

One of those circumstances is her "bitchy withdrawn" reaction to her husband's interest in another woman. Norma Jeane seems more upset about what she is feeling than about the woman in question—or even about her husband. Her "romantic esthetical soul," she suggests, is responsible for making him out to be "some great lover," when, in reality, this is just a situation she has allowed herself to be drawn into. In other words, the entire episode is a projection.

Now at this point, she addresses not herself but "a person who remembers growing up" and who can appreciate how difficult it is for her to establish an "objective, analitical view" without seeming "to pompass" about her "relatively simple thoughts." The misspellings, like her shaky syntax, suggest the tenuous but tenacious dynamic of her effort to understand herself. But what a sense of self she manifests, trying to imagine another person trying to figure out her life. Pardon me, but I feel like she is speaking to her biographer. How many people, even those who become icons, are already notating themselves at seventeen? Does this young woman strike you as the naïve Monroe of most accounts? She is tentative about her self-examination—suggesting that it is not worth much and should be thrown into the wastebasket—but that attitude reminds me of the mature star, who always doubted she had understood her roles and given her best performance.

Characteristically, Norma Jeane is then "sidetracked" by a comment on the perceptiveness of children, an attribute they lose touch with while growing up. This digression is, of course, nothing of the kind, but rather an extrapolation from her own experience. As is so often the case with the woman who would become Marilyn Monroe, I sense her utter aloneness. No one is at hand to take up the connections she is trying to make between herself and the way the world works. Later, her fame would in countless ways prevent her from fully engaging with others.

In her own case, Monroe suggests, marriage to Dougherty cut her off from those insights that develop in adolescence. Or, as she puts it: "My first impulse was one of complete subjection humiliation, alonement to the male counterpart." She began to tremble as she wrote these words, but then stepped back—almost like a psychologist or perhaps a poet—remarking: "I just want to keep pouring it out until this great pot in the mind is, though not emptied, relieved." She is still worried that what she is writing is "crap," but that concern surely is the sign of intelligence, of the doubt that physicist Richard Feynman thought the hallmark of the modern mind.

Of course, *Fragments* does not reveal a great thinker or poet, but the book does show Monroe's affinity for both types, an affinity which, I believe, is what drove her to acting. Like Dana Andrews, another one of my subjects, she was a writer manqué. He kept his own "Fragments," a diary—journal in which he tried to articulate his view of himself and the world. Ultimately, he realized he did not have the kind of concentrated literary power that would make him a writer, but he used that same power in a series of extraordinary performances over a ten-year period, 1944 to 1954. Monroe did much the same thing between 1952 and 1962. One of the attractions of the acting profession for personalities like Andrews and Monroe is that their roles can, at least temporarily, express through the words of others a conception of self and world that is otherwise not within their reach.

Norma Jeane returns to the theme of a husband who has betrayed her, and she is enraged not so much by his infidelity per se, but because it struck a blow to her "unsteady ego." She needs to feel loved, she confesses, and perhaps this desire to be wanted is the only kind of love she feels for Dougherty. But she seems prepared to do without even that much love if it means playing "second fiddle" to another woman.

For a time she thought her husband was honest with her, but then she interjects: "Its hard not to try and rationalize and protect your own feelings but eventually that makes the acceptance of truth more difficult." I think about her mentally ill mother, the various working class families that took care of her, the influence of one of her Christian Science guardians, and none of them came close to speaking this kind of language, or showed this kind of sensibility. Norma Jeane was in her world a nonpareil, although I doubt that anyone noticed as much.

No one has ever offered a better diagnosis of Norma Jeane/Marilyn Monroe than she does in her concluding paragraph: "Its not to much fun to know yourself to well or think you do—everyone needs a little conciet to carry them through & past the falls." Most of us carry with us some kind of illusion about who we are and what we can accomplish. Certainly this is true in my case. I can think of many writing projects that I would not have completed if I had known, from the start, how much trouble they would entail. So imagine the life of a young woman who did anticipate trouble, who could not help but observe herself, and who chose a profession in which she was on display all the time. Her self-consciousness could be paralyzing and was relieved only by moments of acting when she could embody another being. What a relief it would be to act unconsciously and ultimately, to be unconscious, no longer obliged to carry the burden of self, a burden already shouldered by Norma Jeane when she was still three years away from her first appearance in a motion picture. To carry that same burden as Marilyn Monroe was all the more deadly.

4

Hazarding Lillian Hellman:
Discovering the Virtues
of Fair Use

I first became intrigued with Lillian Hellman by reading about her in Joseph Blotner's biography of William Faulkner. I was writing a Ph.D. dissertation that became my first book, *Uses of the Past in the Novels of William Faulkner*. I did not realize then, in 1975, that my interest in Faulkner was leading me to biography, to a concern with how individuals "construct" themselves over time, and how over time the culture constructs *them*, as it happens in *Absalom, Absalom!* How did Faulkner's Thomas Sutpen fashion himself so as to create a figure that haunted subsequent generations? That question was not so different, actually, from Mailer's preoccupation with Marilyn Monroe, or mine with Lillian Hellman.

Faulkner liked Hellman. Unlike most New Yorkers, she understood the Deep South. After all, she had been partly brought up there—to be precise, in New Orleans, site of Faulkner's fraught foray into the shaping of America's multicultural and multiracial identity. Indeed, if you truly want to understand the significance of Barack Obama, you have to read *Absalom, Absalom!*

Faulkner also liked Dashiell Hammett, Hellman's on-again, off-again companion, who was truly her other half. Faulkner read Hammett's hard-boiled detective stories and read mysteries by the ream. He also tried to write them—not too successfully when he followed the formula of pulp fiction, but spectacularly well when he experimented with the conventions of mystery fiction in *Absalom, Absalom!* That novel is an object lesson for biographers because it is about the obsession with knowing what really happened in the past, as well as about the utter futility of ever coming to a final, definitive, determination as to what can be known.

Hellman lay dormant in my mind from about 1975 to 1985, when I

27

was nearing completion of my Marilyn Monroe biography and preparing my dissertation for book publication. Hellman was "hot" in the late 1980s because of revelations about the "Julia" story, made into a motion picture starring Jane Fonda as the intrepid Hellman, courier for her childhood friend, Julia, who was part of the anti–Nazi underground. It became apparent that Hellman's claims about the Julia story could not be verified, which opened up for her critics' questions about the veracity of Hellman's other memoirs. Searching for a subject that my new agent could peddle, I suggested Hellman. "I can sell that," she immediately responded, and she told me to get started. In three months, I had a proposal ready to go, and in relatively short order, I had an offer from St. Martin's Press. I was elated but also terrified. The publisher gave me a 12-month contract and divided the advance against royalties into thirds: one-third on signing, one-third when the book was half done, and one-third upon acceptance of the entire manuscript. It had taken me six years to write my first biography. "Can you do it in a year?" my agent asked. I said yes while fearing the answer was no. I put myself on half-time at Wayne State University, where I was assistant dean of the graduate school, and wrote every morning and took research trips to New York and to archives around the country during semester breaks, summer holidays, and weekends. I did seventy-five interviews and turned the book in on time, cheating only by handing in a third of the book and saying it was half, so that I could get the next chunk of the advance. In the end, this under-the-gun schedule made me a writer working every day and no longer an academic yearning for what they colleagues called "blocks of time" to get their work done.

Hellman had it all, in my book. I grew up in the theater, and she was theater to me. I had always been interested in politics, and she was politics to me. I was obsessed with Hollywood and its history, and she was Hollywood to me. She spent half her childhood in the South, and I was then still steeped in all things Southern. And then there were bonuses: She had a great sex life, and she loved to cook. She traveled to places I wanted to visit. She was endlessly entertaining. When my biography appeared, the *New York Times* reviewer called my book "dishy"; it was the first time I had seen that word in print. True, my book did contain gossip. People loved to talk about Lillian (she pronounced it Lil-yan), and the endless speculation about this entertaining but fearsome woman brought me back to, yes, *Absalom, Absalom!*, a novel which shows how much Sutpen's story depends on who tells it.

With the Hellman biography, I encountered for the first time, the issue of authorization, a rather quaint notion that no modern historian would take seriously. Who gets to tell history? Anyone who sets up as a historian, of course. But at one time, historians did not refer to their sources but to their authorities. They do not use the word nowadays, but vestiges of it remain in that loathsome term, "authorized biographer." Somehow, even now—at least in some circles—authorization is regarded as a good house-keeping seal of approval. Or to put it another way, the unauthorized biographer is driving without a license. The authorized biographer has been vetted; the unauthorized biographer has taken the law into his, or her, own hands. So when I asked Lillian's Hellman editor, William Abrahams, for an interview, he treated me like an interloper and replied that he was "the one and only authorized biographer." It was a very strange attitude for him to adopt, since years earlier he had collaborated on an unauthorized biography of George Orwell.

But Abrahams is not alone. Scott Donaldson, author of an unauthorized biography of John Cheever, became a policeman for the Hemingway estate and wrote me a cautionary letter about not quoting too much from Hem in my unauthorized biography of Martha Gellhorn. In other words, Papa's estate had its eyes on me. When the editor of my unauthorized Gellhorn biography suggested to Margaux Hemingway that I was the perfect writer to help her with her autobiography, Mariel replied, "Oh no, Martha says he is a bad man." And when another editor suggested to Katherine Anne Porter's literary executor that I was the one to write a new biography of Porter, the executor asked what I had written. He mentioned the Hellman biography, and she exclaimed: "I HATE LILLIAN HELL-MAN! I WON'T ALLOW HIM TO WRITE ABOUT KATHERINE ANNE." This reaction would not in itself have stopped someone like me who belongs to the lower criminal classes, but I had to desist simply because the editor would not go ahead without the estate's approval.

Realizing that I would have a hard time with Hellman's estate if I asked for approval to quote from her work, published and unpublished, I relied on the concept of fair use, a concept that many writers and editors still find troublesome and vague. But my reliance on fair use in the Hellman biography became a template for how I was to approach my unauthorized biographies of Martha Gellhorn, Susan Sontag, and Sylvia Plath. My unauthorized biography of Norman Mailer was a different story. I did seek permission to quote from his work. Why I did so, and what resulted, will be explored in another chapter.

Since fair use is a crucial tool for biographers and used even in authorized biographies, the rest of this chapter is devoted to how it can be effectively employed. Fair Use allows biographers, historians, critics, and other writers to quote a modest amount of words from their subject's writings. How modest? A rule of thumb has been to quote no more than 300 words from a full-length book, a sentence or two from a long letter, a line from a poem or a song. But there is no legal definition of how many words can be quoted. Section 107 of the amended copyright act of 1992 describes four factors to be considered when judging fair use defenses raised against claims of copyright infringement:

(1) the purpose and character of the use, including whether such use is of a commercial nature or is for nonprofit educational purposes;
(2) the nature of the copyrighted work;
(3) the amount and substantiality of the portion used in relation to the copyrighted work as a whole; and
(4) the effect of the use upon the potential market for or value of the copyrighted work. The fact that a work is unpublished shall not itself bar a finding of fair use if such finding is made upon consideration of all the above factors.

The last sentence is crucial, and was added in 1992, because several court cases especially a suit that J. D. Salinger brought against his biographer, Ian Hamilton—had virtually destroyed fair use in regard to unpublished work; that is, court rulings made it almost impossible for a biographer to quote, or even closely paraphrase, unpublished writing.

Here is how fair use works in practice: A few years ago, I received a phone call from a distraught biographer. She had been working amicably with her subject's estate for almost fifteen years, and now—quite suddenly— she had been refused permission to quote from unpublished papers. The literary executor had read a part of her manuscript and apparently had reservations. Even worse, another biographer had appeared, a certain gentleman who had been plotting for some years to get control of the estate. I had been contacted because a friend had advised her that I had confronted a similar situation. "What should I do?" the phone caller asked. "Neither my agent nor my publisher has been of much help."

The biography had been contracted with the understanding that the estate would cooperate, and now the biographer—never having squarely faced the issue of authorization—was in a quandary. Just how much use could she make of unpublished material? Did the estate's prior cooperation give her any warrant for retaining her quotations from unpublished sources? She had nothing in writing, no agreement that in any sense "authorized" the biographer.

I did have some advice for the caller that was based on my own experience with estates and with the subjects of my biographies, which I began working on in the late 1980s, just as my wife Lisa Paddock got her law degree and began to explore copyright issues. Our husband and wife collaboration was not merely a matter of a writer getting legal advice from his spouse, but rather a close collaboration in the talking out of what became my narratives, which had to overcome the obstacles biographical subjects and their estates erect to stymie unauthorized biographers. The main weapon, copyright, was not employed to protect the subject's property rights, but to enforce censorship on the biographer and to intimidate him or her—perhaps enough that the biography would be killed. For example, in a case that finally ended happily for the biographer (more about this case later), Margaret Walker's initial contract with Howard University Press for a biography of Richard Wright was cancelled after she was unable to obtain Wright's widow's consent to quote from unpublished material. Walker was seeking permission to quote from letters Wright had written to her. Although the letters were Walker's property, she did not own their copyrights. Robert Newman, author of *Cold War Romance: John Melby and Lillian Hellman* (Chapel Hill: University of North Carolina Press, 1988), confronted a similar situation. Newman had worked closely with Melby and had relied on Hellman's letters to Melby, which were in Melby's possession. Newman assumed that because Hellman's letters were Melby's property Melby could give Newman permission to quote from them. I pointed out to Newman that he would have to seek permission from Hellman's estate. Newman ultimately got such permission, but it carried severe restrictions on the amount of material he could quote. As an unauthorized biographer he did not have the estate's blessing, and this episode provides a clear illustration of the way copyright can be employed in an attempt to limit the scope of an unauthorized biography. Joan Mellen's *Hellman and Hammett* (New York: HarperCollins, 1996) was the first unauthorized biographer to receive unrestricted access to Hellman's papers. Mellen notes Hellman's efforts to prevent the publication of unauthorized biographies but not her estate's previous efforts to perpetuate those efforts.

Before getting to the advice I gave my caller, here is some background on how biographers work and on the legal climate, in which biographers have to weather some highly restrictive rules concerning the use of unpublished materials. To start with the obvious: how a biographer works depends very much on his or her attitude toward biography, and this attitude, in turn, will influence how he or she deals with legalities. Keep in mind the idea of legality. It will be addressed later. Here, in capsule form, is a panoply of biographers:

Biographer A: He has been the editor and friend of the subject for many years. He has never written a biography but he is trusted by his subject; maybe she trusts him because she knows damn well he will never write the biography—so she names him her biographer. There are many authorized biographies that never get written, instead serving the purpose of scaring off other potential biographers.

Biographer B: He is a university professor who develops a special relationship with his subject and with his subject's family. He publishes articles and introductions to books by others and is often quoted in the press, but he never actually produces a biography. The late Carvel Collins, Faulkner's putative biographer and a candidate for top dog in the manger, comes to mind. Collins first announced his biography in the late 1940s. Decades went by as Collins created a mystique about his project, implying that he had inside information unavailable to anyone else. When Collins announced that he was deferring publication until Joseph Blotner's authorized biography appeared, he was praised in the *New York Times* for his forbearance. But even after Blotner's book came out in 1974, no Collins biography appeared. Instead, Collins continued to lecture and to write articles, often pointing out errors in Blotner's official life of Faulkner. When I asked Collins when his biography would appear, Collins said he was still looking for "the figure in the carpet." He retired from the University of Notre Dame and then died without ever delivering on his lifetime promise. So did the late Robert Lucid. Norman Mailer's handpicked man. Through Lucid, Mailer exerted enormous control over how his biography would be written—or, more importantly—not written.

Biographer C: My phone caller. She proceeds for many years believing she is authorized. She has exclusive access to her subject's papers until that moment when her subject or her subject's estate sees the manuscript, and suddenly she is treated like an interloper.

Biographer D: She does not get authorization, but because of the high quality of her work she often gets the cooperation of her living subjects, or, if they are dead, of their estates, who apparently appreciate the value of dealing with a shrewd, responsible biographer. At least they have some opportunity to influence her. Deirdre Bair, the biographer of Samuel Beckett and Simone De Beauvoir, comes to mind. Even Bair, however, ran into trouble with her Carl Jung biography. Jung's estate objected to several passages in her book and requested the unprecedented privilege of refuting in the text of Bair's biography the passages in question. After mounting a press campaign that aroused concern over her German publisher's effort to compromise one of its own authors, Bair brought enough pressure on her publisher to ensure that her text was not tampered with.

Biographer E: The Rollyson/Paddock approach in *Susan Sontag: The Making of an Icon* (2000). My wife and I had no "in" with our subject.

We did not ask for authorization. Although we wrote to her to asking for an interview, we did not secure any special access. We did, however, hear from Sontag's agent, Andrew Wylie, who hinted that Sontag might be available for an interview at some later date if we would, as a precondition, provide him with details as to our sources and methodology. Our vague reply put an end even to minimal cooperation on Sontag's part.

These examples demonstrate that how biographers position themselves has an important bearing on the resolution of legal issues that may arise in the process of writing a biography. I knew, from the start, that I could not obtain permission to quote from Lillian Hellman's unpublished papers. I did what many unauthorized biographers do: I paraphrased and quoted small but lively bits from her unpublished writings. I took a risk, for court decisions of that time (the mid–1980s) severely restricted what is known as "fair use" of unpublished material. I also gambled that my publisher would not submit the manuscript to lawyers for vetting. I won my bet on that one.

Ian Hamilton's attempt to write a biography of J. D. Salinger marks the juncture where life became truly difficult for biographers. "What a great idea," I can imagine Hamilton thinking, "to do Salinger—one of the most private men of letters, a recluse. Everyone will want to read about him." In retrospect, Hamilton's naiveté is comical. He decided he would cover Salinger's life only up to the point when Salinger stopped publishing. Perhaps Hamilton thought Salinger would somehow relent and at least tolerate the approach of a serious scholar and the acclaimed biographer of Robert Lowell. As biographers are wont to do, let's enter further into Hamilton's mindset. Can't you just picture him thinking: "When Salinger sees how careful I've been, how much respect I have for his work, and how much material I've uncovered that he can't hope to keep private any longer, he will realize there's no stopping me." Just the opposite occurred: Salinger read Hamilton's galleys and filed a suit for copyright infringement. See the first chapter of *In Search of J. D. Salinger* (1988) for the biographer's account for his struggles with his subject. A court decision resulted in a severe constriction of the fair use doctrine as it applies to unpublished manuscripts. Salinger was upset about letters written in his youth, which Hamilton both quoted and closely paraphrased. Hamilton argued that he did not need Salinger's permission, since the biographer quoted a very small portion of the unpublished material, and his paraphrasing remained within legal limits. Unfortunately, the court disagreed, instead concluding that Hamilton had merely provided synonyms for Salinger's words—in effect appropriating Salinger's style. Unpublished material could be mined for facts but should not mimic the subject's expression. Hamilton countered that he had quoted and closely paraphrased Salinger in order to convey in the liveliest terms possible his subject's manner. In view of what biographers have done for generations, Hamilton did nothing new, but the court found otherwise, and as a result the use of unpublished material by unauthorized biographers became a questionable proposition.

This bald summary of the Salinger case oversimplifies matters, legally speaking. But I am describing its impact on me and on other biographers. I had to watch every word—even the order of my words—when dealing with unpublished documents from which I had no permission to quote. That the Salinger decision was immediately used to bludgeon biographers I learned from my own experience.

As to my advice to the distraught phone caller: She had at least two options. First, she could try to work out some arrangement with the estate. This would almost certainly mean compromises, writing a book that would have to please the executors. The virtue of this approach would be that at least some quoted material from unpublished sources could be preserved. The other, unauthorized approach, would preserve more of the biographer's independence—although if lawyers had to vet the manuscript, that too would also result in certain compromises.

I recommended the following action:

- Restrict direct quotation from her subject's unpublished papers to less than three hundred words. After the Salinger decision, Beacon Press limited Louise DeSalvo, author of a controversial book on Virginia Woolf that did not have the sanction of Woolf's estate, to one hundred words. St. Martin's lawyers limited me to three words of direct quotation after an all-day session in which a weary counsel gave in to my persistent requests and said: "All right, all right, yes, you can quote Gellhorn's unpublished letter referring to Hemingway's `hot jungle breath.'"
- Instead of paraphrasing quotations line by line, summarize them for their factuality. Where possible, stitch together published and unpublished sources in the narrative so that the two kinds of evidence will seem—as indeed they often are—inseparable.
- When drawing on long, unpublished letters, do not follow the sequence of any given letter from one paragraph to the next. Take the letter as a whole, analyze it as information, and reorder that information in terms of your narrative, thus truly creating your own organization of the material.
- Be more concise than your unpublished source. From, say, a three-page unpublished letter, squeeze out no more than a paragraph or so for your own narrative.

In the years that have passed since this phone conversation, the law regarding fair use has been somewhat modified. Initially, however, courts in the Second Circuit—which includes New York City, home to most publishers—were obliged to follow the precedent the Salinger suit set.

Journalists, historians, publishers, and biographers continued to experience difficulties in performing their jobs and in exercising their First Amendment rights. As a result of their lobbying, in 1992 Congress amended the 1976 Copyright Act by adding a proviso addressing the problem of unpublished work to the section concerning fair use. The long-term effects of the addition of this new gloss on the fair use doctrine have been significant. Unauthorized biographers who need to make some use of their subjects' works, both published and unpublished, now have more latitude. When an attorney hired by St. Martin's Press vetted my Sylvia Plath biography, he was not concerned with counting words but in making sure that what I did quote or paraphrase was accompanied by my own characterization of the evidence. So, for example, when I quoted a few lines from Plath's journal or from a letter, I commented—usually with an adjective. With fair use in mind, I was counseled to write "Plath said dejectedly" or happily, or whatever word fit the evidence. This is called "fair comment." It is the unauthorized biographer's way of saying he has used the quoted or paraphrased material for critical purposes. I was afraid that some reviewers—not aware of how fair use can impact narrative—might criticize me for stating the obvious. In the best of all possible worlds, I would have quoted Plath and let the reader supply the adjective. Fortunately, no reviewer noticed those adjectives I put in to cover myself legally. This relaxation of the restrictions of fair use made it easier to get a contract for an unauthorized biography of Susan Sontag.

Undoubtedly, the burgeoning of electronic publishing has complicated matters. Those who wish to keep abreast of the latest developments regarding fair use can consult an online copyright law archive produced by the Stanford University library in conjunction with the Council on Library Resources. And those biographers who wish to forge ahead despite the unsettled state of the law can fortify themselves with some knowledge of their own rights and responsibilities. I say unsettled, because as the St. Martin's Press attorney told me, determinations of fair use is judge-made law, and what one judge deems a reasonable employment of fair use may seem unreasonable to another judge.

It helps to bear in mind that in the case that started the contemporary fair use controversy, *Harper & Row v. Nation Enterprises*, which the U.S. Supreme Court decided in 1985, Justice Sandra Day O'Connor's opinion for the Court specifically indicated that fair use adheres to all rights protected by the 1976 Copyright Act, including the so-called right of first publication. The right of first publication is the author's privilege of being the first to issue his or her writings publicly, and it is this principle that stands in the way of wholesale copying of unpublished material. In this case the Court found against *The Nation*—rejecting the magazine's defense that its publication of extracts from Gerald Ford's forthcoming autobiography merely made fair use of Ford's explanation of the Nixon pardon, a matter of enormous public interest. *The Nation* may only have printed three hundred words from Ford's lengthy manuscript, but they were the three hundred best words—"the heart of the book," as the Court characterized them. But *The Nation* lost its case not only because it had preempted Ford's right of first publication, causing *Time* to cancel the contract with Ford granting it the exclusive right to print prepublication excerpts, into the bargain—but also because the defendant came into court, as the law so vividly puts it, with "unclean hands." *The Nation* had got hold of the Ford manuscript illicitly. It helps to bear in mind that the First Amendment is a permeable shield and does not trump larceny. Be wary of sources and, wherever possible, acknowledge them explicitly—for the sake of self-protection as well as good manners.

Once an author deposits writings in a publicly accessible archive, however, he or she does surrender complete control over them, and it is the biographer's prerogative to take advantage of this resignation. As L. Ray Patterson and Stanley W. Lindberg state: "the author who presents his or her papers to a library obviously does so in the interest of posterity. Having sought posterity, the author should hardly be able to use the law of copyright to manipulate the judgment of posterity." (See their laudable book, *The Nature of Copyright: A Law of Users' Rights*, Athens: University of Georgia Press, 1991.) And even when others have deposited an author's writings in archives, as in the case of J.D. Salinger, the copyright law does not protect that author's right to privacy. Where Ian Hamilton made his mistake was not so much in using Salinger's letters, but in using too much of them, with the result that the court found that Salinger's property rights had been violated. It seems likely that *Salinger v. Random House*, were it tried today under the revised version of the fair use section of the Copyright Act, would have a different outcome. Salinger does have a First Amendment right to remain silent, which in this context means a right to prevent his works from being published, but this right does not pre-empt the critic's or the historian's or the biographer's constitutional right to make use of them. This right is guaranteed by the First Amendment, by the 1976 Copyright Law, and by the source of this law, Article I, section 8, clause 8 of the Constitution: "The Congress shall have Power ... to promote the Progress of Science and useful Arts, by securing for limited Times to Authors and Inventors the exclusive Right to their respective Writings and Discoveries." Copyrights, like trademarks and patents, protect limited monopolies.

The law, as it is currently interpreted, throws biographers back on their own styles, forcing them to make sources their own in much the way a novelist transforms the raw material of life into a new, vibrant fiction. There are drawbacks, of course. Reviewers ignored the conditions under which I wrote my first Gellhorn biography, when publishers were still cowed by the Salinger case. Reviewers paid no attention to the way a highly restricted reading of copyright law had partly determined the shape of the book, even though I had in a prologue and epilogue made a discussion of unauthorized biography the frame for the biography. Altogether, St. Martin's Press asked me to cut approximately five thousand words. In addition, virtually every page had to be altered, if only in some minor way. The most persistent worry of the lawyers was that I would get too close to Gellhorn's expression, to her manner of saying things—the very thing protected by copyright.

St. Martin's lawyers did such a thorough job of removing Gellhorn's language from my first biography of her that she dropped her allegations of copyright infringement and concentrated on threatening a libel suit, provoking another marathon legal session at my publisher's lawyer's offices. Very little of the text changed that time, and St. Martin's came away from the last skirmish with Gellhorn more convinced than ever of the integrity of my book. I published my second Gellhorn biography, *Beautiful Exile* (London: Aurum Press, 2000), after Gellhorn's death, and the publisher did not have lawyers vet the text. Under a more liberal interpretation of fair use I was able to restore many of the cuts in the biography's first edition.

Such experiences have certainly stiffened my resolve as a biographer, and they prompt me to quote an unpublished line from Hemingway. After having divorced Gellhorn, he wrote long, complaining letters about her to his army buddy, General Buck Lanham. I delighted in quoting some of Hem's most vivid phrases, which the lawyers kept insisting must be cut. One particularly painful bit of surgery had to do with a passage in which Hemingway asserted that Gellhorn was an impossible woman who wanted everything to run smoothly all the time. She would not be pleased, he concluded, unless he could hire for $35 a month "a butler with the probity of Cardinal Newman and the organizing capacity of Henry Kaiser"—in short, the very qualities necessary to today's biographers.

For another anatomy of different kinds of biography, see Deirdre Bair's "The How-To Biography" in James Walter and Raija Nugent, ed., *Biographers at Work* (Nathan, Queensland: Institute for Modern Biography, 1984). A useful discussion of different types of biography authorized (controlled by the subject, the subject's heirs, or the subject's estate), designated (similar to the authorized biography, except that "no authority over the final published manuscript" is exercised), independent (written without the sanction of the subject or of the heirs and the estate), bowdlerized (a miscellaneous, tendentious collection of data sometimes found in popular biographies). Bair also offers good advice on copyright issues and insight into her biographical work on living figures.

5

Martha and Me: The Promise and Peril of Unauthorized Biography

The Promise

I became fascinated with Martha Gellhorn in 1986 while researching my biography of Lillian Hellman. In the *Paris Review* (Spring 1981), Gellhorn published "On Apocryphism," a demolition of Hellman's memoir of the Spanish Civil War. Gellhorn put Hellman in the category of "apocryphiars," writers with self-serving, spiteful fantasies that were retailed by scholars and biographers—no matter how absurd and implausible the printed words. The trend toward "*apocryphism,* a meld of apocryphal story and apocryphiar," was growing at an alarming rate—in other words, the telling of stories by the famous about the famous who in the same breath make themselves more famous.

In her best literary policewoman fashion, Gellhorn tore apart Hellman's chronology and her claims to having shared confidences with Ernest Hemingway. Gellhorn had been *there* and had no trouble contradicting Hellman's fable. Comparing *An Unfinished Woman* and *Pentimento*, Gellhorn discovered instances in which Hellman apparently had been able to be in three places at once: in the Moscow embassy, with Julia, her antifascist agent/friend in Vienna, and in Spain. Gellhorn refuted Hellman's story about reading the proofs of *To Have and Have Not* in Spain. Hemingway had actually read them before leaving for the war. Hemingway and Hellman could not have stood on their balcony in Madrid watching the fireworks from bombing (as Hellman claimed) since the bombs in Spain did not give off light. Gellhorn ridiculed Hellman's "firsthand" description of an air raid. Though Hellman describes children screaming and women running, Gellhorn recalled how impressively quiet Spaniards were in dangerous situations. Is the policeman who pushes Hellman under a bench for protection during an air raid an "imbecile"? Gellhorn asked. What kind of shelter does a park bench afford? That could not be Hellman's attempt at humor, could it? Gellhorn wanted to know. Of Hellman's description of a plane dropping down and setting loose a bomb that "slowly floated … like a round gift-wrapped package," Gellhorn remarked that planes over Madrid flew at a "prudent height," were not dive bombers, and the bombs did not come one at a time floating "like an auk's egg," or a gift-wrapped package. At the most, Hellman had spent three weeks in Spain, Gellhorn calculated, and "her incomprehension of that war is near idiocy."

In Gellhorn's memory of their brief meetings, Hellman was a grumpy sullen presence and no match for her splendid companion Dorothy Parker, who showed none of Hellman's conceit. Gellhorn considered most of Hellman's scenes in her memoirs between herself and Hemingway to be sheer inventions, especially the one in which Hemingway compliments Hellman on her courage, saying she had "cojones" after all. "In my opinion," Gellhorn concluded, "Miss H. has the *cojones* of a brass monkey." The tough talk reminded me of her ex-husband, Ernest Hemingway. "Built-in falsehood, children, is bad," Gellhorn began her article in a fair imitation of Papa.

Gellhorn's wonderful combination of outrage and humor intrigued me. Did she have more to say that I could include in my biography of Lillian Hellman? And so I wrote to Martha Gellhorn. She replied with a short, pithy note, wanting me to know that she had titled her piece "Close Encounters of the Apocryphal Kind," but George Plimpton, editor of the *Paris Review*, "had lost the title and his nerve too…. I just happened to get good and mad, for once: so I wrote that. If one spent life exposing liars, one would have no time to live." She also volunteered that Hellman had been cruel and false to Dorothy Parker and proceeded to elaborate the conviction that Hellman could not be a true friend to any woman because she was "ugly." Of course, Gellhorn conceded there were ugly women like Golda Meir and Mrs. Roosevelt who have been endearing, but these were only major exceptions to the theory.

Gellhorn really did not have much to add to her *Paris Review* article; still I liked her chatty but blunt tone. What she said about Hellman's looks came back to me when certain reviewers claimed I made too much of Hellman's ugliness—even accusing me of clinging to an ideal of beauty exemplified in Marilyn Monroe, the subject of my first biography.

This contact with Gellhorn had a bracing impact, for I should confess that I had her in my biographical sights. Jackie Onassis, then an editor at Doubleday, had already suggested that I write Gellhorn's biography, and after Gellhorn's letter to me, I considered it my destiny to do so. I became quite carried away with my enterprise, musing about editorial lunches with Jackie, envisioning Gellhorn as part of my project to write a series of biographies of notable women. It seemed to me that the times (not to mention the publishing market) would welcome books that followed in the wake of Nancy Milford's landmark biography of Zelda Fitzgerald and Hellman's best-selling accounts of how she had fared in the male dominated worlds of New York theater and Hollywood. As a war correspondent, Gellhorn had had to carve out her own niche among predatory and ambitious males, and she had been the only one of Hemingway's wives to leave him. Writing her biography would take his weight off her.

Even though I indulged in fantasizing about my promising prospects, working on Lillian Hellman's biography taught me that Gellhorn's response to my project would not be positive. Hellman had spent her life crafting a persona that she defended at all costs—whether it meant suing Mary McCarthy for calling her a liar or handpicking her authorized biographer, her Little, Brown editor, William Abrahams. Would Gellhorn, a woman of the same generation and with the same powerful will, react any differently? My ever-optimistic agent, Elizabeth Frost-Knappman, thought so. Gellhorn would be thrilled to have a whole book devoted to her. Elizabeth's response typified what others—even biographers!—said to me: Biographical subjects will be flattered by the attention, and biography is an honorable genre which by its very nature elevates the importance of the individual. The subject's animosity comes as a nasty surprise and induces an aggrieved tone, especially among certain biographers who believe they are doing good and feel injured when their subjects and their subject's supporters suppose otherwise. I remained excited about doing a Gellhorn biography, however, because Gellhorn was such a dynamic figure, and I knew that based on my endeavor to re-create Hellman's life, I would enjoy the contest. Dead or alive, the biographical subject puts up resistance, and there is bound to be friction with a biographer. Call it a conflict of interest theory of biography: there is my interest in Martha Gellhorn's life, and there is her own, and the two can never be reconciled. As David Roberts, Jean Stafford's biographer, writes: "The truest biography is not likely to please its subject."

As I began to assess the resources I would rely on to write Gellhorn's biography, I remembered again the day I learned that the Hellman archive had been closed. Hellman's friend, the poet Richard Wilbur, casually mentioned that "of course" I couldn't rely on that asset. Stunned, I don't think I said a word to him but simply continued the interview. Hellman, by the way, had instructed Wilbur not to speak with anyone but the anointed Abrahams. To Wilbur, her demand amounted to censorship: She was asking him to curtail what he had to say about his life, not just hers. Wilbur, it seemed to me, welcomed my call so that he could assert his own rights. His encouragement bolstered me, encouraged my own sense of independence and my desire to find new and important sources not only in archives but also in interviews. What I could not find in her own letters I re-created in a series of conversations with her friends and colleagues. I believe I became a better biographer by thinking of my sources as creations of my own, so to speak, because they had arisen out of my need to draw on an archive that would not be handed to me. Not enjoying the privileges of the authorized can be a boon.

In all likelihood, I reckoned, Gellhorn would close her archive at Boston University and do what she could to stop me. Working on a living subject is asking for trouble. Hellman had died by the time I began work on her life, and that certainly made it easier for some people to talk. But why not find out? Why not begin interviewing people? Why not call Boston University? Why not write Gellhorn? I did none of these things in the spring of 1988. Even as my Hellman biography came out, I worked up a proposal entitled "Martha Gellhorn: Her Life and Times." I decided that after I had obtained a contract to write Gellhorn's biography, I would contact her and ascertain the status of her papers. It would be too easy for her and others to put me off if I did not have a contract, and I had already determined that even if certain avenues for research closed up, others would inevitably open. I also had in hand Jacqueline Orsagh's Ph.D. dissertation on Gellhorn, a highly useful work because Orsagh had interviewed Gellhorn about her life and work and had identified publicly accessible archives, especially the Roosevelt Library at Hyde Park. What is more, Gellhorn had known so many people and traveled to so many places that the biographical evidence could not be suppressed. An inveterate correspondent, her letters were sure to turn up in other writers' collections. Thus I had done enough preliminary work as a biographer to write the first biography of Martha Gellhorn. I wrote, in other words, realizing that there would be other books about her, but also believing that some of my research could not be duplicated and that the story I told— no matter how much subsequent work modified it—would remain an essential part of her biography. John Lukacs points out in *The Hitler of History* that one of the finest biographies of Hitler appeared in 1935. In *George III and the Historians*, Herbert Butterfield emphasizes that the first biographies of the king continue to influence and remain a part of later, more comprehensive accounts. In *Tread Softly, for You Tread on My Life*, eminent New Zealand biographer Michael King calls the kind of work I had in a mind a "primary biography," the book that has to be "followed by books from later writers ... who colonise the narrative and analytical spaces left vacant by the primary biographer."

But how to pitch the proposal? The first paragraph achieved torque by emphasizing Gellhorn the quester/traveler/protestor and friend of the famous:

> 1908. The American century had turned and Martha Gellhorn rode the streetcars of St. Louis dreaming of better worlds. The daughter of a prominent St. Louis physician, an emigrant from Germany, and of Edna Fischel, a distinguished community leader and founder of The League of Women Voters, Martha Gellhorn has never been content with the status quo. Always an independent minded traveler and reporter, she has found it difficult to stay in one place. As she said to her third husband, T. S. Matthews, "I dislike all governments. And I don't like whole nations at a gulp. I like bits and pieces of every one, some more, some less." Leaving Bryn Mawr after three restless years, she ventured to Europe in the early 1930s to model clothes, to investigate social movements, and to write novels. An early anti–Fascist, she took a French journalist for her lover and first husband, then returned to the United States in the mid-thirties to work for and write about Roosevelt's depression era federal relief program. Her best seller, *The Trouble I've Seen*, brought her to the attention of H. G. Wells and Eleanor Roosevelt (already a friend of Martha's mother).

The second paragraph set up the theme of the no-nonsense beauty and of the only woman who got the best of Hemingway:

> Nearly a perfect beauty, Gellhorn has always bridled at an imperfect world. Hers is a restless quest for an ideal way of life and a pursuit of world-shattering events that have strengthened her personal resolve. She has visited more than half the countries of the world, lived for long periods in seven of them, and as a journalist she has covered every major war from Spain in the 1930s to Vietnam in the 1970s. Much more than her ex-husband Ernest Hemingway, she has been an adventurer. Indeed, she was much too tough a woman for him to handle, and she walked out on him when his talent and his ego were turning to fat. She has always been her own person and has never traded on the reputation of her famous husband or on her own exploits. Rather than emulate the self-aggrandizing example of Papa Hemingway, she has stood alone, viewing herself and her times with self-lacerating and shrewd humor.

Then I quoted Gellhorn's letter to me about Hellman to show that I had her attention and that my subject exemplified the activist writer:

Gellhorn is extraordinary for having accomplished so much fine work without having fallen prey to the blandishments of success. She has written extraordinary novels and journalism that are remarkably faithful and impassioned accounts of her time. She has never become complacent or made herself the object of attention. The excitement of her life lies in the way her forceful personality has come into conflict with her times without overriding social and political realities. In this respect, she was a much more deeply engaged writer than her more famous counterparts, such as Hemingway and Hellman. Gellhorn has gotten "good and mad" more than once at Lillian Hellman, Ernest Hemingway, Madame Chiang Kai-Shek, and many others. Ralph Ingersoll, the publisher of PM, remembered that when he failed to get *The Spanish Earth*—the film Hemingway narrated for the Loyalist cause—widely distributed, Gellhorn "took a whole morning off to give me the most thorough tongue-lashing I can ever remember getting from anybody. I was incompetent, unappreciative (of the sacrifices Ernest had made) and a phony slob."

Overall I wanted to burnish the image of a woman and writer deserving of more attention and respect. I appeared as her advocate—even as her outraged ally—against her more self-regarding contemporaries. In other words, this unauthorized biography would not strip the subject of her glamour; on the contrary, she deserved a bigger build-up putting the preposterous claims of her peers in proper perspective:

Unlike many writers, Gellhorn's talents did not decline with age, although she did suffer from prolonged writer's blocks, and she remained true to her early ideals. As a young woman, Gellhorn thought reporting the truth would help to make a better world. When she saw that her journalism had little impact on public opinion and that her reporting on the dangers of Fascism went unheeded, she was disappointed but she did not despair. As she says in *The Face of War*, her collection of war reports, "the act of keeping the record straight is valuable in itself. Serious, careful, honest journalism is essential ... because it is a form of honorable behavior." Now in her eightieth year, Martha Gellhorn remains on the cutting edge of history.

Looking at my proposal now, I am impressed by how much I wanted to honor and even pay homage to Gellhorn's sturdy independence, endurance, and continuing relevance. But then such layering of qualities is *de rigueur* in enticing pitches. I wonder what reviewers would have made of this proposal considering their automatic assumption that an unauthorized biography is an attack on the subject and that the unauthorized biographer must have unscrupulous aims. But more about my motivations and reviewer responses later. At the time, I had other concerns.

Gellhorn might be an important subject, but she was hardly a household name, and publishers have to be convinced that there is a market for the book, or that a demand can be created. Gellhorn had little standing in the canon of American literature and could not be presented as an unrecognized genius. I could not make a case for analyzing her fiction and nonfiction since she was not taught in classrooms. Even more troublesome, she might—as living subjects sometimes do—use the copyright act as a form of censorship to attempt to halt publication of a biography; that is, she could refuse permission to quote from her published work. I would then be forced to paraphrase and quote very sparingly under "fair use"—then of diminished value to biographers and historians because of the Salinger case. So I had to make a virtue out of necessity, showing how paraphrase, in this case, should prevail over quotation:

> *Martha Gellhorn: Her Life and Times* will be written as an adventure story, not as a literary biography. Her novels and journalism will not be discussed as literary works but as the stuff of her experience. The personal feelings she did not put into her journalism are often dealt with in her fiction, which is heavily autobiographical. For example, Hemingway becomes a character in her novel, *A Stricken Field,* and he is the model for other characters in her short stories. Both her fiction and her journalism contain vivid evocations of the places she has visited and lived in.

I then quoted a passage from A *Stricken Field,* in which Gellhorn presents herself in the thinly disguised figure of Mary Douglas, a war correspondent reporting on the tragedy of Czechoslovakia in 1938. Hitler is about to absorb it into his hideous Third Reich. Mary has learned to be a premier journalist, to be objective, to avoid partisanship. She cannot allow herself to get personally involved in the lives of the displaced people she is writing about; she must not permit herself to act on the love she feels for the families that will be sent to certain death in German concentration camps. Instead she knows she should

> see some big executives, coal and sugar and textiles and God knows what not, and find out how this has hit them; there are politicians to interview too, with quotable sentences; and some high army men; and perhaps even literary celebrities. I've got to get a story, articles, the rounded picture as they say, complete bird's-eye view of tragedy and defeat by our foreign correspondent Miss X.... No propaganda, they would say. We want the inside story. Make it clear, make it colorful, make it lively. If I knew how, I would write a lament. I would tell how I heard the children sing once in Spain, in Barcelona, that cold and blowing March when the bombers came over faster than wind, so that it would all happen in three unending minutes, but if you saw them they were hanging in the sky not moving, slow and easy, taking their time, you'd think, not worried about anything. But usually the planes were higher than you could see or hear, and suddenly the streets beneath them fountained up, in a deep round

echoing underground all-over-the-sky roaring that seemed never to finish, and the windows bent inward and the furniture shook on the floor
and in the stillness afterwards you would hear one voice, wild and thin
and alone, crying out sharply, and then silence. I heard the children at
school, between air raids, sitting obediently on small red painted chairs
& around a low piano; between air raids. The teacher struck chords on
the piano and the children stood and lifted their faces to the dangerous
sky and sang as softly and sweetly as you will ever hear an old song
about being a good child, and sleep now, sleep well. I heard them again
today. It is all the same. So who wanted to know that, and I better get to
work. Be careful, Mary Douglas told herself, you're only a working journalist. It is better not to see too much, if no one will listen to you.

I used this passage as my springboard for showing the primary material
out of which I would compose a narrative that explained why Gellhorn
wrote fiction and why journalism could not entirely satisfy her. As my
proposal noted:

Sometimes Gellhorn has Mary talking to herself; sometimes a third person narrator conveys Mary's thoughts; sometimes the subject is "you" as
Gellhorn gets her readers to imagine what it would be like to cover war
at tremendous cost to our own sensibilities. As Gellhorn depicts Douglas's feelings she simultaneously reveals her reasons for novel writing: it
comes out of the personal anguish she could not put into her journalism.
As accurate as her news stories were, they deprived her of the most intimate and profound feelings. Gellhorn was driven to writing novels for
her own emotional survival. Fiction became a way of recapturing her
deepest sentiments. In fiction she could be true to what she had seen
and heard. Thirty years later, in Vietnam, when Gellhorn tried to report
once more on displaced families and on indiscriminate American bombing that burned, maimed, and killed Vietnamese children, her reports
were considered to be "too tough" for the American public to read. No
American newspaper would take her articles, and she had to publish
them in the English press. A *Stricken Field* proved prophetic: only in fiction would she be able to come to terms with the tragedy of her life and
her times.

For my crescendo, I listed the key action moments:

In re-creating Gellhorn's life and times I will be able to draw very
specifically on her memories of Spain in 1937, of Prague in 1938, of
Finland in 1939, of the Battle of the Bulge, of her years in Mexico, the
Caribbean, Africa, the Nuremberg and Eichmann trials. Gellhorn's
writings will be employed as part of the narrative of her life. My biography, in other words, will read like a novel and will be enjoyed as a movie,
with several scenes unfolding as they occur either in Gellhorn's writing
or in the extensive interviewing and research I will conduct for this
book.

The immodesty is shameless, I know, but my Hellman biography had made the cover of *The New York Times Book Review,* and I wanted to show that the Gellhorn story was even more sensational, although I had no intention of sensationalizing it. I did not have to pump up my story for an audience I described as

> very large and broadly based. First of all, she has lived with such incredible vitality and known so many important public figures, from Hemingway and his cohorts to the Roosevelts, Adlai Stevenson, Leonard Bernstein, and the Kennedys. She is a feisty, independent, beautiful woman who has been willing to risk her looks—indeed her very life—for what she has believed in. Next to her—especially during the years of the second World War—Hemingway seems cowardly. Her energy has been boundless, and she has the kind of complexity found in a good fictional character. She will be easy to identify with. If she has been an intrepid traveler, she has also been a comfort-loving, complaining American. Much of her comic writing involves her admitted fetish about cleanliness, and she is not afraid to show her own fussiness even if it places her at a disadvantage. She sometimes portrays herself as the highhanded liberal brought low by the exigencies of existence everyone must encounter sooner or later. When she writes about her trips abroad in *Travels with Myself and Another,* she reveals her opinionated side and her stupidity in some truly hilarious scenes. As a woman of character, Gellhorn will capture many readers. As a writer involved in many of the significant events of this century, she will attract still more readers.

So the biography would show her self-confessed faults but never lose empathy for its heroine. And (good news for publishers of the biography!) Gellhorn was coming back into print:

> Penguin Virago Books is beginning to reissue her novels. *A Stricken Field* has already appeared in paperback and another novel, *Liana,* is scheduled to be published this year. Atlantic Monthly Press is reissuing *The Face of War* and *The View from the Ground* in November [1988].

The proposal's closing passages are rather repetitive, but then proposals are like commercials: The message has to be crystal clear, the pitch (to use the latest cant) "transparent." I've often said that the best book proposals are platonic; that is, publishers are really buying the idea of the book you want to write. Raising the possibility of difficulties, however, alarms editors. The writer is often advised to minimize any problems an unauthorized biography is likely to encounter. In fact, for the Gellhorn proposal I did not even hint that there might be a problem. Since Jackie Onassis (still at Doubleday) proposed the project, it did not occur to me to raise difficulties that (wishful thinking!) might not arise. In any event, I portrayed the biographical enterprise as a feat, an adventure in itself, following the bold stride of Gellhorn's life. Doubleday bought the book on that basis (though my editor became Shaye Areheart, not Jackie), so I don't know what might have happened if my proposal had had to confront a more critical response from other publishers. I don't know why Jackie did not edit the book, though I suspect that because she knew Gellhorn, Jackie's direct participation would have been awkward, especially if Gellhorn disapproved of the project. A decade later, while revising my Gellhorn biography for British publication, I learned that having Jackie on board would not have made a crucial difference—but that is to anticipate the denouement of this chapter.

The Peril

Contract in hand, I wrote to Martha Gellhorn, enclosing a biographer's gift package (a copy of my biography of Marilyn Monroe and an article on William and Estelle Faulkner I had published in *South Atlantic Quarterly*). I reminded her that we had corresponded about Lillian Hellman a year earlier. I told her about my contract to write her biography. I wanted to interview her. She responded with praise for my article on the Faulkners. I wrote well, but she did not believe writing about the personal lives of artists illuminated their art, and she did not think anyone's personal life was anybody else's business. As for her, she detested the idea of biography and planned to outlive as many of her biographers as possible, for she knew they would do a perfectly dreadful job on her life. Her answer to me was the same answer she gave to everyone: NO BIOGRAPHY. I was not to take it personally. I liked the letter very much and did not take it personally. I was not asking for permission to write about her. I have always had my doubts about how an authorized biographer can maintain an independent point of view. I drafted a reply to Gellhorn's letter, marshaling arguments in favor of the kind of biography I thought she would like, and then I never sent the letter. I realized that I could not please her but should simply write my book.

Gellhorn did not take long to retaliate. As soon as she discovered that my British agent was trying to sell the book, she put the word out in *Vogue* (April 1988), telling interviewer Victoria Glendinning that she was "doing her damndest to make sure there will never, ever, be a biography of Martha Gellhorn." Gellhorn then referred to an "academic kook" attempting a biography anyway:

> I'm writing around asking anyone he might approach to tell him to sod off. I hate modern biographies of writers who are not public figures and

not fair game. The only thing biographers are interested in are your love affairs and your eccentricities. A writer should be read, not written about. I wish to retain my lifelong obscurity.

Although my proposal had emphasized Gellhorn's refusal to aggrandize her life, she surpassed my hyperbole by referring to her "lifelong obscurity." After all, marrying Ernest Hemingway is no way to lead a retiring existence. *Collier's* magazine featured Gellhorn as their blonde and beautiful war correspondent. Eleanor Roosevelt built up Gellhorn in her "My Day" newspaper columns. How many obscure figures get an interview published in *Vogue?* In the *Vogue* interview, Gellhorn referred to herself as "an historic monument."

Certain critics have supposed that Gellhorn's resistance turned me against her. It did make me ask more critical questions about her life and career, but I never resented her opposition to my biography—not only because of my conflict of interest theory of biography, but because her response to my biography contributed to my understanding of her nature. In other words, the very act of proposing to write her biography prompted her to provide me with more biographical evidence. For example, an Author's Guild staffer told me that she called the organization to complain about my book. Couldn't they do something about it? Well, I was a member of the Author's Guild, the staffer told her: "How can we take the part of one writer against another?"

Then I received a letter from Bill Buford, at the time editor of *Granta*, a curious choice to serve as Gellhorn's emissary. According to Gellhorn (*Vanity Fair*, November 1989), Buford

> "did something absolutely terrible to me, and everyone thought I'd never forgive him. He simply stole something from my book, *The View from the Ground*, which was being published in America. He claims he asked me. But when I do business, I expect a letter or something. He just pinched a part of the book and put it in the magazine. I seriously thought of killing him, but I was too busy." Did she sue? "Don't be ridiculous! I called him a monster, a creep, and told everyone I'd never speak to him again. Then came the big bouquet of flowers and the abject letter of apology, full of lies of course. And I was back talking to him within three weeks."

Writing on Gellhorn's behalf, Buford expressed his dismay about my biography. Didn't I know she had an authorized biographer? This did not square with anything Gellhorn had said about her loathing of biographies. No one I had interviewed mentioned an authorized biographer, and I suspected that Gellhorn might be doing a Lillian Hellman—naming someone to write the official, uncontested version of her life. At any rate, the very suggestion that she had one biographer prompted me to wonder why she could not have two.

The Doubleday lawyers advised me to write Buford a short letter simply saying I was doing nothing "actionable"—that is, Gellhorn would have no grounds for a lawsuit. Buford's letter did not seem to disturb my publisher, I thought. But it did contain outrageous claims that I could not use her image and more enforceable threats that I would not be allowed to quote from her writings. Buford specifically invoked the Salinger case, which had virtually wiped out fair use for unpublished material. But I had already worked out my rationale for dealing with hostile subjects and literary estates.

The Buford–Gellhorn axis stimulated my competitive zeal and imagination. I began to write ahead of my evidence (explanation forthcoming). I had already been to St. Louis to interview her childhood friends. I had the good fortune of having an "in"—that is, I had the backing of Delia Mares, a close friend of Martha's mother and a friend of Ann Waldron, my friend and a distinguished biographer. Delia provided me with a list of people to see—all of whom were generous with their memories. I worried that they would question me about Martha's attitude toward my project. But there were few questions. Either my interviewees did not care what Martha thought (many of them had not seen her in decades) or they assumed I had her encouragement, although 1 never pretended to have her approval. They were to varying degrees proud and critical of Martha and fonder of her mother who, unlike Martha, remained affectionately loyal to St. Louis. Washington University in St. Louis had Gellhorn letters in her mother's archive, and other libraries there had important records dealing with her family. The John Burroughs School, which had an important role in shaping Martha's literary interests, supplied me with the school magazine to which she contributed many essays, stories, plays, and poems. A tip from Hemingway biographer Michael Reynolds led to an important cache of Gellhorn letters in the archives of *Collier's* magazine housed conveniently at the New York Public Library. Butler Library at Columbia had an oral history interview with Walter Gellhorn, Martha's older brother, which supplied many valuable details about family life. An online search turned up Gellhorn's letters to an early lover, Joseph Pennell, whose papers at the University of Oregon were copied and sent to me. Carlos Baker had kept his correspondence with Gellhorn and deposited it at Princeton's Firestone Library. Many other archives contained Hemingway/Gellhorn letters as well.

A word from another Hemingway biographer, Kenneth Lynn, sent me to I Tatti near Florence to read Gellhorn's correspondence with Bernard Berenson. That proved particularly important because I had been very curious about Gellhorn's third and last marriage to T. S. Matthews, one of *Time's* editors and her boss (briefly) at *The New Republic,* and about her affair with Dr. David Gurewitsch, which Joseph Lash had described in his book about Eleanor Roosevelt. I had already written a long chapter on the Gellhorn/Matthews marriage based only on Matthews's books, many of them autobiographical (though he did not directly discuss his marriage to Martha), on oral history interviews with Matthews's colleagues available at Columbia, and on what Matthews's *Time* colleagues had told me about the couple. I had no direct testimony, however, from Gellhorn or Matthews in the form of letters or any other documentation. In response to my query about his marriage to Gellhorn, Matthews quoted Macbeth's lines to Banquo's ghost: "Hence, horrible shadow! Unreal mockery, hence!" So I wrote a story of the marriage based on my reading of Matthews's character and on everything I had come to know about Martha Gellhorn. I did not make up any events, but my reading of the marriage's psychological dynamic remained, for the moment, purely speculative.

Imagine my relief and delight to find that in her letters to Berenson, Gellhorn confirmed my view of her marriage to Matthews. My guess had been that she had married him for stability and that he had promised not to interfere with her professional life and her urge to travel. Getting journalistic assignments after World War 11 proved difficult for Gellhorn since she had to compete with younger reporters and had—as she said—lost her place "in the queue" (of journalists and editors called on to cover news stories) by spending so much of the early 1950s in Mexico writing fiction and taking it easy. Much of Matthews's family life and his stuffy idea of the literary world bored her silly, I had supposed in the narrative I wrote before I had the evidence, and she wrote as much to Berenson. I was amazed, in fact, at her candor about this marriage, which looked doomed from the start but which Gellhorn half-heartedly wanted to try because she thought it would give her adopted son Sandy a sense of security, and Matthews so obviously adored her. They made a handsome couple and shared many political convictions, including a pronounced distaste for their native land.

Gellhorn also told Berenson about Dr. David Gurewitsch, a confidant of Eleanor Roosevelt's who fell deeply in love with Martha—much to Mrs. Roosevelt's dismay (as I learned from Joseph Lash's book). Gurewitsch, Martha confessed, was the only man who had truly excited her physically.

He wanted to marry Martha, and Mrs. Roosevelt (also in love with Gurewitsch) watched in dismay as Martha seemed to toy with him, refusing to leave Mexico even though Gurewitsch would lose his practice by leaving New York to join her. Ultimately, Martha backed away and the affair subsided. A later encounter with Gurewitsch again excited Gellhorn, but she did not act upon her feelings for him.

With the Berenson correspondence in hand, I now realized why Gurewitsch's last wife, Edna, had agreed to talk with me and then just minutes before the interview had called me to say she had changed her mind and would not talk. Based on the Berenson letters, Lash's book, and Martha's letters to Eleanor Roosevelt at the Hyde Park Library, I put together the following story, which I outlined to Edna as soon as I returned from Italy:

> Mrs. Roosevelt was shocked not only that Martha had played with Gurewitsch's emotions but also that Martha had preferred to stay in Mexico rather than join the man she said she loved. What is more, this was the Martha Gellhorn whom Mrs. Roosevelt had touted in her columns as an intrepid world traveler and reporter of injustice, especially of cruelty to women and children. Martha seemed to have fallen into a decadent life in Mexico, and Mrs. Roosevelt withdrew in disgust from her protégé.

When I called Edna, I asked her simply to listen to my story and then to comment—if she felt able to do so. When I finished, Edna said, "Well, if you know that much, I might as well tell you the rest." She confirmed what I had surmised and added that Mrs. Roosevelt had been very upset about the way Martha had treated her adopted son Sandy. I wasn't surprised to learn this because I had seen a few of Martha's letters to her mother (Martha had meant to destroy them but somehow missed them when she went through her mother's papers) which complained about Sandy—largely because he was fat and had no discipline or ambition. "Mrs. Roosevelt was very rarely critical about people personally," Edna told me. "But she was critical of Martha." To which I responded, "Then I know why you decided not to talk to me. You did not know Martha, yet you would have had to report what Mrs. Roosevelt's said about Martha." Edna agreed.

Sandy, by the way, I did not contact. I did not want to put him on the spot, and it seemed unlikely that he would be willing to talk to me anyway. For much the same reasons, I did not try to contact Martha's older brother, Walter Gellhorn, or her younger brother Alfred. There were others, of course, who refused to speak to me. Martha had friends in Mexico who had letters from her, but they would not speak to me or part with the letters. General James Gavin, one of Martha's lovers, did not answer my letters. The Hemingway family (Martha had remained on very good terms with them) would have nothing to do with me. I had my share of rejections. But the exhilaration of the chase, so to speak, drove me on, and I never wavered, writing a complete draft of the book in ten months. I turned in my manuscript and awaited word from my publisher.

Nothing Ever Happens to the Brave

And I waited... And I waited... Weeks, then months went by. My editor liked the book, but it had been bucked to the legal department. More weeks went by. My agent had wisely put a clause in the contract obligating Doubleday to accept or reject my book within sixty days. Several weeks after the sixty days—with no word on my book's fate—I asked my agent to take it to another publisher. This is a risky proposition. On the one hand, Doubleday had violated its own contract, which meant I could keep the first half of the advance. On the other hand, how would another publisher respond to an unauthorized biography the subject opposed and the original publisher could not make up its mind about? Fortunately, Toni Lo Popolo at St. Martin's Press had edited my Lillian Hellman biography and wanted to buy the Gellhorn. She had been outbid by Doubleday and could not secure the backing of her boss, Tom McCormick, to increase her offer. Now my agent returned to her, and Toni got editorial board approval during a McCormick out-of-town trip. She had the book she had always wanted and for a price McCormick could not complain about.

St. Martin's had had a rousing success with *Straight on Till Morning: The Biography of Beryl Markham,* and they wanted a title like that for my book. I proposed *Nothing Ever Happens to the Brave: The Story of Martha Gellhorn.* The first part of the title is a quotation from Hemingway's *A Farewell to Arms,* which Martha had used as a kind of motto in one of her youthful letters long before she met him. The phrase captured her intrepid spirit. "Too many words," said the jacket design people. But they found no better alternative and jammed onto the front cover not only the long title but an overbearing explanation, "The Adventurous Life of America's Most Glamorous and Courageous War Correspondent," which also became an ad in *Vanity* Fair—the only ad, I believe, for the book.

St. Martin's hired a law firm to vet the book. I sat through days of consultations with lawyers who excised much of the book's color. Applying fair use I had been very careful to quote only those words and phrases (rarely sentences) of Martha's that captured her vitality. (I will give examples of the excisions when I deal with my revised Gellhorn biography).

But the lawyers were determined to avoid even the remotest possibility of a copyright infringement suit, which is the only kind of suit that could lead to an injunction that would prevent distribution of a book. Before Congress amended the Copyright Act and clearly extended fair use to include quotations from unpublished papers, publishers in 1990 were coming up with various policies that virtually destroyed fair use. The flavor of my interactions with the lawyers comes through in my letter to Toni Lo Popolo (December 1, 1989):

> On the phone yesterday you requested that I send you a letter concerning revisions of my biography of Martha Gellhorn.... I am willing to supply St. Martin's attorney with copies of every Gellhorn unpublished letter I used as a source. My book is fully documented. I have quoted less than 100 words from Gellhorn's unpublished work and used her letters for facts, not for paraphrasing.

I had spent hours on the phone, I told Toni, with an attorney who had suggested hundreds of revisions on the minutest matters concerning not only Gellhorn's unpublished letters but also my very sparing use of unpublished material by other figures. Respected biographies rely on the fair use of hundreds of unpublished sources. To ask the biographer to get permission to quote a few words is burdensome—indeed it is punitive and unprofitable. The main party here is Gellhorn. I do not make enough use of anyone else's work for them to claim invasion of privacy or copyright infringement. I won the argument in so far as I did not have to request permission to quote a few words here and there from sources other than Gellhorn, but even my one hundred words from Gellhorn were ditched.

St. Martin's did not seem so worried about libel. A successful suit in this country would discredit but not kill the book since the burden of proof is on the plaintiff. In England, threatened libel suits often do kill a book because the burden is on the defendant, and publishers and authors start from the premise that they have to prove their innocence. In fact, Martha's threatened libel suit in England doomed publication there.

Just when I thought the legal reading over, St. Martin's got a fax from Gellhorn and a warning from a legal firm she had hired. Although St. Martin's had been careful about distributing advance copies of the book, it is difficult—short of issuing an embargo on galleys—to control their distribution. In this most nerve-wracking of times, I may have contributed to handing over the galleys to Martha—a suspicion that occurred to me only after the book's publication, and which I will explain shortly.

Gellhorn's fax had to do mainly with objections to my handling of her years with Hemingway, of the Gurewitsch–Roosevelt story, and of

Sandy. She left virtually the first third of the book untouched—which is perhaps the most original part and is based on my investigations in St. Louis. She repeated the gist of her attack in a letter (August 26, 1990) to Bill Buford later published in *The New Yorker* (June 22 and 29, 1998): "Rollyson's book is a paean of hate: Hemingway would have adored it." She objected to my using her fiction as part of the narrative of her life— fair enough, since biographies are often censured for confusing fiction and fact, although this is not grounds for a suit. And she called me a liar, though her fax showed that she considered a lie any statement anyone made about her life with Hemingway that contradicted her own version of events. I cannot quote from Gellhorn's fax, but here is the rebuttal I sent to St. Martin's lawyers on August 30, 1990:

> I am in receipt of Martha Gellhorn's objections to my biography of her. I will reply to them by taking her paragraphs in order.
>   **Paragraph 1.** I did not write my book in spite, and I do not hate Martha Gellhorn.
>   **Paragraph 2.** I did not make a "proposal" to Ms. Gellhorn, which she then rejected. I wrote her a letter stating I had been offered a contract to write a biography and that naturally I would like to interview her. I was not asking for her permission, and my biography was never meant to be authorized. She had no foundation for believing the matter of a biography was "closed." I never said or implied that I would do the book only with her permission. She dislikes my interpretation of her letter [the one she sent saying she did not want a biography written], but I do not see any reason to make any changes in that interpretation.
>   **Paragraph 3.** Contrary to Ms. Gellhorn's belief, I had access to many papers and correspondence. Even so, it is not unusual for other papers to be restricted or for biographers to have limited use of archives. A literary biography of Marianne Moore was just published which is based on limited use of her archives. The biographer did no interviewing for the book. Again, this is not unusual. Many biographers—distinguished academics like Charles Molesworth (Moore's biographer)—must labor under certain limitations.
>   **Paragraph 4.** Ms. Gellhorn's assumptions about professional biographers are erroneous. Many unauthorized biographies are written without the cooperation of their subjects and their families. Indeed, I shudder to think what biographies would look like if they had to have the sanction of their subjects. My methods for my book on Ms. Gellhorn were no different from those I employed for my biographies of Lillian Hellman and Marilyn Monroe. Ms. Gellhorn says she has not read the Hemingway biographies, yet she is sure she is portrayed as a "hateful personage." I have read these books, and I do not think she is portrayed as "hateful"; nor is she treated that way in my biography. I also see nothing wrong in hoping that the "large Hemingway public" she mentions will be inter-

ested in my book. She says I have a "personal hatred" for her. I do not. She says "I cannot leap to conclusions," but that is exactly what she has done. Certainly she is shown to have some faults, but this hardly makes my book an exercise in spite.

Paragraph 5. Ms. Gellhorn levels several charges: "incorrect facts, distorting spite, provably untrue gossip, absurd unfounded conclusions, dishonest manipulation of facts, libelous gossip (usually from 'confidential' sources), or libelous commentary by Mr. Rollyson." In subsequent paragraphs I will reply to Ms. Gellhorn specific instances of her charges. But here let me say that Ms. Gellhorn never defines what she means by the term "libelous" and that I do not believe I have libeled her in any way. My manuscript was very thoroughly checked by Szold and Brandwen, and I see no point in putting Ms. Gellhorn to the task of three or four days of work.

Paragraph 6. This paragraph objects to my methods as a biographer. This paragraph is an interesting exercise in literary criticism, but I do not see any cause for changing any passages in my biography. I am not the first biographer to employ the methods Ms. Gellhorn deplores, and I am sure I will not be the last.

Paragraph 7. Ms. Gellhorn objects to the theme of my biography and characterizes it in a certain way. Whether she is right or not, I don't see any reason to change my book.

Paragraph 8. "The entire book is defamatory and intended to be," says Ms. Gellhorn, leaping to another conclusion. I don't see anything "defamatory and libelous," and Ms. Gellhorn does not define those terms.

Now for the specific passages she cites by page number from my uncorrected proof:

p. 94. My source for passage describing Hemingway and Gellhorn as "kissing and carrying on" is a book by James McLendon, *Papa: Hemingway in Key West* (Miami, Florida: E. A. Seeman Publishing Company, 1972), p. 166. This book was published almost twenty years ago and has been cited by other biographers, and I cite this source in my notes to the biography. I don't see why this is a "libel," as Ms. Gellhorn claims.

p. 98. Ms. Gellhorn is correct. The sentence she quotes is from Jeffrey Meyers, and I do cite Meyers in my notes. I see no libel.

p. 99. 1 do not say Hemingway and Gellhorn were lovers before Spain. If I had, Ms. Gellhorn would surely have cited that passage. She also does not quote the rest of the paragraph, which is about Hemingway's "expertise" in war. It is not about their love life.

p. 210. The passage Ms. Gellhorn objects to is from a taped interview. I don't understand why it is "libelous gossip." It is something a husband told his wife, and where, exactly, is the libel?

p. 218. Ms. Gellhorn means the passage on page 238 beginning "There's no need...." This is not from a confidential source. My notes plainly indicate that my information is taken from Jeffrey Meyers's biography of Hemingway. Once again, I do not see her grounds for charging "libel."

p. 241. Why is [Gellhorn] making "cutting remarks" about Mary Hemingway a "libel"? Ms. Gellhorn's marks no pages but protests my "personal conclusion" about David G.[urewitsch] and Mrs. R.[oosevelt]. My interpretation does not differ markedly from my source, Joseph Lash, and the Roosevelt family authorized his work.

p. 248. The paragraph beginning, "Finally, no longer willing to wait..." and ending "no reply to this astonishing letter" is all from one source, Joseph Lash's book on Mrs. Roosevelt. It is true that I do not cite a specific source for this paragraph, but the paragraph is clearly part of the story I got from Lash's book.

p. 276. Ms. Gellhorn objects to my characterization of her friendship with Mrs. Roosevelt. I listened to Ms. Gellhorn on tape at the Roosevelt Library and I had a transcript of the tape. It sounded to me as though Gellhorn "complained that Roosevelt did not visit her anymore." The rest of the paragraph is a confidential source, a source I found to be reliable, and I have this source on tape. Ms. Gellhorn calls the passage "false therefore libelous." I do not believe these two terms, "false and libelous," are synonymous, and I do not think the passage is false or libelous.

p. 281. I do not say Gellhorn abandoned Sandy. Earlier I do say she put him in boarding school. I don't "bring in Sandy," as she says. She herself wrote an article in a national magazine about her adoption of Sandy. Readers will naturally want to know about him.

p. 298 Saying Sandy did not have an easy childhood is not the same thing as saying Gellhorn was a "bad mother," which is what she alleges. I don't use such labels. I don't say Gellhorn was a good mother, a perfect mother, and I certainly don't say she was a bad mother. There is nothing libelous in what I said.

p. 301. Ms. Gellhorn seems to have some quarrel with Ms. Symington [a Gellhorn friend in St. Louis who spoke about Hemingway]. I see no reason to change the passage Ms. Gellhorn dislikes. I have my interview with Symington on tape. Indeed, all my interviews have been tape recorded.

p. 322 Ms. Gellhorn objects to a passage in my Epilogue to the biography. Let the record show that I deleted this passage a few weeks ago when I saw the "first pass" pages of my book. The references to *Mommie Dearest* and Anthony West were deleted then (I had compared Gellhorn's tense relationship with her son to Rebecca West's upbringing of her son Anthony).

p. 324. The "confidential source" Ms. Gellhorn objects to is stating an opinion, an opinion I heard from more than one person who knew Gellhorn. I don't see how it is a libel. Ms. Gellhorn does appear in a Hollywood feature on celebrities. I have the videotape of Hedda Hopper's film of Gellhorn at Sun Valley with Hemingway.

p. 326. Ms. Gellhorn objects to my listing her in my Acknowledgments. All I do is acknowledge people who reply to my letters of inquiry. I do not say these people actually gave me information. This is my practice in all my books. As a biographer, I write many letters that people do not answer. I am grateful when they do—even if they do not offer help or information. In fact, in Gellhorn's case, she did provide me with information that I used in the prologue to my book. I also make clear in that prologue that the book was written without her cooperation and that it incurred her displeasure. Surely I have been honest and forthright in citing my sources. I don't see any reason to change a word of my book. Any time any sort of criticism of Gellhorn is raised she calls it false and libelous. This is stretching the meaning of those words so widely that it amounts to excising from the book every interpretation of her behavior that she disputes.

I stand by the accuracy of my book.

To my surprise, Gellhorn's fax made little impression at St. Martin's—perhaps because Gellhorn alleged no copyright infringement and the charges of libel were so flimsy. The book had already been vetted, and after one more meeting I agreed to change a few words which did not alter the facts but simply paid deference to Gellhorn's injured feelings. So far as I know, the publisher never heard another word from Gellhorn or her lawyers and the book appeared as scheduled, published on Pearl Harbor Day, December 7, 1990.

Reviews and Suspicions

In my experience, reviews of biographies (perhaps of all books) vary so widely as to make one cynical about their value as assessment, literary or otherwise:

Rollyson frames a picture of her courage, contrariness and complexity, and in the process further dismantles the Hemingway legend [*Publishers Weekly*].

A worthy and highly readable attempt to limn one of the memorable characters of the American century [*Kirkus Reviews*].

Rollyson ... chums out prose that is one part academic cannon fodder and two parts *People* magazine schmaltz [*Los Angeles Times*].

If he seldom sounds inspired, he achieves an impressive portrait all the same, especially of his subject's childhood and her forebears [*Washington Post*].

[Gellhorn] knows, better than most women, that we must never let the men have the last word. They always get it wrong [*The New York Times Book Review*].

But the war that is most engaging in Rollyson's otherwise clodhopping chronology is the battle of the sexes [*Philadelphia Inquirer*].

These excerpts roughly reflect the mood of reviewers, and since they were not startlingly different from the mixed reception of my Lillian Hellman biography, they made little impression on me.

Then my publisher sent me a review from the *Portland Oregonian* that included comments by a scholar working, the reviewer said, on a biography of Gellhorn. The scholar mentioned that she had "talked with Gellhorn recently" and volunteered that "Martha is 82 now and suffers from arthritis." In the summer of 1990, this scholar contacted me on the recommendation of a friend of mine. She said she was working on Martha Gellhorn's fiction and thought that my biography might be of some help to her. I told her about my galleys and my reluctance to show the book to her before publication. There had been difficulties with Gellhorn, and I was obliged to be cautious. But on the phone I decided to send the galleys to her as a courtesy to a fellow scholar along with an agreement stipulating that they were only for her use, that she was not to make copies, and that she would return the galleys after she had read them. In our phone conversation, she mentioned nothing about writing a biography. What is more, she never returned the galleys or the form she agreed to sign. I sent a letter of protest to her department chair.

I got a quick response from my fellow scholar. My letter to her conveys the gist of her defense:

> At the end of your letter you express a "hope that upon receiving" your "clarification" I will "see fit to clear" your name of my "harsh accusations in a subsequent letter to my department head and dean." I regret that I cannot comply. You say that you never received a form to sign and that you did not know that you were to return the galleys. I was not there to open the package you received, so I cannot say what happened to the form. What I know is that we discussed such a form in your initial call to me. I told you I was very concerned about limiting the distribution of the galleys and that I would need a signed guarantee as well as the letter you sent to me. We made an agreement then. That you may not have received the form does not absolve you of the agreement.
>
> You are right that my "suspicion and anger" was "aroused" by the Paul Pintarich review of my book. Here is why: Except for your letter of June 13, 1990, I have had no response from you about my galleys. I had no idea how you were going to use them or how your project was developing. Then I read about you in the newspaper, and it says you are writing a biography of Gellhorn and that you are "mildly critical" of my book. Put yourself in my position. I have written four biographies. Like you, I have relied on the generosity and graciousness of colleagues in researching my books. Two scholars are currently using sources I developed for my Hellman and Gellhorn biographies. They have been in communication with me. I know how they are using my work. If the Pintarich article

embarrassed you, why didn't you contact me? Did you seriously think I would not see the review? And I think it is a poor excuse to blame the reporter. What is he expected to think when you say you just got off the phone with Martha Gellhorn? Most literary critics do not communicate in this way with the subjects of their scholarship. Some do, but how would a reporter be expected to make that distinction, especially when you use such loose language—that you are "working on" Gellhorn. I placed a call to Paul Pintarich, which he has not returned. So I don't have his version of your conversation. Again, what I find really strange was that you were anxious to clarify things with members of your department but not with me. Is this the action of a responsible and scrupulous scholar? Having not heard from you, how could I not be suspicious? Even now, all I get from you is the galleys with passages marked in ink. In my exchanges with scholars there has been some discussion or at least some attempt on their part to inform me of the progress of their work. I am not used to getting my reports about them in the newspapers.

I have in hand a very strong letter of support from your department chairman. I take his remarks very seriously, and I am heartened to know of your high reputation in your department. But I cannot, under the circumstances, do what you ask: clear your name. I don't have all the information necessary, and I don't think you treated me fairly—especially in failing to write me about the circumstances of the newspaper review. Had you written Pintarich some kind of correction and sent that to me immediately or made some other effort to demonstrate your good faith, I would not have felt it necessary to write a letter to your department chair. I am perfectly willing to believe that you have acted appropriately with other scholars. In my case, however, you did not.

I really did wonder what use this scholar had made of my galleys during the time she had them in her possession.

The Cold War

In the next decade Gellhorn sought to denigrate my biography and manipulate scholars and journalists who sought to interview her. I would get calls—usually from women—who had discovered Martha Gellhorn. Often they would get in touch with her—usually by phone. Initially she would be gracious, but then as they asked her more questions and touched on sensitive topics, she would explode and cut them off. Then they would call me and compare notes. The relentless ones remained in touch with Gellhorn and learned how to cope with her volatile moods. Here is a typical case of a scholar—this time a male inquiring about Gellhorn's novel, *A Stricken Field*, set in the period just before Hitler invaded Czechoslovakia.

Richard Crane, then working on his Ph.D. in history, dared to admit to Gellhorn that not only had he contacted me but that we were both on a panel that would discuss her work at an academic conference. Fair use will permit me to quote a sentence from her letter (November 28, 1994) to him: "Dr. Rollyson seems to have turned me into a sort of cottage industry which is interesting as a feat of imagination."

My callers wanted to share their fascination with Gellhorn's life and work and their frustration that she could be so prickly. One person who did not call me was journalist Loral Dean, who began a correspondence with Gellhorn in 1991. Dean did not desist, even when she found Gellhorn "imperious." The testy Gellhorn acknowledged Dean's persistence, and the two women corresponded until a year before Gellhorn's death. When they met, Dean found Gellhorn "congenial," and Gellhorn relaxed as soon as she realized Dean intended to become her megaphone. Gellhorn complained that I had given her one marriage she never had, Dean reported in "A Writer's Life" (*Ottawa Citizen*, June 14, 1998). But my book questioned the legality of the marriage to Bertrand de Jouvenel, even though Martha's mother (as several Gellhorn friends told me) announced the marriage, which St. Louis newspapers duly reported. Dean asked: "Why would Gellhorn—renowned for her uncompromising honesty—lie to me, a virtual stranger, about an early marriage?" Dean might as well have asked why Gellhorn made up a story about a lynching so convincing that a congressional committee called her to testify about anti-lynching laws. Why did Gellhorn try to suppress the existence of her first juvenile novel? Dean, like certain reviewers of my book, never even suspected how deeply Gellhorn, like most of us, wanted to remain in control of the narrative of her own life. When I came to revise my biography of Martha Gellhorn, I was to learn that even after her death, her estate and certain friends would do everything in their power to discredit any version of events contrary to her own.

Beautiful Exile

Martha Gellhorn died on February 15, 1998. I immediately began to work on a proposal for a revised biography, restoring the quotations cut by the lawyers and adding materials I had subsequently gathered from additional interviews and archives. Since the early 1990s, when I began work on a biography of Rebecca West, I kept re-crossing Martha's path. She became a friend of Rebecca in the early 1980s, and Martha's letters to Rebecca were in the latter's collection at the University of Tulsa. Several of Rebecca's friends were Martha's friends—notably Victoria Glendinning, herself a Rebecca West biographer, who had also conducted that *Vogue* interview in which Martha had denounced me as an "academic kook." After Glendinning wrote an admiring review of my Rebecca West biography, I wrote to her saying that one day I would revise my Gellhorn biography and if Glendinning had spotted any errors in my account I would be grateful to get her corrections. She replied that she doubted there were errors; Martha simply did not want her biography written. When I subsequently met Glendinning for dinner in London, I told her that the idea for the Gellhorn biography had initially come from Jackie Onassis. "Oh," Glendinning lit up, "I'll tell Martha. Perhaps that will make a difference." Alas, it did not.

Researching Rebecca's relationship with John Gunther, I found Martha's letters to him in his archive at the University of Chicago. Speaking with Rebecca's friend Raleigh Trevelyan, I discovered he had been Martha's editor at Michael Joseph. Rebecca's niece, Alison Macleod, relayed to me Rebecca's impressions of Martha. Researching the West—H.G. Wells's relationship, I found passages in Wells's unpublished autobiography relating to Martha—about which more in a moment. Thus material came flooding my way without my really trying to find it—even letters from readers like a German doctor who had known Martha's father and had met Martha in Germany when she was twenty (he enclosed photographs of her then) and shocked the Germans by smoking on the street.

Martha's death was much bigger news in London than in New York. After World War II, she spent much of the remainder of her life in London and Wales, except for interludes in Mexico, Italy, Africa, and reporting trips to Poland, Israel, Central America, and other places. Although my Gellhorn biography had a respectable sale in the U.S. (15,000 copies), as soon as my American agent started sending round my new proposal, it became clear a revised biography, even with much new material, evoked surprisingly little interest, even though Gellhorn's novellas had been reprinted in a handsome omnibus volume in the early 1990s and her reportage was featured in two Library of America collections. W. W. Norton, which had just published my biography of Susan Sontag, showed no interest—perhaps because Gellhorn had given them a very rough time over their publication of Bernice Kert's book, *The Hemingway Women.* They still thought that if not Gellhorn, then her estate, would be a problem.

So my British agents, Rivers Scott and Gloria Ferris, helped me rework my proposal for the British market, calculating that they could get a pretty good advance for a biography never published in Britain if we gave the British publisher world English language rights. I began the proposal with a resumé of Gellhorn's career and then described the restored and new material that would make a British edition appealing, concentrating on my most dramatic discovery, the typescript of H.G. Wells's autobiography, in which he speaks candidly about his affair with Gellhorn and compares her with his other lovers—even considering briefly whether he should marry her and calling her one of his "last flounderings towards the wife idea." This account was suppressed in the publication of Wells's memoirs (it was written shortly after Gellhorn married Hemingway). Gellhorn later tried to squelch the rumor of an affair with Wells, but his circumstantial account is buttressed by the correspondence between them.

Wells describes making love to Gellhorn on a visit to the United States in 1934, when she was working for the Federal Emergency Relief Administration. "We liked each other, mind and person," Wells wrote, vowing to help Gellhorn's career in any way he could. (He wrote the preface for her second book, *The Trouble I've Seen*). At least one Hemingway biographer had speculated privately to me about a Gellhorn–Wells affair, but I was the first biographer to discover the evidence. Gellhorn stayed in Wells's home in 1934, and they continued their affair on another Wells visit to the U.S. in 1936. "We too had a very happy time together for a week, making love, talking, reading over her second book," Wells recalled, even relishing the lively hour they spent in Connecticut digging a car out of a snowdrift: "Martha in ski-ing trousers with her shock of ruddy golden hair in disorder, her brown eyes alight and her face rosy with frost." Later in New York she "flitted" in and out of his hotel room, alternating sex with theatre-going and parties. Throughout his reminiscences Wells is affectionate, approving of Hemingway and admiring him after their only meeting, which Gellhorn had engineered.

Wells numbered Gellhorn's letters among the liveliest he ever received, and the specimens I have collected bear him out. She often sounds like the wisecracking women of 1930s screwball comedies—but one that is uncensored, who refers to herself as a "bitch," a "girl-author" who sometimes writes "on one foot" for money that will support her trips abroad. This is the uncensored Gellhorn. To another of her intimates, Alexander Woollcott, Gellhorn describes a fellow writer as a "little man with a mouth which I like to think looks like a hog's ass in fly-time." The lawyers for St. Martin's Press made me expurgate such lively and amusing material because Gellhorn threatened a libel suit. Much of the ribald character of the book could now be restored, including the sex scenes, such as the one where Martha arrives home to find Ernest greeting her at the front door without a stitch of clothing on. He liked to come home and immediately drop his drawers and everything else he had on. Gellhorn considered him quite a pig—something else I had to downplay because of the St. Martin's attorneys.

The proposal revealed my evolving picture of Gellhorn, especially in her last years, because I had collected more information and, of course, Martha could not sue me. My later words, compared to my original proposal, have a harder edge, a skeptical thrust:

> A handsome woman who never lost her sexual allure, Gellhorn kept her chaps (her word for them) in thrall. She knew how important sex was for most men, and she used it not only to please men but to get good stories. She slept with generals; she had one-night stands with ordinary soldiers who might not survive the next day. She dressed elegantly, used makeup skillfully, flirted, and coaxed men to do her bidding. If employing a bit of glamour helped her on her way, Gellhorn played along— whether it was modeling French designer dresses in Paris when very young, or posing like a Hollywood starlet for the jacket of an early novel, or playing the *grande dame* in her later years. She hated publicity and the world of self-promotion that her second husband, Ernest Hemingway, succumbed to, but Gellhorn used the machinery of celebrity when it suited her. She thought she could turn it off, and it always perturbed her when others still wanted to play the fame game with her long after she had tired of it.

What really fueled the British proposal, however, was my reaction to the obituaries that presented a rather simplistic portrait of a pure altruist:

> What is missing in the British obituaries of Gellhorn is an acknowledgment of her ambition. One would suppose from reading the encomiums that Gellhorn was fired only by outrage at injustice—whether it was Margaret Thatcher putting down the noble miners, or America bombing North Vietnam (as was often said at the time) back into the Stone Age. Outrage plays well, especially in the press. Gellhorn got rave reviews for saying trust no government, suspect all politicians. In the context of her melodramas of good and evil, such statements have enormous appeal. The trouble is that they also shut down thinking, allowing reporters to withdraw from a complex reality to report only what they see. And this was Gellhorn's advice: "Write what you see. I never believed in that objectivity shit." Well, she was a remarkable observer, but the testimony of the eyewitness is never enough. Reading all of her reports on Spain, for example, with their impressive evocation of events on the ground, one would never suppose that the Stalinists were systematically eliminat-

ing all opposition, that the brave Spanish Republic that Gellhorn so loved would have been swallowed into the Soviet maw if the fascists had not devoured it first.

Biographies are necessary to remedy the sentimentality that creeps into obituaries and the lionizing that inevitably follows the death of a figure as legendary as Martha Gellhorn. It takes nothing away from her achievement to document how cannily she made her way in the world. Her fierce drives were every bit as political as those of the politicians she deplored. Her careerism was just as intense as Hemingway's, even if she rejected the idea of mythologizing her life. Indeed, she went to the opposite extreme, supposing that she could threaten and sue (if necessary) anyone who produced a version of her life that did not accord with her own. It is a very strange position for a reporter to take. And it is a very controlling attitude—one which is understandable in writers who want to command the narratives of their own lives. Gellhorn's success writing her own story is reflected in those obituaries and memoirs that flooded the press. She is always pictured as an opponent of cant, always in the right place at the right time. What the obituaries never ask—what her friends fail to note—is how Martha Gellhorn got there.

I then dropped the bomb that would later cause me the most trouble in reviews of the revised biography:

> Case in point: the maligning of Ernest Hemingway. In my first biography of Gellhorn, I gave Gellhorn the benefit of every doubt. Although she described my book as a "paean of hate," it is painstakingly objective. If anything, it blackened Hemingway and brightened Gellhorn. He was the beast who would not let Martha be Martha, who could not stand competing with her as a writer, who wrote journalism inferior to hers, who wrote a World War II novel, *Across the River and into the Trees,* which is no match for her stunning war novel, *The Wine of Astonishment* [published in 1948 and reissued in 1989 under the title she always preferred, *Point of No Return*].

But how is it that Gellhorn married such a "brute" (the word Rebecca West would use after she and Martha became fast friends and Martha told her all about that horrid Hemingway)? My biography told part of the story, but not the whole story because Gellhorn threatened a libel action and because certain evidence only became available during my research on Rebecca West, when I met West's and Gellhorn's mutual friends.

All the obituaries and the memoirs said that Gellhorn "met" Hemingway in Key West. Sought him out is more like it. Visiting Miami with her mother and brother, she changed their itinerary to include Key West. She "just happened" to walk into Hemingway's favorite bar, a site already well known to Hemingway aficionados. Hemingway was all the rage among her high school and college classmates. When she realized that he was giving her more attention than his wife Pauline, she stayed put in Key West, sucking Hemingway in deeper with Gellhorn guile.

But then, Gellhorn had been through this sort of romance before. When she met the man who would later become her first husband, Bertrand de Jouvenel, he was already married. He was also Colette's stepson and well connected to the literary and journalistic community in France. She traveled in his company in Germany and then wrote her first novel, *What Mad Pursuit* (1934), which features (no surprise) a feisty female reporter destined for greatness. Curiously, though, she is on the look-out for "one grand person," who will make the whole world worthwhile. First it was Bertrand de Jouvenel, then it was Hemingway. No wonder Gellhorn did not want this nakedly autobiographical first novel republished.

In her old age, Gellhorn made her friends—mostly adoring males half her age—think that de Jouvenel and Hemingway were her youthful follies. Poor Bertrand, poor Ernest, these yearning males wanted sex with her, and she obliged. What she omitted from the story was her overwhelming need for a male hero, a need that made her gush over John F. Kennedy and take the dashing paratrooper general, James Gavin, to her bed. Men were a HUGE disappointment, but Gellhorn still went after them like Hemingway after big game.

Though Hemingway found Gellhorn enticing in Key West, he did not pursue her. Instead, he left for Spain. Gellhorn expected an invitation to the war and safe passage there. Hemingway proffered neither. So she showed up on her own, angry at Hemingway, but determined to snag him nonetheless. Hemingway was not a fool; he knew this was a woman intent on goading him into action. Although he responded to her gambit, he also—well before they married—captured the conniving side of her character in his play, *The Fifth Column.* His portrait of her has been treated as sour grapes, but it was written before the couple married, when Hemingway was smitten but no sucker. He was neither as self-involved nor quite as needy as Gellhorn made him out to be. In retrospect, with a hoard of Hemingway biographies treating him as a lout, it has been far too easy to accept Gellhorn's denigration of his character.

Of course, Hemingway could be a boor, and his best work was behind him. He wanted to retire to Cuba. What did he have left to prove? He was approaching middle age, and he had had enough action. One can admire the restless Gellhorn without having to denigrate Hemingway for declaring his separate peace. When she finally prodded him into action, he treated her like a competitor, to be sure, grabbing the assignment at *Collier's* that should have been hers. But he thought he was playing her game. War was rough, and it was for keeps, as he might have said.

I had given a different slant in the original biography, but I was again (this time unconsciously) writing ahead of my evidence. Eventually I would discover that the John Fitzgerald Kennedy Library, which houses a huge Hemingway collection, had just released letters Hemingway had written to Martha and to her mother. These letters revealed a man trying very hard—if only intermittently—to provide a home for Gellhorn in Cuba that would measure up to her demanding standards. The letters also showed a cuddly, charming, and certainly loving side as well as the more familiar brute. This new evidence convinced me that I had to provide a more subtle, more nuanced view of the marriage. If Hemingway was a beast, he was also an aging, vulnerable beauty.

My British agents had no trouble selling the book to Aurum Press, which acquired (as expected) world English language rights. Aurum wanted a new title to emphasize how much of the book was new. I proposed *Beautiful Exile: The Life of Martha Gellhorn* to allude to this attractive woman's life-long search for the perfect place, to the irony of her not finding it, and to the resulting sense of isolation, which she never overcame no matter where she lived.

I did a year's intensive work of interviews and searching for new letters (some new ones in private hands came my way), during which I received a letter from Sandy Matthews, the son of T. S. Matthews, Gellhorn's literary executor. This Sandy, Gellhorn's stepson, is not to be confused with Sandy Gellhorn, her adopted son. It is important to get this elementary fact straight—as will become apparent in the sequel. The said Sandy warned me sternly that I would be denied permission to quote from Gellhorn's published and unpublished writings. I wanted to reply "a little late in the game to scare me off, don't you think?" But I refrained. His letter reminded me that I could expect some kind of attack as soon as my book was published.

Conflict on Every Front

Aurum held the first serial rights and had offers from the *Daily Mail* and *The Times*. The former offered twice as much money, but my publisher (consulting me) selected *The Times* since he feared that the tabloid would sensationalize the biography while *The Times* would more likely reach readers actually interested in buying the book. I concurred. But in the event,

The Times hired a writer to do a flashy article in their magazine that ended up vulgarizing the biography anyway. "Conflict on Every Front" (April 8, 2001) ignited an incendiary from Gellhorn's forces, who could not wait to read my book but launched a pre-emptive attack based on the potboiler adaptation. I dare not quote their letter in *The Sunday Times* (April 15, 2001), but my reply, published April 22, contains the gist of their charges:

> H. G. Wells describes in detail his love affair with Gellhorn in a long-suppressed memoir. Nowhere in my book do I suggest Gellhorn was afflicted with self-hatred. What I say in the book about Gellhorn's attitude toward her adopted son Sandy is a mild paraphrase of the much harsher verdict explicitly stated in her letters. While I did not have access to all of Gellhorn's papers, many of her letters were available in archives—all of which are cited in my biography.

The *Times* letter, signed by Betsy Drake, James Fox, Alfred Gellhorn, Sandy Matthews, and John Pilger, accused me of lack of evidence (especially concerning the H. G. Wells affair), although it was apparent that they had not read my book. It is fascinating to note that Sandy Gellhorn did not sign this letter and did not put his name to any of the subsequent onslaughts on my book. Pilger, on the other hand, attacked me in *The New Statesman* and on "The Woman's Hour," a popular BBC program on which I also appeared. But Pilger and Co. got sidetracked into a quarrel about whether or not Martha was a feminist, allowing me to state ruefully, "You see how difficult it is for a contemporary biographer when even Martha's friends fall out on this crucial issue." Pilger notwithstanding, *The New Statesman* later ran a highly favorable review of my book. Indeed, the reviews, in the main, were much better than the American reviews of *Nothing Ever Happens to the Brave*:

> [Rollyson] has done honour to her in establishing her place in history, and given the rest of us the gift of an absorbing account of a life spent at the centre of a century's turmoil [*The Irish Times*].

> This perceptive, well-researched and well-written book covering almost a century, leaves one full of admiration for a woman so plucky, so witty and so talented [*The Literary Review*].

> Gellhorn, although dismissing Rollyson's first biography, in 1990, may well have secretly enjoyed this more thorough attempt. She was no sycophant [*The Independent*].

Of course there were negative reviews:

> I have never read a biography like this before, in which the biographer clearly can't stand someone he regards as an appalling human being [*The Spectator*].

Rollyson offers us a desiccated Martha interested in little more than self-advancement. More dimensions please, professor [*Evening Standard*].

But the reviews were easily two to one in the book's favor, and perhaps this is why Gellhorn's troops tried another assault using a *Guardian* reporter to advance a new allegation—this time deploring my inaccuracies rather than my lack of evidence. On April 26, 2001, the *Guardian* published my reply:

> The headline reads "Gunning for Martha—Audrey Gillan Investigates" (April 24). Apparently that investigation did not include attempting to contact me.... Gillan reports that Gellhorn wrote 25 pages of notes about my errors.... Gellhorn's "friends" have had 10 years to seriously refute the first edition of my book and they have not done so. Nor did Gellhorn force any changes in the first edition. She only threatened a legal case.

The 25 pages, I'm sure, are Gellhorn's fax to St. Martin's Press, which did not result in changing a single fact in the book.

Finally, on May 15, 2001, Sandy Matthews granted an interview to *Daily Telegraph* reporter Cassandra Jardine. By this point, surely, he could at least have read my book. Instead, he was clearly responding to the reviews that had confused him with Sandy Gellhorn. (A few hasty reviewers may have been relying on my book's index, which I did not prepare or have the opportunity to proofread, and which did confuse Sandy Gellhorn with Sandy Matthews, putting all entries on Sandy under the name Matthews.) Since Sandy Matthews had written me a threatening letter, and since the narrative in both editions of my book is clear on the difference between the two Sandys, I can only conclude that Matthews deliberately misled the *Telegraph* reporter who did not bother to check with me when she said I had "muddled up" the two Sandys. I wrote a two-sentence letter of clarification which the *Telegraph* printed.

The oddest response to *Beautiful Exile* came in mid–April from Hemingway biographer, Scott Donaldson. He wrote to me care of my publisher, and on behalf of the Hemingway estate, pointing out that the *Sunday Times* magazine article contained a "couple of quotations that ran to a length that made me think they went beyond the parameters of fair use." I was astonished, since what had been quoted amounted to fewer than two sentences from different letters out of dozens I had consulted for the biography. It also seemed extraordinary that a biographer—one who had himself published a biography of John Cheever which had been hampered by the Salinger decision effectively eviscerating fair use—should conduct a sort of pre-emptive strike on behalf of an estate. Like the Gellhorn battalion, he had fired before even reading my book. Were literary estates now hiring biographers to police other biographers? Donaldson had to be aware that I was no neophyte. If I had needed permission to quote, I would have done so. If he had read my book and thought I had exceeded fair use, certainly an objection—not just a query—would have been in order. But Donaldson was putting me on notice—even suggesting in a subsequent email that if my book were to be published in the U.S. I would have to secure permission to quote.

I immediately responded with a terse note: "My quotations from his [Hemingway's] letters are minimal and fall well within the parameters of fair use." Not willing to give up his bone, Donaldson emailed me a clarification noting that the estate was "particularly vigilant where quotations from unpublished letters are concerned and the 'fair use' doctrine can hardly be made to apply." Aghast at his ignorance, I pointed out that after the Salinger decision Congress had specifically amended the copyright act to include unpublished material under fair use, adding that my wife, an attorney, had advised me carefully about the law. Settling down for a good chew, he then wanted me to send him the relevant statute! I did, but like one of those dogs who is adept at walking backwards as well as forwards, he added that the "point I was stumbling toward making was that fair use is as I understand it severely limited when it comes to use of unpublished work." And so he wanted to "avoid difficulty ... by reaching agreement about permission in advance of stateside publication." As Rebecca West used to say, "What impertinence!" We (writers, publishers, estates) all have a sense of "fair use"—admittedly an elastic term and meant to be so; otherwise it would be impossible to quote anything without securing permission from the copyright holder. Imagine a writer using hundreds of sources and quoting a few words from each consulting other writers, publishers, estates and having them determine for that writer what constitutes fair use. In effect, this was Donaldson's position, although I'm sure he did not adopt it when doing the Cheever biography. His officiousness felt like a holdup. But I refused to show my hand, and his emails ceased.

Is There a Happy Ending to This Story?

Well, U.S. publication arrived—sort of. The British edition, distributed by Trafalgar Square Books, was reviewed in *Publishers Weekly*, which repeated the disinformation campaign waged in the British press. The negative review, I later learned from the editor of *PW*'s forecasts section, had drawn directly on false statements made by British reporters about my book. After a firm letter from me, *PW* ran a retraction on June 10, 2002:

> Correction: In our review of Carl Rollyson's *Beautiful Exile: The Life of Martha Gellhorn* (Forecasts, Apr. 8), we stated that "Gellhorn's successful lawsuit ... forced (Rollyson) to retract portions of his first biography of her *(Nothing Ever Happens to the Brave)*, published in 1990." In fact, there was no such lawsuit, nor did Rollyson retract any portion of the biography. P W regrets the error and apologizes to Mr. Rollyson.

The damage, of course, has been done, and I expect to read other reports repeating how I had to retract. Like the *PW* reviewer who did not bother to check if I had replied to fallacious press reports, *PW* readers will accept the "facts" of the review. Stating there has been a successful lawsuit sounds like a fact, not an opinion, which is what makes such malicious reviews especially damaging.

Fortunately, *Beautiful Exile* received a decent review in *The New York Times Book Review*. But the best American review provided a bittersweet sendoff, for it encapsulated both the book's appeal and its doom: "This fascinating account presents a well-rounded portrait of a woman whose writings are fast disappearing from U.S. consciousness" (*Choice*, June 2001).

Postscript

In 2005, Caroline Moorehead published *Gellhorn: A Twentieth Century Life*. "The first major biography of Martha Gellhorn," her publisher announced. The minor biographies, I had to conclude, were my work. They were not included in Moorehead's "sources and select bibliography." The Gellhorn estate had authorized her, and that meant I had become the nonbiographer.

I learned a good deal from reading Moorehead's book—chiefly how Gellhorn viewed her own life—in letters that only her authorized biographer has been allowed to read. Gellhorn was more critical of herself than I had imagined, acknowledging that she put all her skill into reporting. She had a great eye and ear, but she had no gift for analysis. I knew that Gellhorn could only write about what she had seen and heard, and that she was no thinker, but I did not realize that she herself came to this same conclusion after fruitless efforts to complete books about the Spanish Civil War, Cuba, and Vietnam.

I was delighted to see descriptions of Gellhorn's austere London flat, virtually a mirror of her astringent mind; to discover that she was very pleased with her long and narrow feet and had Ferragamo made shoes especially for her; and to learn that "new words made her laugh with sudden delight." From Plutarch to Boswell and beyond, good biographers have given us such details and anecdotes to make their subjects live again.

Moorehead studiously avoided any use of my material and repeated Gellhorn's charge that my work is riddled with errors. Moorehead need not have trusted my books. By using almost any of the Internet search engines, she could have found my archive at the University of Tulsa, open to any researcher who wants to examine the notes, correspondence, and tape-recorded interviews I used in my two biographies of Martha Gellhorn. I eagerly read Ms. Moorehead to see what I got wrong, but her biography only confirms what I believed: that Gellhorn's charges had no merit.

When she got mad, she lost all perspective. Gellhorn was mad at her own native land and lived most of her life away from it. She was mad at the Palestinians and would not brook a single word of criticism of Israelis. She loved the Spanish republic and never wrote one word about how the loyalists committed atrocities or how the Stalinists eliminated all elements of the left that did not hew to Moscow's line. Moorehead sees this side of her subject—but only selectively. Hers is one of the most anti–American books I have ever read. Moorehead repeats without comment every hysterical charge Gellhorn made against the United States. The biographer is only dismayed when Gellhorn does not give equal consideration to the Palestinians or to the Germans, whom Gellhorn did not believe would ever create a democratic country.

As a biographer, I'm shocked at how little attention Moorehead devotes to Gellhorn's St. Louis background. True enough, the relationship between Gellhorn and her mother Edna is sensitively rehearsed, but Edna's work as a reformer in St. Louis and the manner in which that reforming spirit energized Gellhorn is not portrayed. Her grandmother, a provocative social reformer in St. Louis, is not even mentioned! Gellhorn conducted a life-long campaign to distance herself from St. Louis and hurt her mother terribly by giving no credit to the city's progressive ethos; Moorehead writes in the same vein—as if she were writing not a biography but completing Gellhorn's autobiography.

In general, this biography is out of tune with what made Gellhorn, for all her anti–Americanism, an American figure. It is out of sync with her effort not to sound American: I was astounded by Moorehead's reference to Gellhorn's "accent as unmistakably still of the American Midwest." No American friend of hers I interviewed heard any trace of St. Louis in her mature speech. On television she always sounded like a posh mid–Atlantic confection, combining British and aristocratic East Coast elocution. Perhaps she saved the Midwestern "drawl" to entertain her British friends.

Still, Moorehead does deliver the news—with much to say about Gellhorn's lovers, from Bertrand de Jouvenel to Ernest Hemingway to General James Gavin, and many more. Crossed off the list, however, is H.G. Wells— primarily because Gellhorn denied the affair and was "scrupulous," Moorehead asserts, about identifying her lovers. Maybe so, but H.G. said they did make love. Having done my own extensive research on this randy writer for a biography of Rebecca West, I see no reason to dispute his account.

Has Moorehead's work changed the basic shape and significance of Martha Gellhorn's life as I described it? I don't think so. And for that I'm grateful.

In 2006, Caroline Moorehead published *Selected Letters of Martha Gellhorn*. The Spanish Civil War, World War II, and Vietnam are brought to vivid life in her lucid and precise prose. Besides letters to Hemingway, we have her exchanges with Eleanor Roosevelt, Leonard Bernstein, H. G. Wells, and a host of other important literary and cultural figures.

One of Gellhorn's correspondents thought that her letters constituted her greatest achievement. Certainly they are as striking as her journalism, more engaging than much of her fiction, and full of the energy that led her to visit and write about something like half the countries of the world. She was always avid to be off somewhere, since nowhere ever quite fulfilled her idea of paradise—not Italy, Mexico, or Africa, to mention just the dozen or so homes she established in the course of her peregrinations. She was, as I implied in the title of my biography of her, a "beautiful exile" in search of a beautiful exile.

Martha Gellhorn lived in a nearly perpetual state of dissatisfaction, which sometimes made her a bore, but often made her attractive precisely because she was so demanding. She could also be very, very funny about her naïve search for the perfect world. *Travels with Myself and Another*, for example, is a comic masterpiece, one of the truly great travel books of our time.

But just how wonderful are these letters? And perhaps more to the point: How can we trust them? Gellhorn was writing about real people, events, and places. So unless her correspondence is regarded as fiction masquerading as fact, inevitably the nature of her perceptions has to be explored and analyzed.

The trouble is that Caroline Moorehead is ill equipped to render this sort of service. As in her authorized biography of Gellhorn, Moorehead simply gives her subject her head. If Gellhorn denies she had an affair with H. G. Wells, Moorehead drops the subject. That Gellhorn wrote the sort of ingratiating letters to Wells that have prompted the suspicion of more than one Hemingway biographer; that Wells himself wrote quite directly about his affair with Gellhorn, means nothing whatever to Moorehead.

How much the editor of Gellhorn's letters ought to say about them is, of course, debatable. An editor who is constantly correcting or augmenting her subject's text might very well annoy some readers. But in this case, both Gellhorn's own skewed accounts and the provenance of these letters are cause for concern.

What Moorehead's reticence and the letters themselves reveal is Gellhorn's fierce desire to define history solely on her terms. She adopted an attitude toward biography and history that essentially eviscerates both forms of writing. She believed exclusively in eyewitness history. If you weren't there with her at the Spanish Civil War, if you were not a friend of Dorothy Parker, then how could you possibly know anything? Thus Gellhorn writes as follows to the esteemed Parker biographer, Marion Meade, who had sent a letter inquiring about Gellhorn's friendship with Parker:

> Dear Miss Meade; Have a heart. I could talk to you about Dottie for hours, I knew her well ... but I can't write a whole chapter for you. I haven't time to live let alone write letters.

Of course, Meade was not asking Gellhorn to write a chapter for her (I know, I checked with Meade), and besides Gellhorn loved writing several letters a day. The real point of the letter, of course, was to put Meade in her place. Gellhorn was forever writing such letters to biographers.

In a letter to Alan Grover, one of Gellhorn's lovers, Gellhorn enunciated her lifelong distaste for biography: "I think it is barbarous, and the mark of microscopic minds, to confuse the man and his work; as long as the man, in his own life, is not the enemy of the commonwealth." This letter written in Cuba sometime in 1940, when Gellhorn was living with Hemingway, conveys the dread she felt in anticipating the public attention that would inevitably follow her marriage to one of the kings of American literature.

But Gellhorn was a part of history and had no trouble, when it suited her, promoting and to writing about herself—as she did in *The Face of War* and *The View from the Ground*. She squirreled away her letters in the special collections department of Boston University's Mugar Memorial Library, presided over by the late Howard Gotlieb, who aggressively sought the papers of celebrities and literary figures. Gotlieb was quite willing to make his devil's bargain—in this case, promising Gellhorn that her papers would not be available to anyone until 25 years after her death (she died in 1998).

But if Gellhorn wanted no biography, why not destroy the papers? Why leave an estate free to hire an authorized biographer? Why allow Moorehead to edit the letters *now*? Why let her make a selection that no other scholar/biographer can check since the Gellhorn collection is still closed to other researchers? Moorehead mentions, for example, that she has chosen a few pages from a 40+-page letter that Gellhorn wrote to her lover David Gurewitsch. Perhaps those are the best pages of that letter, but what is the principle of selection? What are we really reading when only parts of letters appear?

Gotlieb justified his deals by saying that in order to preserve history he had to accept the terms he was offered. He also suggested that Gellhorn was trying to prevent the kind of "pop biography" that would appear before there could be any perspective on the events she participated in. But Gellhorn said she did not believe in perspective. The perspective argument is fallacious, since history and biography occur all the time. To be sure, there is perspective, but there is also the immediacy of biographies written on the spot, so to speak while the evidence is still hot, or at least smoking.

So by all means, enjoy Gellhorn's letters, but *caveat emptor*! What to make of a writer who thought the Spanish Civil War had been the only just war fought during her lifetime? Or what about this passage on Alger Hiss, written on April 11, 1982:

> The man is 77 now, and with hurt eyes, still trying to restore his good name. And though he doesn't understand why Whittaker Chambers and Richard Nixon were out to kill him, I do; he was the very embodiment of everything they were not and could not be, the educated upper class American, an American gentleman; they hated him. It had nothing to do with Communism; it was like a private vendetta.

This passage can be easily turned on its head: Whittaker Chambers is dead now, and the old lefties cannot let go of vilifying him. I know why: he was fat and Conservative and worked for *Time* magazine and had none of Hiss's elegance and education. How could someone as well spoken and with the right opinions possibly be a traitor?

Reducing history to such psychology and ideology is repugnant.

There may be a grain of truth in it, but to make such explanations dominate, as Gellhorn does, makes her a very unreliable correspondent. Why didn't Moorehead at least include an introduction that explored the nature of Gellhorn's prejudices and blind spots? She mentions Gellhorn's Jewish background, yet makes no connection with Gellhorn's staunch support of Israel and how she related to Jews. Gellhorn made a Jew discovering the horror of Dachau the main character in her novel, *Point of No Return*, yet she never commented on how that character's sudden awakening to his Jewishness reflected her own obsession with protecting Israel.

Or did she? Since we only have a selection of letters we cannot know for certain. This half-baked collection is certainly better than not having a loaf at all, but what will arise from a complete and uncompromising publication of the letters remains to be seen.

6

The Biographer Who Came In from the Cold: Becoming Rebecca West's Authorized Biographer

"This is your last job…. Then you can come in from the cold."—Control to Alec Leamas, *The Spy Who Came In from the Cold*

We all compose novels of our own lives. The plot I have chosen for myself most closely resembles that of a John Le Carré novel. I used to be taken with the idea of the biographer as a detective. But then what is the crime the biographer/detective is investigating? And who is the criminal? In contemporary fiction, the criminal is usually the biographer. He is the spy in William Golding's novel *The Paper Men*, caught by his subject in the act of rifling through his subject's garbage.

My spying began in 1980 with biographical research for *Marilyn Monroe: A Life of the Actress*. Although working on this book remained a pleasure, two episodes proved to be deeply disturbing. When I called Whitey Snyder, Marilyn's favorite makeup man and confidant, he treated me with scarcely veiled hostility. He had spoken to too many biographers already, he said. I tried my usual ploy: I was an academic especially interested in her work as an actress, an approach to Monroe that biographers had not handled very well. I tried asking a few innocuous questions just to get him warmed up. I tried mentioning names of people I had already interviewed and who I knew he respected. I tried and tried in an agonizing phone call that lasted perhaps five minutes—with me doing most of the talking—and then I gave up and said goodbye.

There is nothing very remarkable about this rejection in itself, except

77

that most biographers do not dwell on their rebuffs. Although they may feel rather aggrieved that someone has decided not to cooperate with them, biographers cannot afford to be too introspective—especially while working on a biography. To brood over the nature of biography as a rude and transgressive genre might result in abandonment of the project. Biographers are intruders—that was the message Whitey conveyed to me. And I do not believe I have made a single phone call to an interviewee since my call to him without a considerable degree of reluctance. I have been told off a few times or made to feel like an interloper. Indeed, many biographies have never seen the light of day precisely because the biographer cannot stomach the opposition that arises as soon as he or she begins asking impertinent questions.

I know biographers who have avoided this troubling aspect of biography by dealing with figures who are long dead and do not have surviving friends or family who might be interviewed. But that is really a dodge. You can be sure that Leon Edel and Richard Ellmann would not have had the blessings of Henry James and James Joyce. The latter novelist called my colleagues "biografiends," and the former not only burnt his letters to foil future biographers, he wrote two works of fiction that expose biographers as a breed of skulking spies. Just recently the estate of Ted Hughes has attacked Jonathan Bate's biography of Ted Hughes, citing numerous errors and accusing Bate of presumption. Bate a distinguished scholar of Shakespeare and author of other groundbreaking books has already said he will confine his future work to authors who are long gone.

In *The Aspern Papers*, the better known of James's two broadsides against biography, an erstwhile biographer of Jeffrey Aspern, an early 19th-century poet, visits Venice hoping to acquire the correspondence between Aspern and his mistress, Miss Bordereau. Insinuating himself into Miss Bordereau's life, the biographer takes her niece, Tita, into his confidence. After Miss Bordereau catches him searching through her desk, he leaves for a few days. When he returns after a fortnight, he finds that she has died. Tita has fallen in love with him and intimates that only a relative can be permitted to examine the papers. Alarmed at this proposal, the biographer leaves, only to find at his next meeting with Tita that she has destroyed the letters. This is the story in which James coins a memorable term for the biographer: a "publishing scoundrel."

In "The Real Right Thing," George Withermore, an inexperienced young journalist and critic, is flattered by an invitation from the widow of the great writer Ashton Doyne to write her recently deceased husband's biography—especially since she gives him complete access to Doyne's papers and puts him to work in the writer's study. Withermore immerses himself in Doyne's archive, and at first is encouraged by the almost palpable presence of his subject, and then he begins to have second thoughts.

James wrote the latter tale while embarking on a biography of the American poet and sculptor, William Wetmore Story. As Leon Edel suggests in his biography of James, the novelist seems to have wondered whether he was doing the right thing in abandoning fiction for biography. "The Real Right Thing" reads like a Gothic ghost story, with the biographer portrayed as a kind of grave robber, awakening the spirit of the deceased. James, of course, did not invent this attitude toward biography: "Biography is one of the new terrors of death," wrote John Arbuthnot (1667–1735). But James blackens the biographical quest as if to shrive himself. In fact, "The Real Right Thing" is cloaked in black. Doyne's widow greets the biographer in her "large array of mourning—with big black eyes, her big black wig, her big black fan and gloves." She encourages the biographer to work in the evenings "for quiet and privacy." But those evening sessions reveal that the biographer is working in the dark. It is on such a "black London November" that Withermore begins to doubt he has the right to plumb Doyne's life: "What warrant had he ever received from Ashton Doyne himself for so direct and, as it were, so familiar an approach?" Yet for nearly a month the biographer labors to believe in the "consecration of his enterprise." Words like warrant and consecration suggest just how badly biographers want to believe that they are blessed.

Biographers are moles and burglars—as James dramatizes by having Withermore "dipping, deep into some of Doyne's secrets." The biographer delights in "drawing curtains, forcing many doors, reading many riddles, going, in general, as they said, behind almost everything." Biographers go for the back story, the hidden side of the subject's face, as Edel himself acknowledged with relish when he changed a Jamesian term, "the figure in the carpet," to describe the biographer's quest to find the "figure under the carpet." That banal cliché about sweeping things under the carpet becomes a Gothic horror in the biographer's mission. So deluded is Withermore at one point that he imagines Doyne's presence as a kind of breath of the holy spirit lingering over the "young priest at his altar." It does not occur to the biographer, so dedicated to resurrecting a life, that to others he is creating a kind of Frankenstein, a semblance of a human being, but certainly not "the real right thing." His enterprise is not right morally and not right aesthetically.

It is precisely at the moment of his exaltation that Withermore senses Doyne's withdrawal from him. The biographer's "protected state"—largely a figment of his imagination—disintegrates, and doubts about his business begin to gather. Now the biographer experiences the "monstrous oppression" of his subject, "who becomes a burden the biographer cannot tolerate. Suddenly the widow appears as "the tall black lady." Withermore no longer feels in league with her but rather on the other side, so to speak— that is, on the side of his subject, who is signaling through Withermore's uneasiness Doyne's wish that the biography should proceed no further. "I feel I'm wrong," the biographer tells the widow. Rather than giving his subject a new life, Withermore contends that in writing about Doyne, "We lay him bare. We serve him up. What is it called? We give him to the world." Exposing his "original simplicity" as a misunderstanding, the biographer concludes, "But I understand at last. He only wanted to communicate. He strains forward out of his darkness; he reaches toward us out of his mystery; he makes us dim signs out of his horror." The uncomprehending widow replies, "Horror?" Withermore explains: "At what we're doing.... He's there to *save* his life. He's there to be let alone." The widow, thinking only of the precious biography, "almost shrieked": "So you give up." Like a character in a Gothic tale, she exclaims: "You *are* afraid!" And indeed, the biographer is terrified, telling her that Doyne is "there as a curse!" And the curse carries moral and spiritual weight: "I *should* give up!" Withermore emphasizes.

The widow has seen the biography as a gift to her husband, a tribute to his importance. But then the biographer essays one more attempt to climb the stairs to his subject's study, only to return to say Doyne is on the threshold "guarding it." So Withermore did not enter? she asks. "He forbids!" Withermore says in such a commanding voice that after an instant the widow concedes, "Give up." Then she decides to mount the stairs herself but returns, acknowledging that her dead husband still blocks the way. "I give up" are her last words.

By and large, biographers who do not give up do not wish to confront the harrowing aspects of biography. I have heard biographers joke about their work in archives, saying they like to read other peoples's mail. I think they find it comforting that those documents are housed in a public repository, as if such institutions sanction their research. Even better if the biographer gets a grant, another sign of approval. But the truth is biography remains invasive, however you dress it up. As Leamas says to his East German interrogator, "We're all the same, you know, that's the joke."

But there is another side to the problems of prying biographers— which leads me to the second episode that disturbed my equilibrium while exploring the life of Marilyn Monroe. After a few years of working on the biography, I had formed a tight circle of friends/interviewees who had come to believe in my book and who wanted to do everything in their power to assist me. Two of these people—I shall have to call them X and Y—gave me a sense not of the movie star and the actress but of the day-to-day woman. In late 1984, toward the end of a conversation with X, she began to discuss Marilyn's last days. She lowered her voice: "You know Y was very good to Marilyn and always wanted to help. Unfortunately, that help sometimes took the form of drugs." To this day, I have not seen this aspect of Monroe's biography addressed, for most of the talk of her taking uppers and downers involves her doctors. I could see no way then to tell what I knew without divulging the identities of X and Y, who were already present in the biography but not directly implicated in the story of how she died. Now that both X and Y have died, I will reveal that X was Steffi Sidney and Y was Ralph Roberts.

What is the point of writing biography if you cannot tell the secrets you learn? I felt not only deeply frustrated, since I wanted to enrich an appreciation of the circumstances in which Monroe died, I also felt like a spy who was expected to hold back information in order to present a cover story, so to speak. That this remained the only story I had to hold back for this biography did not make me feel any better, and my suppression of part of the story continues to rankle. I decided then never to submit to such a self-imposed gag order again. Or so I thought.

In both episodes with Whitey Snyder and X and Y, I had to confront the unseemly side of biography that most biographers—like good spies—do their best to conceal. Have you ever noticed how over-the-top the acknowledgments sections of biographies tend to be? The biographer does not just thank everyone (and the list can go on for pages and pages) for their generous help, those acknowledgees are made to seem heroic, kind, thoughtful—you name it—paragons of virtue. (For a state of the art example of what I mean, read the Acknowledgments in Blake Bailey's biography of Richard Yates.) I suppose biographers should not be blamed for this sort of flattery. It is right to thank people, of course, and who knows when some of those folks will come in handy again? Laying it on thick is one of the ways a biographer builds up a network of contacts that might become useful for the next book. (Researching Marilyn Monroe provided me with invaluable Hollywood sources I called on while working on my biography of Lillian Hellman.) But if you are a biographer, you know that some of those people the biographer so fulsomely thanks cannot possibly be *that good*. In our contemporary language, we'd have to say those acknowledgments just do not compute. I have to hand it to Jerry Oppenheimer, biographer of Martha Stewart, for using his Acknowledgments in a novel way to thank some of his interviewees: all of the people "Martha stepped on along the way." Jerry might be mean-spirited, but he is also therapeutic. Debunking biographies often release the passions other biographers may feel but dare not express in their books. In his overrated biography of John Kennedy, Robert Dallek, for example, is quite happy to exploit Seymour Hersh's revelations about Kennedy's sex life in *The Dark Side of Camelot* while writing an introduction that sanctimoniously refers to his "balanced" view of his subject and the need to rise above all the debunking biographies. Without Sy the Spy, a superb interviewer who ferrets out the nitty-gritty, Dallek's soporific book would lose what little steam it has—as I show in *Reading Biography*.

Reading acknowledgments, when you have done the job yourself, becomes an exercise in decoding. The biographer, like a good spy, simply cannot reveal how he got all those people to talk. Some are willing witnesses, of course, but all of them? It all fell into place because the biographer is such a good guy, a stand-up woman? Dallek does not even refer to interviews—just to talks and conversations. How deceptively comfortable it makes biography seem. No one had to be coaxed, flattered, or pressured? What the acknowledgments do not tell us is how the biographer manipulates his sources and vice versa. Janet Malcolm is one of the few writers to be candid about this jockeying for position between interviewer and interviewee. In *The Silent Woman*, she makes us privy to what she is thinking as she talks to the principals in Sylvia Plath's life, and what she is thinking is, "How can I get the information I want?"

In *The Blood Doctor*, Barbara Vine (Ruth Rendell) provides a rare insight into the biographer at work. Martin Nanther cajoles, bites his tongue, and does whatever the situation requires to keep his interviewees talking. "I nod sympathetically," he notes—not because he is sympathetic to what is said but simply to further the conversation, to establish a rapport with the interviewee. Meanwhile Martin withholds what he is really thinking and does not contradict the witness when she is mis-stating or even lying. Sometimes Martin lies to protect the information he already has. One interviewee asks him not to mention a certain party to another and Martin agrees, already knowing that he will break his promise because it is the only way to elicit the information he seeks. In another case, he violates an agreement that his interviewee thought was implicit in their conversation, and Martin comments: "I remind him that when he asked for an undertaking I didn't answer him."

Martin's behavior is not surprising to me. When I decided to write my biography of Martha Gellhorn in the spring of 1988, I made a strategic Martin Nauther–like decision. I flew to St. Louis to interview every one of her childhood friends and schoolmates I could find, as well as friends of her parents. Some of these witnesses were still in touch with Martha; many had not heard from her in decades. Only a few asked me if I had her cooperation. To them, I simply said that I hoped to get it. I did not go into any detail, and to my relief they asked no more questions.

The trip to St. Louis became exhilarating as I gathered new material from interviews with people in their eighties who might not be available for biographers awaiting Martha's death. It is curious, by the way, that it is the unauthorized biographer of the living figure who becomes an object of hate. Those biographers who lie in wait, or conduct deathwatches, anticipating that moment when their subject is no more so that the biography can proceed apace, are, strangely, regarded as the responsible types. Agnes DeMille waited decades for Martha Graham to die so that she could publish the biography of her friend. It had been all ready to go the moment Graham departed this world. "That was rather sneaky of me, wasn't it?" DeMille said to her biographer Carol Easton. Am I alone in thinking there is something ghoulish about Scott Berg's grave-robbing memoir/biography, published less than two weeks after Katharine Hepburn's death? Well, there are those of us who spy on the living and those of us who dig up the dead.

In countless interviews, Berg presents a picture of biographer and subject that is positively homey. But I have never made a trip like the one to St. Louis without feeling at some point a profound deracination. It usually occurs at night in a hotel room when I realize I am all alone, *adrift*— that the only one really supporting this adventure is me. A fellow biographer once confessed to me that she also had such moments, and they made her feel suicidal. The unauthorized biography is, among other things, a tremendous act of will. At such Alec Leamas moments, I vow that this will be my last job and now I can come in from the cold.

Much of my life has been spent working on unauthorized biographies of subjects who have treated me with suspicion, contempt, and hostility. Arthur Miller, for example, did not answer my letters asking for an interview about Marilyn Monroe. In desperation, I attended a Hopwood Festival celebration at the University of Michigan, where Miller, once a student winner of a Hopwood for one of his earliest plays, was the featured speaker. He spent a portion of his talk reminiscing about his former wife. During a reception for him after his talk, I entered the circle around him and introduced myself, reminding him that I had written to him and that

I wanted to ask him a few questions about Monroe. He stared at me and solemnly asked: "What is your question?" I began to stammer at the thought of ONE question, and as I began to formulate it, a woman, book in hand, barged in asking for his autograph. He smiled at her, took the book, and majestically turned his back on me. I suppose I could have tapped him on the shoulder and said, "Hold on, here's the question!" Instead, I slunk away.

After completing a draft of the biography, I sent it to Miller, saying only that I thought he should see it. I hoped, of course, that he would comment. I hoped that he would see my book was serious, see that I had treated him with respect and compassion. I hoped he would appreciate that I had avoided Mailer's rather mean spirited portrait, in which he remarks on Miller's parsimony by observing that no one could remember Miller ever picking up the check after a meal. I dreamed the playwright would grant an interview. I fantasized that he would blurb the biography. Miller did send a short reply, which said only that as with all manuscripts that came without a self-addressed envelope and postage, he had thrown my work into the wastebasket.

I have been treated with benign neglect and sometimes with threats of lawsuits. I do not have the slightest feeling of remorse or regret for my actions. Like Alec Leamas, I am case-hardened. I don't believe that the authorized biographer has any moral superiority over me; in some cases, quite the contrary. Authorized biography often strikes me as a put-up job. I began as a spy, and I have remained a spy, although I was "turned"—to use the language of spies—and became a kind of double agent, which is how I think of authorized biographers. They have an inherent conflict of interest. On the one hand, they spy on their subjects, dipping into the secrets a la Withermore. On the other hand, they are spies for their subjects, searching out evidence that promotes their subjects. What else could authorized mean, whether you are a biographer or a Toyota dealer?

The turn toward authorization began in the spring of 1987 while I was at work on my second biography, *Lillian Hellman: Her Legend and Her Legacy* (1988). I read Lillian Hellman's review of *H. G. Wells and Rebecca West* by Gordon Ray. He had contrived a narrative around letters H. G. had sent to Rebecca between 1913 and 1923, the period that encompassed their intense and stormy love affair. H. G. destroyed Rebecca's correspondence, but she could not bear to obliterate his sexy, funny, and provoking prose, which he embellished with amusing illustrations. Ray's book is a little gem, marred only by Rebecca's heavy supervision—the price of gaining exclusive access to her archive at Yale. Hellman did not like this lopsided aspect of the book, and she twitted West for allowing Ray to write about her lover's letters. Hellman's reservations amused me, since she had made a career of writing about her thirty-year on-and-off affair with Dashiell Hammett, and she had not been averse to revealing the intimacies of their relationship. Hellman's review also had a subtext: As a Stalinist she bitterly rejected West, a vehement anti–Communist. But more of that when I come to the early stages of how I became (most improbably) Rebecca West's authorized biographer.

Hellman's review kindled my interest in Rebecca West, for I could tell even from Hellman's jaundiced attitude that Rebecca had a wonderful life full of lovers, literary achievement, and fascinating political involvements. Sooner or later, I thought, I would make her my biographical subject. But I had to finish with Hellman, and the final phases of that biography inevitably led to my biography of Martha Gellhorn.

After Gellhorn, I wanted to do West, but there was a problem. Victoria Glendinning's well received, if brief, biography had been published in 1987, and West's Yale archive remained closed until the death of her son, who was still very much alive. Not willing, however, to abandon Rebecca, I proposed doing a book called "Counterfeit Lives," which would include chapters on the liaisons between Hammett and Hellman, Hemingway and Gellhorn, and West and Wells—plus a few other couples (the cast kept changing as I tinkered with seven different versions of a proposal my agent was never able to sell). The premise of the book had to do with how these writers had re-invented themselves in these relationships, thus producing lives that resembled works of art. Some editors thought I would be merely cannibalizing my biographies; others simply thought the material too well worn. They asked, instead, for another biography of a single subject.

Ultimately I decided on what became *The Lives of Norman Mailer: A Biography.* Mailer adopted many different guises and wrote about himself in the third person, so he constituted a fitting example of my interest in the ways writers re-create themselves. I had already published studies of Mailer's work, and I felt certain that because two biographies had already been published, he would not try to obstruct my unauthorized effort. The first one, by Hilary Mills, a well-done life, was not a critical biography—that is, other than summarizing reviews, she made no literary assessment of Mailer. The second one, by Peter Manso, was essentially a tape-recorded book, an oral biography skillfully organized. Manso had a falling-out with Mailer—but not before he had interviewed Mailer's mother and most of the key players in his subject's life. Again, however, this book did not deal with the nexus between the work and the life. I proposed a much more interpretative and literary biography, and that is what my publisher, Paragon House, bought.

Mailer had an authorized biographer, Robert Lucid, who never published his projected multi-volume work. Lucid once praised a paper I gave on Mailer at a Modern Language Association meeting, and I decided to contact him—hoping that since he held all the cards, he might be generous enough to retrieve a few out of Mailer's vast archive that might be useful for my biography. I presented Lucid with a modest list of requests. He promised to see what he could do, although I never heard from him again. I think he was spying on me and thought I was spying on him, trying to find out how far along he had progressed with his authorized opus. Maybe he thought I had some nerve asking him to act as a reference when I applied for a grant to support the Mailer biography.

Mailer responded courteously to my letters asking for an interview. I was surprised that he did not simply say he had committed himself to Lucid, an old friend, and that therefore he had no time for me. Instead he asked me to send him my Lillian Hellman biography, so that he could assess what side I was on. He did not explain, but I presume he was curious about my politics. Evidently Mailer had forgotten or chose not to acknowledge that he already had one of my books. I had sent him my biography of Marilyn Monroe before it was published, hoping for a blurb from him. I did not hear from him again until my altercation with his agent.

In 1990, my correspondence with Mailer had to do with his agent's request to vet my biography, insisting that if I received permission to quote from Mailer's writings, such permission would be tantamount to endorsing my biography. I found this position absurd and told Mailer so. He stepped in and not only directed that I be allowed to quote from his work but that I should be charged the lowest possible fee. Perhaps because of his own work as a biographer and authorship of an espionage novel, he took my spying as merely part of the game he himself had been playing for decades.

I wish I could say that episode constituted the happy ending to my work on Mailer. First Peter Manso objected to my editor that I had stolen material from his book. It is true I quoted extensively from Manso's interviews, but they were not his words; he did not own them. He could not claim copyright in these words—as my wife, Lisa Paddock, an attorney, told my editor, who, fortunately, accepted Lisa's argument. Manso made a few more threatening phone calls and then dropped his feeble complaint.

Another controversy ensued when William Styron attempted to recant the testimony he had given for my biography. The contretemps concerned a story Styron told me about an editor (a friend of his and Mailer's) who had stabbed his girlfriend in an incident that occurred seven or eight years before Mailer stabbed his second wife, Adele. I tape recorded Styron murmuring how amazed he was to hear Mailer whisper his admiration that the editor had the guts to commit such an act. Mailer and Styron closed ranks, telling the *New York Post* that I had "sensationalized" the story. In fact, I had faithfully reproduced Styron's own wording of the episode and said so to the reporter who duly noted as much in his piece on my biography.

If I seem to digress in this discussion of *The Lives of Norman Mailer*, it is only to emphasize once again the solitude of the unauthorized biographer. Styron had told the story about the stabbing to Hilary Mills. But her version of the story is rather less explicit than mine. Mills was Styron's friend, so he counted on her not to go too far. Why he thought he could count on me, though, is a mystery. A few years earlier I had written him to ask for an interview about Lillian Hellman. He sent a courteous card saying he would like to help but had promised Lillian (practically on her death bed) that he would speak only to her authorized biographer, William Abrahams. Perhaps Styron wanted to be helpful this time, and then had second thoughts, because after our interview he rescinded his offer to grant me access to his archive. Mills, by the way, abandoned a biography of Hellman because she found that even her friends (like Styron) would not consent to interviews about Hellman.

As I was completing my biography of Mailer, I put in a call to Vincent Giroud, curator of Rare Books and Manuscripts at Yale's Beinecke Library to see if there had been any changes in the restrictions put on the Rebecca West collection. He informed me that Anthony West had just died. Beginning in the fall of 1991, I started making the trip by train from New York City to New Haven every Friday to begin the arduous task of reading through an uncatalogued collection of a literary career that spanned over seventy years and a life that lasted to the age of ninety.

I spent nearly a year reading through a good portion of Rebecca's Yale papers, which were a mess. Hundreds of boxes of material had been buried in a Beinecke vault it took a staff member over three hours to locate on my first day trip. Subsequent trips were frustrating because of the rudimentary finding guide to West's papers. Only one staff member seemed to be able to locate items in the order I wanted to follow. But such delays only whetted my curiosity—as did my discovery that the guide was not always accurate. I found the most amazing stuff stuck in those boxes. In the midst of some correspondence from the 1920s, I found a cache of love letters Francis Biddle (FDR's attorney general and a prosecutor at Nuremberg) wrote to Rebecca in the 1940s.

I thought for sure that anytime that year someone would show up and provide some competition. If anyone had done so, I would have hurried to write my book proposal. I usually put together my pitches after about three months of research; in this case, I spent a year researching before submitting a proposal to my agent. The idea of devoting so much time and money on a book that a publisher might not buy and that my agents (in the U.S. and the UK) showed no enthusiasm for, struck me as the biggest risk I had ever taken with a book. Much of Rebecca West's work was out of print in the U.S. She had not made it into anthologies taught in college classrooms. Widely read in her own time, she now appeared mainly in the histories and biographies of her period. So why did I persist and take so long in formulating my proposal?

For one thing, my skeptical but tactful agent said that my proposals were so good that she could sell whatever I felt passionately about. And I passionately believed Rebecca West belonged in the canon and that the full story of her life and career had not been told. My Rebecca West proposal would have to be the very best sample of what I could achieve—a pitch not only for my book but also for her. For another, I realized that the Yale collection would provide a significant new cache of material that in itself would be a huge selling point. Finally, I wanted to show just how steeped I was in the archival sources before I began trying to interview people about Rebecca. I had done only American subjects, and I would somehow have to make my way in London literary circles—with some aid, however, from Gellhorn's London friends, who had helped me in spite of her maledictions, and from my London agents. However, I knew no one in Rebecca's family and had no idea how this deeply divided clan (split between those who were related to her son Anthony, whom she had cut out of her will, and her nephew Norman Macleod, who inherited her estate) would react to me.

I had to get the proposal and myself, so to speak, off to a rousing start. I wanted to show, in one paragraph, both the vitality and incredible range of her biography. The first sentence would have to justify my subtitle: A Saga of the Century. Out of Rebecca West I would fashion an emblematic figure:

> The life of Rebecca West (1892–1983) not only spanned a century, it was an invention of a century in the making. In the year before West's birth,

George Bernard Shaw published *The Quintessence of Ibsenism*, an argument for a new conception of society and self, socialist in its political orientation, feminist in its demand for equality. Born with the name of Cicily Fairfield (what could sound more Victorian, more like a character satirized by Oscar Wilde?) an eighteen-year-old properly brought up young woman, already steeped in the suffragist struggle, having marched and protested for her rights since she was fourteen and struck in the throat by a policeman during a demonstration, already having failed at a career on the stage, already having died (so to speak) in the throes of adolescent ambition, never minding the pain and ridicule, prepared herself to become a new woman, Rebecca West, Ibsen's defiant heroine, the embodiment of a new age.

I felt I needed to confront in a second paragraph those editors in New York unfamiliar with Rebecca's work and had no visual image of her. (Rebecca would be more recognizable to London editors but she would not be thought of as bankable, and so I needed a sale in North America first to obtain substantial British backing.) At least Rebecca had appeared in an important film, and her greatest book, *Black Lamb and Grey Falcon*, was still in print, so I tried to anchor a view of her in whatever meager knowledge an editor might already have:

Rebecca West would be her life long role as a voice of history—as she would come to seem, discoursing on the Russian Revolution in Warren Beatty's film, *Reds*, looking the part she had in fact been awarded in 1959, Dame of the British Empire. This Dame had helped create the era of John Reed and books such as *Ten Days That Shook the World*. In her words, in the chiseled brightness of her sagging but undaunted face, one can trace her passage from Cicily Fairfield, to Rebecca West, to Mrs. Henry Maxwell Andrews to Dame of the British Empire, to the whole woman who was all these things, who plunged into the politics of Central Europe, not at all fazed by the chaos of the Balkans, the upheavals of Yugoslavia that did not merely presage the Second World War, but the world today which is again dividing itself into ethnic enclaves. To remain only a private person, not to engage oneself with world history was, in Rebecca West's view, the equivalent of being an idiot, of not noticing, for example, that the price of peace in the Western world had been bought at the cost of the Eastern Europe's enslavement—first to the Turks and later to the Communists.

Now a third paragraph could work in her agonizing family drama and psychological complexity while emphasizing the Anglo-American trajectory of her career and her cultural and political importance:

A displaced person herself, part Scotch, part Anglo-Irish, a product of genteel poverty, dark complected and self-conscious about her appearance, West was at home in a world of minorities struggling for self-determination, and an arch opponent of Communism and of every orthodoxy that denied human differences and individual autonomy. She was a marriage of contradictions, a feminist, a mistress, and a dutiful wife, who stood on the margins of society and detected the fault lines running through America and Europe. She partied with Paul Robeson at the Cotton Club in the 1920s and fascinated Huey Long in a famous interview he gave her on the Capital steps in Washington, D.C. She reported on the Nuremberg trials and afterwards set off on the trail of spies and traitors, realizing that betrayal and disloyalty—the things that had split apart her early home life, disrupted her career during her affairs with H. G. Wells and Lord Beaverbrook, and saddened her married years—were the very stuff of history. Not to know about espionage was tantamount to knowing less about one's own life, about the secrets and the lies and duplicities of one's mates and offspring. Her lifelong struggle with her son, Anthony, and her older sister, Lettie, over the meaning of her life, of her relationship with Wells (Anthony's father), was nothing less than an epic engagement over a family's identity, over who Rebecca and Anthony were—not only to each other but to themselves, to their friends, and to the public which became privy to this familial quarrel, with the roots of it all going right back to Rebecca's ambivalent feelings about her father and mother and to Anthony's sense of illegitimacy.

Rebecca was fascinated with spies and wrote riveting prose about them. She had friends who spied on Anthony, and Anthony had friends who spied on her. I could have made more of that, I see now, re-reading this proposal. A biographer herself, an expert interviewer and confidant with friends in the CIA and the British intelligence services, Rebecca knew the art of deception well and reviewed biographies better than anyone has ever done. But all this I would learn only much later after years of research.

What I did already realize, I'm happy to say, is what a good role-player she was, and how closely her writing and her life coincided. It is as if she gave herself code names and assumed identities:

> In this saga of the century, the political and the personal, the literary and the historical, fuse in the biography of a character named Rebecca West, a character invented once by a playwright and invented again-and-again—by the woman herself, who could know herself only by the roles she played, who spent her whole life regretting that she had not stuck to the stage, who wrote a novel, *Sunflower*, casting herself as an actress, who was devastated by her son's novel, *Heritage*, which also cast her in the role of insincere actress, and who finally made it to the screen in *Reds*, speaking not as another's character but as her own, a summation of all the roles and casting calls she had devised for herself.

I doubted that there were many editors who could place Rebecca in literary history and say what her contribution had been. So I supplied a quick overview, being careful to show that she had received critical attention:

> As a novelist, biographer, historian, and critic, who can match West in encompassing so many different forms of expression? As critic Motley F. Deakin remarks, West had an unrivaled command of "libraries of literature"—from the "patristic fathers to the most recent best sellers" and wrote close to a thousand book reviews. Her impact on literary and political journalism was immense, and for a period she divided her time between London and New York, befriending Alexander Woollcott and Harold Ross (she thought of him as a brother) and many *New Yorker* writers, publishing regularly in the *New York Herald Tribune* and *The New Republic* as well as in the most important British newspapers and periodicals. "I doubt whether any such brilliant reviews were ever seen before; they certainly have not been seen since," wrote Frank Swinnerton in *The Georgian Scene* in an effort to characterize West's influence in the 1920s and 1930s.

But that was a long time ago, and I was keen to build up West not merely as a historical monument but as a timely figure:

> In her biography of St. Augustine she created a figure like herself, deeply self-aware—at the same time extraordinarily self-deluded and capable of creating plots and fictions she was so adept at foiling in others. It is in her autobiographical novels, in the unfinished trilogy that she reveals how her father's abandonment of the family led to a devotion to art which gave back to her a possible world his departure seemed to have denied. In her criticism she spoke of it as the "strange necessity," meaning the peculiar craving for an art that can put a finishing touch to life that life itself lacks. Her accounts of history—particularly of Central Europe—were as necessary as her art. Indeed, she made an art of that history by fusing a displaced peoples' quest for identity with her own, taking her husband along with her as a necessary companion, for he had also had his experience of displacement, having been an Englishman of German heritage interned by Germans in the First World War. "My husband" she is fond of saying in *Black Lamb and Grey Falcon* as a kind of refrain and backstop to her own perceptions, making out of her marriage a union of disparate ideas. *In The New York Times Book Review* (February 10, 1991), under the front page headline, "Rebecca West: This Time Let's Listen," Larry Wolff shows just how prescient and how relevant West's life and work is for today.

In a last paragraph which concluded the "concept" section of my proposal—a section which is the equivalent of the "pitch" screenwriters give when they have an idea for a film—I wanted to convey the idea that justice had not been done to such a profoundly important figure:

> Rebecca West read many languages and wrote in so many different genres that the totality of her achievement has hardly yet been recognized.

She turns up as a figure in many books of her period, for she befriended and antagonized and corresponded with the greatest personalities of the twentieth-century: H. G. Wells, Bernard Shaw, Noel Coward, Dorothy Thompson, Diana Trilling, Alexander Woollcott, Paul Robeson, Bernard Berenson, John Gunther, William L. Shirer, Arthur Schlesinger, Jr., Virginia Woolf, Ford Madox Ford, Violet Hunt—the list could go on for pages and pages. And it is in her biography, in the depiction of how Rebecca West became herself, the actress who felt driven to take on so many parts, that the astonishing range of her achievement can be captured. Her career was truly the work of a century.

I then provided an 80-page chapter outline, working in many references to the letters and other documents I had found at Yale and at other archives including the New York Public Library, Boston University, the Library of Congress, the University of Texas and the University of Tulsa. Through Arthur Schlesinger, Rebecca's friend and my colleague at the City University of New York, I made contact with a few members of her family and could quote them in my proposal. A detailed chronology, an annotated bibliography, an account of published and unpublished biographical resources, and a brief history of how my other biographies had been received rounded out a proposal that ran to 109 pages, about three times as long as my previous ones.

Only a handful of New York trade houses seemed interested in my biography. I did not consider a university press or a smaller publisher because I knew I would never get the kind of advance that would allow me to do the extensive traveling I still needed to do for the book—let alone compensate me for all the expense I had already incurred. Fortunately, Erika Goldman, an editor at Scribner's (a part of the Maxwell empire then and with its apostrophe still intact), bought the book when another eager editor, Don Fehr at Atheneum, could not convince his boss to do so (the boss had edited Victoria Glendinning and could not see the need for another biography). Without Erika, I'm not sure I could have obtained a contract.

My American agent, Elizabeth Frost-Knappman, then showed my proposal to Rivers Scott and Gloria Ferris, Elizabeth's co-agents in London. I had met with them on previous trips to London when they tried to sell my biographies of Gellhorn and Mailer. At one of those meetings sometime in 1988, I had broached the idea of a Rebecca West biography, and Rivers scotched it. He thought it was too soon after Glendinning's book. He mentioned casually that he had known Rebecca, but I did not then inquire further. Now (in early 1992) he told me he had been her editor at the London *Sunday Telegraph*. He also said that Stanley Olson, whom

Rebecca designated to write an authorized biography much longer than Glendinning's, had died without making any substantial progress on his book. Had I known these facts, I would certainly have put them in my U.S. proposal, since, as I was to learn, Rivers had extraordinary contacts with Rebecca's friends and publishing associates. And as I later discovered from Rebecca's diaries, Rivers had been her favorite editor—more than that, he was a kind of surrogate son. He now helped me tailor my proposal for the British market and won for me a sensational hardback/paperback contract with Hodder & Stoughton, soon to become Hodder Headline. My editor there, the aggressive and brilliant Richard Cohen ran the Cheltenham Literary Festival. But he was promptly fired, and Erika left Scribner's, and my orphaned project passed from one editor to another (seven in all).

However, I felt nothing like an orphan because I had entered a world quite different from those I had ever experienced before as a biographer. I had always been an outsider in every sense of the term. With each biography I had been forced painstakingly to build up a network of contacts, relying chiefly on the way I could put the idea of a book to them and not on whom I knew or who could vouch for me. It was very hard going, and my victories had always seemed miraculous to me. I was astounded, for example, when one day Walter Matthau called me up to talk about Lillian Hellman. I had simply looked up Matthau's professional address in some reference book about actors. As I recall, I had to write to him care of his attorney. I did not expect a reply but felt I had nothing to lose and even suggested to Matthau which days were best to call me! Near the end of our interview, I could not help asking him: "Why did you call me?" "Because," he replied, "you wrote one of the most interesting letters I have read in the last decade." Such responses sustained me as I encountered many more rejections. Now, with Rivers's help, I began to feel like an insider. He almost immediately put me in contact with Alan Maclean, who for many years was Rebecca's editor at Macmillan. She liked Maclean and trusted him—a remarkable fact since his brother Donald was part of the famous spy trio that included Guy Burgess and Kim Philby. Alan had nothing to do with spying, but his career had been somewhat blighted by his brother's treason, which had, in part, provoked Rebecca's classic study, *The Meaning of Treason.* She was very keen on the concept of loyalty in both public and private affairs, and she had concluded that Alan deserved her trust. She made him one of her literary executors. I wanted to interview Alan not only about his memories of Rebecca, but also about his contacts in the publishing and literary world that my subject thrived in.

I met Alan not far from my agent's office in a pub on the old Brompton Road in South Kensington. I remember it as a warm enough day for us to sit outside and have a pint. A friendly Alan asked about my previous work. When I mentioned I had published a biography of Lillian Hellman, he ignited. "You know Rebecca and Lillian hated each other," he remarked. He had edited one of Lillian's memoirs but had been careful to steer clear of any conversation about it with Rebecca. This made Alan a kind of double agent, I thought. Perhaps that is why I felt emboldened to raise a subject I probably otherwise would have skirted, especially at this first meeting. "How do you feel about what Rebecca wrote about your brother?" I asked. "Brilliant writing, absolutely brilliant," he replied, "and *wrong*." I did not feel confident enough then to press him on the point. I already knew that Rebecca had keen perceptions and amazing insights, but she could badly misinterpret people she did not like.

Then Alan dropped what felt like a bomb on me. "I'm a good friend of Billy Abrahams, and I promised him I would edit his biography of Lillian when he finishes it." I gulped. I'm surprised I did not choke on my beer. In the preface to my Hellman biography I had mentioned writing to Abrahams asking him to allow me access to Hellman's papers at the University of Texas. Not only did he deny my request, he had gratuitously written that he was the "one and *only* authorized biographer of Lillian Hellman." His response seemed pompous and only made me more resolute. I had quoted him in the preface and made fun of the idea of a number of biographers who went around claiming to be authorized. Rehearsing this history in my mind I heard Alan say, "Why don't you send me a copy of your Hellman biography? I'd love to read it."

I felt done for. Should I say anything to ameliorate the situation? How would Alan react when he read my outlaw biography? Unauthorized biographies are certainly undertaken in England, but they are deeply discouraged by the literary community and the biographer is often shunned and pilloried in the press—as Stephen Spender's first biographer, Hugh David, had been. The stigma of the unauthorized cannot be obliterated—as I found when Michael Foot, who had agreed to my doing a biography of his wife Jill, told me he had received calls from friends doubting the wisdom of allowing me to go ahead.

"Of course, I'll send you the book," I said to Alan, and said no more. I thought it best for him just to read the biography and let him make up his own mind. I did not want to weight the book with the baggage of explanations. Excerpts from my letters to him during this period explain what happened next:

May 14, 1992

Thank you for your letter of May 7. I'm pleased your first impression of my biography is favorable, and I hope it holds up as you read through it.... I do think I would benefit from the designation of "authorised" in that it might, as you say, open a few doors and take care of the permissions problem. Indeed, it would be a great convenience to me now because Tulsa will not photocopy any of West's letters or other unpublished writing without permission from the literary executors.

June 24, 1992

Thank you for your letter of June 17. I'm so pleased you liked the Lillian Hellman biography. Your reaction is what I hoped for, and I'm gratified to say that some of Hellman's friends wrote letters similar to yours.

Whew! Alan never mentioned William Abrahams again. He did, however, express one reservation to Rivers, who relayed it to me. "Do you think," Alan asked Rivers, "an American chap will be able to do right by Rebecca?" Rivers, then in his mid–60s, an affable man and a shrewd negotiator, immediately scoffed at the question. He had read my proposal—better yet, he had massaged it to perfection—and he firmly rejected even the possibility that I might get the story wrong. Agents can do much more than sell a book; the right agent can become a stalwart ally in tight spots.

I don't know, however, if Alan really ever warmed to me. Another American, Stanley Olson, had been designated as Rebecca's biographer of choice. A Midwesterner, Olson had come to London when still a young man and made himself over into the epitome of an eccentric Englishman. He dazzled the likes of Alan Maclean and the Bloomsbury diarist Frances Partridge. Stanley entertained Rebecca with extraordinary literary gossip he would cull on his rounds in London. A charmer, a good literary politician, he befriended Frances Partridge and Rebecca who did not like each other. Indeed, in the quarrel between Anthony and his mother, Frances took Anthony's side, and Rebecca responded by calling her a "goose down to the last feather."

When I met Alan or Frances or Gwenda David, who worked for Viking in London as a liaison with Viking in New York (Rebecca's American publishers), I sometimes felt their wistfulness. It should be Stanley doing the job, not me. Gwenda, I think, felt his loss most keenly. One day she called up Rivers and complained that I was bothering her. The bother simply had to do with my request for a second interview. Everyone knew I came to get the goods for my biography, and then I would be off. Stanley, on the other hand, had parked himself and would have remained for the long haul. He had planned a ten-year project for a biography of 300,000 words. I was a 150,000-word man (although I first turned in a 200,000-

word-plus manuscript) and would get the job done in three years at most. Stanley, overweight and a gargantuan smoker, suffered a stroke at 42 (my age when I started my biography of Rebecca) and died a few years later. (I felt I got to know Stanley through his cousin, Phyllis Hatfield, who published a biography of him and with whom I talked frequently, since she, too, had Rebecca stories Stanley had told her.)

Back in the U.S., I still had plenty of work to do at Yale. I had already spent a fortune on photocopying. There was just too much material to take notes on during my one day a week at the Beinecke. I applied for a short-term fellowship that the Beinecke offers to researchers who require an extended period of residence, but I felt I would be successful only if I secured a letter of recommendation from Alan Maclean. He had earlier tried to persuade Yale to open its collection to Victoria Glendinning. Yale refused because of the restriction that Rebecca had put on the collection regarding her son, who was still alive when Glendinning was at work. That Glendinning was authorized did not change the terms of Rebecca's stipulation. An angry Maclean suspected Yale was upset that Rebecca's substantial collection of literary papers (three times the size of what Yale already had) had been sold to the University of Tulsa rather than given to Yale. At any rate, after first agreeing to write on my behalf, Maclean realized he could not do it. He remained angry about the earlier rebuff. I was left feeling, once again, out in the cold.

I doggedly returned to my one-day-a-week trips to Yale while also fitting in nine research trips to Tulsa, and teaching my usual full time schedule. I interviewed Rebecca's friends as well as her son Anthony's family and friends in New York City and in Connecticut. I was able to secure by mail Rebecca's correspondence from various British libraries and archives. But I still had to make nine trips to London and other parts of Britain. One of my best sources, Kitty West, Anthony's first wife, lived a bucolic existence in Dorset. She welcomed my visits and letters and wrote close to two dozen letters filled with her memories of Rebecca and Anthony. Kitty, a remarkable painter and an independent woman, remained in love with Anthony even after he divorced her and remarried. She was on good terms with his second wife, Lily, who could not have been more encouraging to me.

When I first contacted Kitty, however, she said she had received a phone call from someone telling her not to speak with me. The someone was Dachine Rainier, a poet Rebecca had first befriended and then come to regret knowing. Rebecca watched in dread as Dachine proceeded to set herself up as a kind of Rebecca West expert, egging on Viking to do an anthology of Rebecca's work that Dachine would edit and introduce. The publishers did not like Dachine's writing, and Rebecca felt embarrassed by it, but Dachine persisted. Rebecca gradually withdrew from Dachine's company, but her withdrawal did not stop Dachine from publishing reminiscences of Rebecca from time to time. I knew this much from reading Rebecca's correspondence, her diaries, and letters to and from her publishers. I had written to Dachine asking for an interview. She had written me a curt note calling Rebecca a great liar. I, poor chap, would not have a clue as to how to sort out fact from fiction. I drew a line across Dachine's name on my list of people to interview. In retrospect, I can imagine how infuriated she was that an American interloper thought he could just show up and write Rebecca's life.

Of course, I asked Kitty: "What did you say to Dachine?" Kitty replied: "I told her to mind her own business!" Kitty was not in the habit of being instructed as to whom she should see. "Well, that's all right then," I said with a laugh as I fell into a Britishism. Kitty and I liked to stay up late talking about Rebecca and everything else, too. In her very cozy and quiet Dorset cottage I slept the sound repose of the authorized biographer. It was too good to be true. Surely someday I would rue this proximity to my subject, but I never had to. As good as her word, Kitty never asked me to change what I wrote.

After allying myself with Alan Maclean, Kitty, Anthony's family, and then with Alison Macleod-Rebecca's niece who had a treasure trove of family documents and letters—all seemed to be falling in place. Alison had been a Communist and for many years she and Rebecca had fought bitterly. Every time I visited Alison, her husband Jack would remind me, "I used to play chess with Earl Browder [head of the American Communist Party]." Jack was the only one I ever found who called Rebecca Becky, which seemed to amuse her. Alison, a journalist of considerable accomplishment, also enjoyed a successful career as an historical novelist. She shared with Rebecca a sarcastic, humorous side that came out when I discussed my research. When I brought up H. G.'s playful letters to Rebecca, whom he called Panther while signing himself Jaguar, Alison commented dryly: "They weren't quite human, were they?"

As successful as I had been so far, there was one key witness and center of power, so to speak, that I had to win over: Alison's brother, Norman. I had delayed contacting him because, in a sense, he could make or break my biography. He was Rebecca's heir and chief literary executor. I would need his permission to photocopy the extensive Tulsa files and to quote from Rebecca's writing in my biography. I wanted to quote a good deal because she is such a striking and amusing author.

Norman was also a flashpoint for other members of West's family—especially Kitty, who believed that Anthony had been done out of his inheritance. She found it galling that her two children by Anthony, Edmund and Caroline, received their legacy from Rebecca as administered by Norman. All along, I wondered how I could write a book that would please the Anthony/ Macleod sides of the family, especially when what divided them was money!

Norman, is the son of Rebecca's favorite sister, Winifred (Winnie). Norman achieved the higher degrees and settled family life that Anthony (very bad about money) never attempted. Anthony had become a good literary critic and a novelist of indifferent reputation, but he had spoiled his relationship with Rebecca by writing novels and articles about her that made her look like a phony. When Anthony's son Edmund wanted to attend medical school, Rebecca suggested that Anthony contact Norman for advice. It was always Norman! thought a disgusted Anthony. Norman, the paragon of virtue.

So I wondered what Norman was like, this ideal relative who never gave Rebecca trouble. And how would he treat me? I turned to Alan Maclean for help. He wrote to Norman on my behalf, and then Norman invited me to visit him at his cottage in the Lake District. We had a very pleasant visit, and he assured me he liked what I had to say about my approach to Rebecca. There did not seem to be any issue about which he was touchy. He made no stipulations, expressed no demands, and seemed quite content not only to approve my book but also to extend his aid. This he did, for example, by encouraging Anne McBurney, one of Rebecca's secretaries, to speak with me. McBurney had already refused me once.

Even with Norman's encouragement, however, I remained somewhat uneasy. When I asked him about permission to quote from Rebecca's writing, he deferred to Rebecca's agent, Michael Sissons. "So I should apply to Sissons for permission?" I asked Norman. "In the first instance, yes," he said. I remember that phrase distinctly because I did not know what he meant, and rather than pressing him, I decided to see where I stood with Sissons. I thought he might prove to be another obstacle. I was well along with my book before I met him, and I think he expected writers to apply to him much earlier in the process of their research. In effect, I contacted him with the book half done. I was also wary of him because I knew Rebecca did not like him. She had a decades-long relationship with her agent, A. D. Peters, and Sissons inherited Rebecca when Peters died. It remains unclear to me why Rebecca disliked Sissons (perhaps for no better reason than that he was not Peters), and I did not know if Sissons was aware of her dislike, or whether it mattered to him. I still don't know. There are some questions even I won't ask.

I also worried that Sissons would give me permission but charge a hefty fee for all the quotations I wanted to use. Well, all that worry went for naught, since Sissons turned out to be as obliging as Norman. He simply signed off, so to speak, on my project—although that is only a matter of speaking, since I never obtained, in writing, any sort of permission from Norman Macleod or Michael Sissons. When I completed a presentable draft, I sent it to them and waited to see what they said. I was never charged a thing. Norman pointed out some factual errors and had plenty of comments to make on how Rebecca had chosen to tell her story. Like Dachine, Norman scoffed at some of Rebecca's stories. Rebecca was fond of calling other writers mythomanes, but she did pretty well in that department too. But Norman seemed amused rather than aghast at his aunt's prevarications. And he knew quite well that Rebecca had been a difficult mother for Anthony. Rebecca was hard on her family and very critical—rarely of Norman, but she certainly had harsh words to say about his wife and other family members. So Anthony's bitterness did not offend Norman, even if Norman did not believe Anthony handled his grievances very well.

On the other side of the water, Anthony's American friends and family felt his anger over his childhood was amply represented in my book. Consequently, I did not suffer from the family conflicts I had anticipated when I first spoke with Kitty. Anthony's son, Edmund, acknowledged his father's paranoid strain. Edmund, once Rebecca's favorite, had also experienced her disfavor when he divorced his first wife (a Rebecca favorite) and married his second (a Rebecca *bete noir*). Everyone in the West family had been insulted by her at some point or felt her sharp tongue had abused a family member.

I found one similarity between Rebecca West and Lillian Hellman. I occasionally contacted people who refused to speak because they felt they could say nothing good about Rebecca or Lillian. In the latter's case, playwright Ruth Goetz refused to be interviewed, but she could not help but whisper fiercely over the phone: "She was a *viper!*" (I have just let out a secret, by the way, because I did not identify Goetz in my biography.) Christina Byam-Shaw, a West relative appalled by Rebecca's treatment of her eldest sister Lettie (or so I heard from other family members) would not meet with me. Here is the approach I took in my third letter to her:

October 8, 1993
Dear Mrs. Byam-Shaw
   I feel uncomfortable about not having seen you. I have read various comments about you in Rebecca West's correspondence and in her diaries, and I would like to balance these with an interview with you. I note that Victoria Glendinning thanks you in her acknowledgments, and like Glendinning I will certainly be covering the period during which you knew Rebecca West.
   I have conducted more than one hundred interviews with Rebecca West's friends, family, and employees and read more than five thousand of her letters. I am now writing my biography, but I expect to make one more trip to England—probably next autumn when I should have a complete draft but will still be seeing a few people I have missed on previous trips.
   Is there any chance we could meet?

I don't believe I got a reply to this third letter. I usually give up after three tries.

   I certainly presented Rebecca's dark side in my biography, but I have never worked on a subject who was more entertaining or who had better friends in spite of her failings. She was generous and amusing and astonishing in her range of interests and in her talents as a writer of journalism, fiction, biography, art criticism, and travel writing.

   Did I leave out anything because I was an authorized biographer? Nothing, I do believe, that would have altered my portrayal of Rebecca. Rivers asked me to leave out a bit of Rebecca's diary in which she said she thought of him as a son. He seemed embarrassed by the comment and said his colleagues might make fun of him. I could also have included one bit of testimony that would have made clearer why Rebecca preferred Norman to Anthony. I interviewed Norman's three children about their memories of Aunt Cissie (as she was called in the family). Helen, Norman's youngest child, is an unabashed Rebecca admirer, a writer who aspires to be worthy of her example. Fiona did not like Rebecca much, especially because Rebecca treated her Aunt Lettie so terribly, even making her an object of derision in stories and novels. Norman's son Graham also disliked Rebecca, but he couched his unflattering view in terms of his disappointment with his father. "Rebecca was the only person I ever saw my father pander to," Graham said. I could have winced, but like Martin Nauther I maintained my biographer's mask. At that point, I had become very fond of Norman and impressed with his acute perceptions about my subject. I knew from letters I had seen that he had had arguments with Rebecca—though mostly about literary preferences. Here was another side of him, playing the good son, and getting his reward. I do not know how Norman would respond to his own son's criticism. I will never ask him. Because I did not ask him, I did not feel I could put Graham's comment in the biography. To make this confession now reveals the sense in which biography is an intrigue, a keeping and a divulging of secrets.

Above all, Rebecca liked intrigue. I think that is why she found biographies—especially biographies of spies—irresistible. She once criticized contemporary biography as a "blood sport," although she relished the contest between biographer and subject—as her own biographies and reviews of biographies show. Working on her may have increased my own paranoia. My books have always received a high proportion of mixed to negative reviews, with reviewers hostile to my unauthorized approach. Even with my Rebecca West biography, I always thought that in the end I would get the knife, suffer exposure, or be shot attempting to make my escape over the wall every biographer has to climb to get at his subject. In *The Spy Who Came In from the Cold*, Alec Leamas is shot near the Berlin Wall. He could have made it back to the West. But he turned around to try to rescue his companion, a woman he had fallen in love with— although the ruthless Alec would not have used that term. When he looks down from the top of the wall and sees his love has been shot, he descends and gets hit.

Like Alec Leamas, I have been a loner. So it came as a delightful surprise when reviewers almost uniformly approved of my biography— including Victoria Glendinning, who might have seen me as a rival. I have made relatively few friends out of the contacts I have made when researching my subjects. Rebecca West, however, has been an exception. She brought me friends like Michael Foot, Jill Craigie, Kit Wright (she hosted Rebecca during her stays in Mexico), and many others, including virtually all of Rebecca's family (who I continue to see and who have visited me). They provide a degree of warmth I have not otherwise experienced as a biographer. For better or worse, I've always been one of those biographer/ spies who does not look back.

7

Susan Sontag: The Making of a Biography

Summer 1995: two biographers in search of a subject. My wife and I wanted a figure who dovetailed with my previous subjects. The choice was not hard to make, especially since we had both met and been charmed by our subject during our stay in Poland in 1980. But the obstacles were formidable and had to be addressed squarely in our book proposal. We had to entice a publisher by taking on a powerful writer even as we had to allay fears that she would find ways to block our book. The book proposal, an art form in itself, had to promise more than any book could possibly deliver. The best book proposals are platonic; that is, publishers are really buying the idea of the book you want to write. Raising the possibility of difficulties, however, alarms publishers. The writer is often advised to minimize any problems an unauthorized biography is likely to encounter. We did just the opposite: we built up our project's scary side and made it part of the project's appeal, showing how the obstacles would in fact work to our advantage. If our subject was formidable, we presented a front that was anything but timid.

The first paragraph of the proposal revved up:

Lillian Hellman (the most daring and controversial playwright and auto-biographer of her generation), Martha Gellhorn (America's most glamorous and courageous war correspondent and Hemingway's third wife), Rebecca West (the most feted and feared feminist, reporter, historian and critic of her day)—where does a biographer look for figures to replace them? Where are the women who have adopted a pose, struck a nerve, and dominated the literature and politics of their age who have not been done to death by other biographers? What woman has an image both as a woman and as an intellectual battleground, as a person and as a cause, who is history but who is also very much alive? The answer is inescapable: Susan Sontag.

We quoted Carlos Fuentes, the Mexican novelist, playwright, and diplomat. This litterateur who commanded the colossal range of contemporary world culture had called Sontag our Erasmus: "I know of no intellectual who is so clear-minded with a capacity to link, to connect, to relate. She is unique."

We called Sontag our culture's Simone de Beauvoir, attacked from the Right, first championed, then vilified by the Left, fighting and making up with the likes of E. L. Doctorow, Norman Mailer, and the other major literary lights. We noted that she had been repudiated as a sham feminist by Adrienne Rich and a lapsed exponent of popular culture by culture maven Camille Paglia, and also lionized by the literary establishment (she was a past president of American PEN). We recalled that Sontag had enthralled and enraged her peers and several generations of readers since the appearance of her first controversial collection of essays, *Against Interpretation* (1966).

Publishers always want to know which of your subject's books is still in print; we emphasized that her publisher had *never* allowed her work to go out of print. We played up her successes. *The Volcano Lover* (1992) had been on the *New York Times* bestseller list for several weeks; this romantic historical novel won Sontag a new following. We made great claims for *Illness as Metaphor* (1977), her classic book-length essay, which demolished the mythical link between disease and personality types and revolutionized the medical profession's thinking about cancer, provoking doctors to be more candid with their patients and to enroll them in the fight against the disease. We described how Sontag's bombshell of a book grew out of her own prolonged bout with breast cancer. Doctors gave her a less than a ten percent chance to live, but she aggressively took control of her own treatment, experimenting with new forms of chemotherapy as well as surgery. Virtually every reviewer, including some of her fiercest detractors, hailed *Illness as Metaphor*. It had been reprinted ten times.

Then we cut to the chase:

> Writers have not investigated Sontag's resolute image making—or her complex and not unrelated sexual life (reports of her lesbian affairs in the New York literary community have circulated for years). Susan Sontag has been ballyhooed, but she has yet to receive the in-depth attention of a probing biography—one that is sure to excite and outrage her friends and enemies and intrigue her legion of readers, an impressive contingent that cuts across the generations from the sixties to the present. Her books fill college bookstores, appear on school reading lists, and are debated not only in journals such as *Partisan Review*, *The New York Review of Books*, and *The New Criterion*, but in mass circulation publica-

tions such as *The New York Times Magazine* and *People*. Sontag herself
has appeared in publications as diverse as *The London Review of Books*
and *Vogue*.

From this evocation of the writer as intellectual celebrity we segued
to the conception of the writer as myth and cultural symbol:

> *Commentary* editor Norman Podhoretz has called her the dark lady of
> American letters; critic Walter Kendrick has anointed her its unofficial
> hostess. Susan Sontag's success has surely stemmed from her writerly
> accomplishments, but she also bridges a gap in the culture. As Podhoretz
> observes, there is always a slot available for such a woman. In one gener-
> ation it is Mary McCarthy; in another it is Susan Sontag. McCarthy her-
> self recognized the prototype: "So you're the one who is supposed to be
> the next me," she remarked to Sontag on their first meeting.

Then we aligned the cultural symbol with the careerist:

> It takes nothing away from Sontag's achievement to say that she has been
> groomed for the part. She has had only one publisher, the redoubtable
> Roger Straus. He has squired her through the labyrinth of New York's lit-
> erary environs and orchestrated her published appearances with aplomb.
> (She lives within walking distance of his office.) He has been seen as pro-
> moting her (doing only what a publisher should do), while she retains
> her *gravité*. Edmund Wilson caught on to the game, grumbling in his
> diary about Roger's touting of this new girl, who wrote a tad too preten-
> tiously for Wilson's taste. (The aging Wilson may also have been jealous
> of the younger Straus, fabled for his womanizing and still in shape to
> shepherd a female writer as Wilson had groomed Mary McCarthy.)
> Straus even tried to canonize Sontag in mid-career, raising the eyebrows
> of not a few reviewers when *A Susan Sontag Reader* appeared in 1982.

Still, we needed an overarching term that would unify all the elements
of our subject's success:

> Sontag has gained the status of an icon. She shows up at watershed
> events. Hanoi in 1968, the Arab-Israeli war of 1973, the Town Hall meet-
> ing to protest the suppression of Solidarity in 1982, Sarajevo in 1993.
> With her olive skin, dark hair, and dark clothing, Susan Sontag is the
> dark lady of literary desire. The black-and-white photographs of her that
> appear on book jackets and with articles conceal as much as they
> reveal—and there is almost always a photograph. She does not show off
> her figure; she does not give much away, except the occasional smile. She
> can seem both forbidding and feminine, formal and casual, the very
> archetype of the talked-about writer. "Even her nursery-rhyme name,"
> critic Mary Ellmann observed, "seems designed for dropping." Ellmann
> remarked that when Sontag won a Merit Award for her first novel, *The
> Benefactor* (1963), from *Mademoiselle*, her "somber posture in the maga-
> zine was splendid. Barbra Streisand appeared no more exemplary as

Singing Comedienne, or Valentina Tereshkova as Cosmonaut, than Susan Sontag as Writer." Aristocratically tall and composed, with that streak of silver-white just above her forehead, Sontag can appear aloof and elitist. But she is also nonchalant and accessible, clothed in jeans and devoid of makeup. Her photographs trade on these contradictions, for like all mythic figures she must be seen as a union of opposites. She is a handsome woman—not plain, not pretty, not beautiful. She is neither too feminine nor too masculine.

Having established Sontag's importance and explained why she was an intriguing and saleable subject, we turned directly to the kind of biography we would write:

> An authorized biography of Susan Sontag? Surely such a project would be self-defeating. Sontag has never shown any interest in biography and is unlikely to cooperate with a biographer. To protect herself, she might buck biographers to Roger Straus, counting on him to deflect biographical inquiries. She might authorize a biography or, like Martha Gellhorn, pretend to have given her blessing to an authorized biographer as a means of discouraging the unauthorized. Any successful biography of Sontag will have to be not only a pioneering but a buccaneering work, willing to press on no matter how many times the subject, her publishers, or her coterie try to ambush it. The only biography of Susan Sontag worth writing is an outlaw biography. In the long run, the unauthorized biography will attract sources and supporters precisely because its authors are nonaligned and owe nothing to any camp.

We expressed the hope that Sontag would provide some limited cooperation, but we were not counting on it. Collaboration, we thought, compromises biographers, especially biographers of living figures, who may think themselves fortunate to have selected material doled out to them by the subject and the subject's friends. Inevitably, such biographers become fearful of alienating their subjects and other important sources—worse yet, biographers can become their subjects' friends and begin keeping the secrets and confidences biographers are supposed to expose. The best outcome would be a series of interviews with Sontag but no sanction from her.

We described our qualifications and the way we worked together. I had published five unauthorized biographies and was used to dealing with reluctant and even hostile subjects. Lisa, a member of the New York bar with a Ph.D. in English, had edited my books and advised me on copyright and libel issues. She had also written biographies of Emily Dickinson and Thurgood Marshall for the juvenile market, as well as a history of the Supreme Court and a critical study of William Faulkner.

We argued that a joint biography of Susan Sontag would have several advantages. We had done many interviews together and found that in certain instances, especially with women, Lisa's presence yielded invaluable information that might not otherwise have been revealed (later this contention would be proven when we interviewed *Partisan Review* editor William Phillips and his companion Edith Kurzweill). We contended that a husband and wife, with legal and literary training, working on a contemporary woman writer, made for an unusual configuration and would draw attention and cooperation that a single author was less likely to attract.

We conceded that as with all unauthorized biographies, there would be people who would refuse to talk. But Sontag had so many acquaintances and had traveled so widely that sources of information would hardly be lacking for this biography. We identified Sontag letters in the archives of contemporary writers. Even better, we had complete access to her publisher's archive at the New York Public Library. Indeed, the Farrar, Straus collection was the bedrock of our biography, since it included the correspondence of Roger Straus, Susan Sontag, Robert Giroux and other important figures, as well as memos documenting books sales, promotion, and publicity concerning Sontag's books.

We had already done several preliminary interviews, starting more or less at the periphery, gradually building up a network of contacts. The next step was to secure a publisher and to seek out major figures for interviews. This is the Robert Caro procedure, the one he used for his Lyndon Johnson biography. He knew that many important figures would not speak with him if he approached them immediately, so instead he turned first to figures of lesser importance, cultivating them, and parlaying the information they gave him into interviews with major sources.

Similarly, we had interviewed figures such as Ralph Schoenman, organizer of the Town Hall protest against the suppression of Solidarity, at which Sontag managed to alienate many of her supporters on the Left. Schoenman befriended Sontag and her son, David Rieff, but he was not an intimate member of their circle. We also cited the assistance of other biographers—one of whom had put us in touch with a Sontag schoolmate. In the proposal we presented a list of potential interviewees which read like an all star cast, pointing out that Sontag seemed to know everyone from photographer Richard Avedon to writers like William Gass, Milan Kundera, Joseph Brodsky, Norman Mailer, and Arthur Miller, to dancers like Merce Cunningham, and movie stars like Warren Beatty and Jane Fonda.

The very fact of having a contract for a Sontag biography, we emphasized, would also make a significant difference. Interviewees want to know that the biographer has a publisher and that the biography is the "real thing." Subjects are the same way. Sontag was more likely to extend some limited cooperation if she knew the biographers had a contract and that they were not going to go away. In my experience, people who had turned down interview requests two or three times eventually came around when they realized I was drafting a book and they might be featured in it without having had a chance to have their say.

Then we put a question that we thought would arise when we requested interviews: Why a biography of Sontag *now*? What point is there in doing one while her career is still in progress? Why do it if there would be difficulty obtaining information, or if there were people who would not cooperate? The answer, we replied, was that Sontag passes the visceral test. When we told others that the subject of our biography was Susan Sontag, people gasped. Just the announcement of a Sontag biography was greeted as an act of daring, as though Susan Sontag were untouchable.

"This is indeed the moment for a Sontag biography," we declared. She had reached a peak in her career. Perhaps she would produce greater work, but a biography *now* would capture Sontag's moment of triumph and show what it looked like to her contemporaries. The verdict of posterity might be different, but the point of first biographies is that they embody an epoch in the subject's life and in the life of the world she helped to shape. First biographies show this epoch from the inside in a way that subsequent biographies cannot. Some of the witnesses to the trajectory of Sontag's career would soon be dead. This is what happened with my biography of Martha Gellhorn. By the time my book was published, several of Gellhorn's friends—especially her childhood schoolmates—interviewed for my work had already died. The difficulties an unauthorized biography faces are no more troublesome—in many ways less so—than those encountered by the authorized biographer who comes generations after and has fewer people to interview but more archival material to wade through and difficult literary estates to placate. (On this subject, see Ian Hamilton's *Keepers of the Flame* and Michael Millgate's *Testamentary Acts,* and my *A Higher Form of Cannibalism? Adventures in the Art and Politics of Biography.*)

We mentioned that we had met Sontag at a pivotal point, when we were living in Poland in 1980 and reassessing our views of the Cold War period and Communism. Sontag was doing much the same thing and would later pay heavily for the change of mind and heart she evinced during her Town Hall speech in 1982. We brought the immediacy of witnesses, not just the hindsight of historians.

Fall 1995: Elizabeth Frost-Knappman, our agent, offered our 118-page proposal (which included a detailed chapter outline and an annotated bibliography) to several publishers. Five or six seemed quite interested. Scribner, Carl's previous publisher, was not. Scribner publisher Susan Muldow told Elizabeth that the company could not possibly publish a biography of Susan Sontag because Sontag was a friend of Muldow's. In the cozy world of the New York book trade, there was hardly an important figure that Sontag did not know.

It quickly became clear that only one editor really understood our proposed book and would risk the opposition of Sontag and her allies. Before he made an offer, he called us. Only Lisa was at home. In a half hour of intense grilling Gerry Howard, then an editor at Norton, covered every area of concern. How would we handle fair use? (He had already concluded correctly that we would be denied permission to quote from Sontag's work.) How could we be so sure we could get people to talk to us, and how would we penetrate Sontag's inner circle of intimates? He wanted to know why she and her son David had been so upset over their caricatures in Edmund White's novel *Caracole.* He brought up the issue of libel in the context of the Mary McCarthy-Lillian Hellman suit and how it had ruined Mary McCarthy's later years. Lisa replied the case for summary judgment favoring Hellman had been wrongly decided, and because it was no notoriously misguided, something like it would probably not happen again in New York. Although Lisa's area of specialty was copyright law, Howard pressed her, evincing a good deal of skepticism. How much information he really wanted from Lisa, and how much his questions were really a form of testing her toughness, is hard to say. He sounded interested and wary. Perhaps it was in this conversation, or in a later one when both of us spoke to him, that we made the key point that sold the book: We wanted to tell the story of how Susan Sontag became Susan Sontag. It did not matter if we got to know the intimate details of her sex life. It did not matter if her closest friends did not speak with us. It did not matter if we could not quote at length from her work. Of course, we would explore all of these questions and try to interview every important source, but our main task was to show how she had become an icon. And for that approach we had the Farrar, Straus archive—the inside word on how Sontag's career had been promoted and tended to with exquisite care and determination.

After Howard had satisfied himself, he told us that he now had to sell the book to his colleagues. Norton is the last of its kind: an independent publisher. Editors there work closely together and think of their books as a collective enterprise. Howard liked our book because he did not think we had sensationalized Sontag. We were not basing our biography's appeal on lurid revelations, but rather on the story of how she had become a public figure. Howard was well aware that in the literary community Sontag had a privileged place—backed to hilt by her powerful publisher, Roger Straus. Howard expected Straus to personally intervene in hopes of stopping our biography. After he had sold his colleagues on the merit of our proposed book, Howard called us and said: "I'm very excited and very scared."

We were thrilled and heartened by Howard's words. He was the first editor we had dealt with who understood the peril and the promise of an unauthorized biography of a living figure. The more usual dynamic is for a house to buy such a book and then—after the initial exhilaration of acquisition has subsided—to panic when the subject's lawyers initiate the first legal threats. Thus Doubleday dropped my Gellhorn biography when Gellhorn hired a Manhattan law firm to put the publisher on notice.

Along with our signed contract with Norton, we agreed to sign on to a special insurance policy to protect us and our publisher in case of a libel action. There was a high deductible. We might have been responsible for up to $16,000, but on balance we thought that amount would be acceptable. It was not so high as to bankrupt us, and in the event of any kind of extensive litigation (which might well have killed the book) the insurance policy seemed a prudent measure.

Howard also arranged for us to meet with Vic Schmalzer, then executive vice president at Norton, so that we could all review what would constitute fair use when we quoted from Sontag's work. We agreed that if we quoted in total somewhere in the neighborhood of 5000 words from the body of her work (published and unpublished, including correspondence), that would be an acceptable amount for a 130,000-word book. This agreement was only a rule of thumb since copyright law does not specify how much can be quoted under fair use. For individual works such as novels, for example, 300 words is fairly standard; for poems, no more than two lines (Norton's policy, not ours). For us, it was not the rule of thumb in itself that was important but rather the publisher's desire to work out these matters beforehand. In our experience, no publisher had ever approached an unauthorized biography with so much deliberation and understanding of the authors' problems.

Spring to fall 1996: Our next major step was to write Susan Sontag. Lisa thought there was just the possibility that Sontag would see us—if only to gauge our commitment and qualifications and perhaps to co-opt us through some form of limited cooperation that would keep us in line, so to speak. I thought Sontag would react negatively and forcefully. The idea that we would in any sense take her measure in a biography would displease her, and like many literary figures she would regard a biography as a sign that she was losing control of her life myth, one that she had brilliantly crafted in the course of countless interviews conducted over several decades.

In early March we sent Sontag a letter with a bull's-eye opening:

> Dear Ms. Sontag
>   We have just signed a contract with W.W. Norton to write a biography of you.

We reminded her that we had met her at a literary conference in Warsaw. We described our publications. We explained why the "time is right for a biography of you." We singled out her role as public intellectual, her independence and freedom from academic sectarianism, her landmark essays and innovative novels, and the need to write a full scale life since there were only two introductory books that hardly did justice to her evolving sensibility, "which can only be essayed in a biography."

We tried not to be presumptuous. We certainly did not count on her cooperation when proposing the biography to our publisher. But we would obviously profit from a meeting with her—"not only to gather information, but to help us evaluate what we learn from other sources." We conceded that the biography of a living figure cannot be definitive, but we added "what biography can ever be definitive anyway?" Instead, we wanted to "establish a ground on which other biographers and critics can build." We quoted Herbert Butterfield on the importance of first biographies that capture materials otherwise lost to history. We quoted a phrase from my biography of Norman Mailer: "Sometimes one can, with a pen, get a purchase on the future." We ended our letter by offering to send Sontag copies of our publications and saying we looked forward to hearing from her. In the meantime, we continued interviewing figures on the periphery, deciding that until we heard from Sontag it would be best to keep a low profile and not rile her by trying to approach those closest to her before we knew for certain what her attitude was going to be.

In early August, still not having received any word from Sontag, we sent her a brief note saying that perhaps she had not had the opportunity to reply to us or had not received our first letter (a copy of which we enclosed). Then on September 12, we received a letter from Andrew Wylie, Sontag's agent. He thanked us for our letters to Ms. Sontag, and he said she had asked him to write on her behalf. He reported that they were "intrigued" with the idea of a biography but that because she was writing a new novel she did not have the time for an interview then. For future reference, he wanted to know more about our "approach," what sources we would use, and how long we expected to work on the book. He looked forward to hearing from us.

We talked this letter over with Gerry Howard, who relished discussions of strategy and tactics. If there was anything surprising about Wylie's letter, it was the mildness of his reply. Wylie had a ferocious and formidable reputation in the New York literary community, and we expected (when we saw the envelope with his name on it) a far more intimidating response. But we realized that his strategy was shrewd: he wanted to find out what he could without offering anything in return except a vague possibility that Sontag might see us. At the time, we followed Gerry Howard's advice and our own inclination to say as little as possible:

> September 18, 1996
> Dear Mr. Wylie
> Thank you for your letter of September 12 regarding our biography of Susan Sontag. We are in the preliminary stages of research, having done some interviewing and research—for example, we have consulted the Farrar, Straus archive at The New York Public Library. As with other biographies of living figures we have worked on, our approach, proposed sources, and even the amount of time we spend on this project, will depend, in part, on the subject's availability for an interview. We are delighted to hear that Ms. Sontag is working on a new novel. One of our aims is to give a full account of her career as a writer of fiction. We hope that when the pressures of writing the novel let up, she will have the time to be interviewed for our book.

We never received a reply to our letter, but Wylie's silence gave us a slight opening. When interviewees asked us if we had Sontag's cooperation, we could say, in good faith, that we still hoped to secure it, and that Andrew Wylie had written an encouraging letter. I think we must have sounded naive to the hardened New Yorkers we began to contact—writers like Jill Johnston who seemed to think we were born yesterday. In New York, seeming naive can take you a long way, though, because people are sure to underestimate you and your persistence

Certainly we had not penetrated her inner circle and perhaps—as often happens with the subjects of unauthorized biographers—she and her set presumed we would eventually lose heart. But she could not have thought so for long, since on October 6, 1996, *The New York Times* published a profile of unauthorized biographers that featured an interview with us. We were photographed sitting in chairs back to back, our picture several times larger than the one of Sontag that also accompanied the piece. The article mentioned our literary and legal backgrounds and reiterated our view that the public had a right to read about "subjects who have created these images of themselves and who seem to feel entitled to project this as history ... the public is entitled to understand how that is done." We hoped to send a message to Sontag that we would not give up or feel humiliated—as some biographers do—when their subjects won't cooperate with them. "I feel my subjects are entitled to their anger," I commented. "I can certainly understand why someone would be nervous that there is someone around inquiring into her life. They have no control over this person. Who *is* this person?"

The *Times* article was very gratifying, especially since *The New York Times Book Review* had not printed our authors' query. Over a three-year period, we submitted the query three times, but it was never printed—and that seemed very strange since Sontag was such a New York item. Who at the *Review* was protecting her? If that sounds paranoid, remember that the New York book crowd inhabits a very insular world and that they protect their own. When John Simon gave Norman Mailer's novel *Harlot's Ghost* a less than enthusiastic appraisal, the *Review* gave Mailer almost as much room as Simon for rebuttal. Yet my biography of Mailer (published shortly after Mailer's novel) got no nod from the *Review*. Such is the skewed world of *The New York Times*.

The New York Times Book Review later published a letter from Doris Lessing's agent attacking her unauthorized biographer. Plenty of room for that kind of missive, but not space enough for a three-line author's query. It was very odd since the *Review* had published the query for my Rebecca West biography twice. A former *Times* book editor had discouraged Janny Scott from publishing her article about us, but fortunately she persisted.

The *Times* piece attracted the notice of Edward Field, a fine poet who had been a friend of Alfred Chester, a writer close to Sontag in the 1960s. Chester had profoundly influenced Sontag's work, and as Chester's literary executor Field was able to give us access to letters and other materials that documented the first stages of Sontag's career. Just as important, he persuaded Harriet Zwerling, one of Sontag's early lovers, who watched her develop into a great literary figure, to talk to us. Others also approached us because of the *Times* article, and this sudden spurt of activity emboldened us to begin writing to Sontag's closest friends. Many of them, like playwright Maria Fornés, another former Sontag lover, did not answer our letters. Others, like poet Richard Howard, sent disingenuous replies. He wrote that he did not feel "qualified" to comment on Sontag's life, although he had no such difficulty years later when he appeared in *Regarding Susan Sontag*. Still others did speak with us but only off the record or on a not for attribution basis. It was remarkable to us that even tenured professors at Columbia, the City University of New York, and New York University, would not speak for the record. Sontag & Co. had pretty well cowed the literary/academic establishment.

It was generally thought that Sontag had immense power and access to high-powered attorneys who could make life difficult for those who cooperated with us. Rumor had it that she had threatened to sue Edmund White over *Caracole*. She *had* sued *Soho News* for printing her remarks at Town Hall. But in large part impressions, not facts, predominated. One story from a writer who had taken a course from Sontag at City College sums up the absurdity of these fears. The story is so incredible we decided not to put it in the biography, believing that reviewers would simply dismiss it as paranoid and a sign of bias against our subject. Yet the story was not so different from others we had heard and it bears repeating here as the kind of parable that evokes what might be called the New Yorker's dread of the Sontag ascendancy.

At a National Arts Club event, biographer Carole Klein spoke with a woman who told Klein that she had had a terrible experience in Susan Sontag's writing class. Carole, a friend of ours, asked the woman if she would be willing to speak with us. "Oh yes," she replied. She was so eager to tell us about this horrible episode that it seemed she was expecting a catharsis. We phoned her to set up an appointment. The first note of hesitation could be heard when she said she did not want her name used. "You see, I'm coming out with a first novel, and Susan can see to it that the book will be reviewed badly." We did not argue with her, except to ask mildly, "Do you really think she has that much power?" But the question was not discussed; we simply agreed to terms. Ten minutes later she called back. Her husband had advised her not to speak with us. She simply could not risk the possibility that Susan would associate her with the story. I responded that she had put us as biographers in an awkward position. We had been given to believe that she had a terrible story to tell; she had, in effect, alluded to evidence that as biographers we were obligated to investigate whether she was willing to speak with us or not. Could she not consider her story as deep background? It was important for us to hear the story even if she forbade us to use it. She agreed. We reconfirmed the time of our appointment with her. Ten minutes later she called back again. No, she just couldn't do it. She only wanted to extricate herself from a career-threatening situation. This incident increased our sympathy for Sontag, now a victim of a paranoid writer who was willing to say that Sontag had done a terrible thing but Sontag herself was such a terrible person that the story of her terribleness could not be told or she would do something even more terrible. Later we discovered the following passages in Vivian Gornick's *Approaching Eye Level* and Kathy Acker's *Great Expectations:*

> "Susan Sontag has a stranglehold on the intellectual press. Without her say-so nothing gets accepted."
> "You don't really believe that, do you?"

> Dear Susan Sontag,
> Would you please read my books and make me famous?

In his memoir *I Can Give You Anything But Love* (2015) Gary Indiana reports Sontag's annoyance when she happened upon Acker's exhortation. Sontag never wanted to be reminded of her status or that she had some kind of power, even though she was forever touting certain writers, introducing and blurbing them in such a forensic, authoritative way, that made budding writers seek her blessing.

January to July 1997: *The New York Times* profile and our steady stream of letters to Sontag's confidants set the Sontag legal team in motion. On January 10, 1997, Donald S. Lamm, chairman of W.W. Norton, received a letter from Russell E. Brooks of Milbank, Tweed, Hadley & McCloy, a Manhattan white shoe law firm. The letter stated that we were "unknown to Ms. Sontag" and that she had "no reason" to believe we were "qualified to write such a biography." The letter expressed the concern that Sontag's privacy and the privacy of her friends would be violated in a book that aimed to "provoke controversy." The letter put the publisher "on notice." Our book would be scrutinized and Sontag's rights "meticulously defended."

"Well, now we know where we stand," Gerry Howard said when he called us. He did not seem at all daunted by the letter. In truth, we had at least half-expected the day when the legal intimidation would begin. Gerry told us that Roger Straus had also called W.W. Norton to complain about our book to editor Starling Lawrence, who had published with Straus's firm. Straus alleged that Norton had bought our book only because Farrar, Straus were their competitors and Norton was trying to get back at him. He called biographies of living figures "a mug's game." After our book was published we learned from a *New Yorker* profile of Straus that he had said to Lawrence, a propos of our book, "kill the fucker." When Lawrence did not do so, Straus promptly dropped Lawrence's forthcoming novel from the FSG list.

On January 29, Vic Schmalzer replied to Millbank, Tweed:

Dear Mr. Brooks,

   This is to acknowledge receipt of your letter of January 10 to our Chairman, Donald Lamm, concerning a biography of your client, Susan Sontag, and to assure you that we and the authors intend to do a responsible job of publishing the work.

Our confidence in the project grew as it became clear that Norton would back us. Gerry Howard, through his contacts in the press, also began to tell the story of attempts to suppress our biography. Soon there would be an article in *The New York Observer*, but first I have to explain an intervening controversy with Sontag and her collaborators that I made into a public issue.

   In the fall of 1996, we interviewed Victor Navasky in his office at *The Nation*. His magazine had published responses to Sontag's controversial Town Hall speech, as well as her rebuttal. David Rieff, then acting as his mother's editor, protested a critical review of *A Susan Sontag Reader* published in *The Nation*, alleging that it constituted revenge for her attack on the Left. But Sontag subsequently published an article about Bosnia in *The Nation*, and Navasky told us that she had told him it was one of her favorite magazines. Navasky was cordial and helpful, not only answering our questions but also making suggestions about other avenues of research. He asked us if we had read the PEN board minutes during the period of Sontag's presidency. We looked at each other in chagrin. It was such an obvious thing to do, and we had not thought of it. Under the title "PEN's Iron Curtain," I reported in the May 1997 issue of *The New Criterion* what ensued.

   In October 1996, I called PEN American Center to request board minutes for 1987–1989 when Susan Sontag was president. An office assistant said they would get back to me. I called a week later and was informed that PEN's attorney had advised that my request be denied because I had not been a member of PEN during Sontag's presidency. I replied that such reasoning seemed disingenuous for an organization created to promote openness, freedom of expression, and understanding among writers.

   Between November 1996 and January 1997, I sent three letters to Karen Kennerly, then PEN's executive director, requesting the minutes. She finally replied on January 3, stating that the new board would consider my request later in January. I wrote again in late February but received no reply. So on April 16, 1997, near the end of a long PEN meeting on openness and democratization in PEN, I spoke briefly about the iron curtain that had descended on my request for board minutes. The members laughed raucously when I pointed out that it had been easier for me to obtain Lillian Hellman's FBI file than to get an answer out of PEN. Clearly angry that I had raised the issue at a public meeting, PEN's new president, Michael Scammell, asked me if I had Susan Sontag's permission to write her biography. I replied that I had every right to write her biography, just as she had every right to oppose it. His remark suggested to me that he felt he needed Sontag's permission to release the board minutes—an odd position for the unauthorized biographer of Alexander Solzhenitsyn to adopt. After the meeting, I asked him: "What if I were writing a history of PEN? Would you still refuse me the minutes?" Changing the subject, he replied that he did not appreciate my hijacking the meeting to vent personal grievances. Then a former PEN board member told me that in 1986 the board had gone on record stating that minutes would be available to any member who requested them. Finally, a member of PEN's Freedom-to-Write committee told me that he was aghast that I had not received the minutes: "Our committee was all for you." Only PEN staff members were against approving your request. In fact, at the Freedom-to-Write committee there had been a vote, 13–1, in my favor, with the lone dissenter Leon Friedman, an attorney for Sontag's publisher, Farrar, Straus.

Eventually, from several eyewitnesses who prefer anonymity, we were able to piece together what had happened in the Freedom-to-Write committee. Karen Kennerly addressed the committee, saying PEN had a very difficult problem on its hands. A writer named Carl Rollyson doing a biography of Susan Sontag wanted access to board minutes dating from the period when she was president of PEN, and she was opposed to his request. Kennerly wanted to get a reading from the committee about what it thought. With an ex-president of PEN present, Kennerly suggested it was an especially good time to bring the issue up. Kennerly smiled at Tom Fleming, one of her old friends. She then pointed to an irony, which made some committee members think she favored granting permission, especially since she said the irony made her feel "uncomfortable." PEN's records dating from before the period Sontag became president had been sold to Princeton Library, where anybody could consult them, "including those about you, Tom," she said. (Later, we discovered that the records for Sontag's first six months as president were available at Princeton.) Fleming said he could not imagine anything that happened while he was president that he would want to conceal. But even if he could, he did not see how he could say no. "We are an organization that stands for freedom-to-write and free access to information. And we're defenders of the First Amendment. We try to strike down censorship. The principle is so glaringly obvious."

Kennerly wanted to hear from other committee members. There were a few Sontag friends in the room, and they expressed sympathy for her opposition to an unauthorized biography. But the committee nevertheless supported Fleming, except for Leon Friedman, who went through "various circumlocutions," as one committee member put it, to rationalize Sontag's position. Kennerly said that under the by-laws the Committee did not have the power to release the board minutes but that she would report the strong sense of the meeting back to President Scammell.

One former board member we interviewed did believe board minutes should be kept secret. How else, he said, could business get done? How could PEN officials keep confidences or explore positions that would be made immediately public? But we wanted access to minutes now nearly ten years old. We were doing nothing that could possibly jeopardize a sitting president's effectiveness.

My *New Criterion* article was followed by Celia McGee's "Susan Sontag Stonewalls Norton's biographers" in *The New York Observer* (July 21, 1997). She began her article by noting that Roger Straus had just announced an edict:

> No biographies of living people allowed. The cause? Susan Sontag.... The usually garrulous, expletive-spewing Mr. Straus would only say that he would "under no condition talk to anyone about this policy, a result of seeing how it (being the subject of a biography) affects our author."

McGee then described PEN's refusal to give me copies of the board minutes. Scammell told McGee that he did not feel like "adjudicating" that matter. He said that he was a good friend of Sontag's, and he was certain she had good reasons for opposing the biography. But McGee, at least, faced the issue squarely, observing that the "close-knit, status-conscious New York literary elite are alert to the storm signals transmitted from the intellectual Mount Olympus occupied by Ms. Sontag and her circle." McGee noted that Sontag is the "reigning deity of a particularly incestuous literary scene."

McGee's article quoted Starling Lawrence expressing his respect for Straus's view, but adding: "I don't think of Norton as the publisher of kiss-and-tell biographies, and this is a serious book." Gerry Howard shrewdly observed that it was not a biography per se that was Straus's concern: "There's just this sense that if a biography is to be written about Ms. Sontag ... it should be written by somebody in the fold; an authorized biography, with all it implies." McGee noted that we had not written for *The New York Review of Books* or the other outlets Sontag favored. She quoted Andrew Wylie, who used precisely the words I had used to describe Sontag's probable reaction to her biographers: "I don't know who these people are."

Sharon DeLano, a New York book editor and a member of Sontag's retinue, said of us: "They've told people that they're writing a hostile book. It's sordid and mean-spirited." Ira Silverberg, then editor-in-chief at Grove Press, scoffed at such charges and added: "Roger Straus is the aging buffoon of the business.... His arrogance precedes him. He makes publishing decisions to protect his friends." To Silverberg it was obvious that Sontag "has always been motivated by a manipulative desire to become, and stay, famous." To our amazement, Silverberg quoted a letter from Alfred Chester: "Susan is going to be terribly famous very soon because Roger Straus, her publisher, is mad about her."

After *The New York Observer* article appeared, we tried to put pressure on PEN by enlisting the support of Norman Mailer, E. L. Doctorow, Pete Hamill, and Victor Navasky. None of them answered our letters or pursued the case, so far as we know. Doctorow's silence was especially disappointing, since he had reacted in outrage when I told him (in early 1997) that I had been refused access to the minutes. "Write Scammell," Doctorow advised, assuring me that the president would clear the way. Scammell made a show of openness by airing the controversy in the November–December 1997 issue of the PEN newsletter. He argued that the First Amendment had its limits. How could any organization simply throw itself open to members and nonmembers alike? Trying to complicate my request for records nearly a decade old, he wondered, "When does the past becomes history?" He treated me like a firebrand and reserved for himself the role of philosopher of history.

My reply to Scammell appeared in the January–February PEN newsletter and noted that Scammell had a "timid idea" of independent intellectual and biographical inquiry if he believed that one needs permission to deal with public figures—"no less the President of an organization." I ventured the observation that Scammell had an "extraordinarily genteel view of the genre that I don't think the membership will support." In fact, the newsletter never printed a single letter supporting Scammell's position, although it did print several that opposed Scammell.

I traded more letters with Scammell, pointing out that PEN had not done me the courtesy of even supplying information already in the public record, such as press releases dating from the Sontag's presidency. Scammell replied saying he was sure that this had been an oversight, and if I would write to Karen Kennerly again, I would have the material. Kennerly never answered my letters. I made one final try with Michael Roberts, the new executive director of PEN, writing to him on January 4, 1999. Roberts never answered the letter.

We were prepared to do a book that tested this hypothesis: How far would a figure like Susan Sontag go to suppress a biography? Her reaction would say a good deal about her personality. It was telling that she never answered our letters directly. She occupied, as McGee put it, Mount Olympus. Millbank Tweed, Roger Straus, and later other powerful figures acted for her. By contrast, Martha Gellhorn had written me a direct, forthright letter saying she did not want a biography written about her. What bothered Sontag most was the *fact* that we were doing her biography. It did not matter that it was not sensationalized; it did not matter that the book would carefully describe her writing and her career; it did not matter that we treated her as a serious cultural figure; it did not matter that we had a reputable publisher.

Certainly a number of writers like George Garrett, Edmund White, and Yoram Kaniuk (who appeared in Sontag's film *Promised Lands*) took our project seriously—as did Richard Sennett, Sontag's colleague at New York University's Institute for the Humanities. All of them provided important testimony. Sennett was especially eager to put us in touch with writers like White and with William Phillips, the longtime editor of *Partisan Review*, which had published "Notes on 'Camp'" and other important Sontag essays.

Our interview with Phillips provided one of the more amusing and revealing episodes of our research. We told Sennett that we had written to Phillips but had received no answer. Sennett urged us to write another letter and use his name. We did. Phillips took our mention of Sennett as a sign that we were Sontag's authorized biographers, although we had not stated or implied that such was the case. He had evidently received a call from Sontag shortly before we arrived at his Lincoln Center apartment for an interview. We encountered a recalcitrant figure that, at first, could not be budged—until I hit upon the idea of asking him about his *Partisan Review* memoir. He agreed to comment, but he became increasingly upset as I focused on page references to Sontag. His companion, Edith Kurzweil, seemed more sympathetic: "Talk to them, William," she kept saying. But Phillips had checked with Sontag and was on orders not to talk. As we were preparing to leave Kurzweil took a phone call and waved goodbye, but I remained concentrating on Phillips, attempting to pry answers out of him. Lisa was paying attention to Kurzweil. Lisa realized that the telephone call was from Sontag and heard Kurzweil running down the list of people we said we had interviewed and some of the questions we had posed to Phillips. Even with this crusty witness to Sontag's life, we obtained good material—not only about Sontag but about Roger Straus.

We were face to face with Sontag perhaps a dozen times during the course of our research on the biography. A frequent speaker at arts events in Manhattan, Sontag was always a fascinating study, entering a room with an entourage, and then exchanging kisses, and other elaborate greetings with well-wishers. At one event in an NYU auditorium we saw a man actually genuflect and kiss her hand. At The Drawing Center in Lower Manhattan, we ducked out of a panel on Artaud after she had delivered her remarks. As I began to analyze Sontag's performance, Lisa looked behind her, and there was Sontag, just a few paces behind us. Did she overhear what I said? It probably would not have mattered to her, since I'm sure she had often caught what audience members said about her. That she was right behind us was also revealing. She tended to make her star appearances and whisk out of the room before anyone could stop her.

Throughout the arduous process of researching and writing our biography, Gerry Howard proved a constant source of support. He helped to secure important interviews and relayed stories he heard about Sontag's cronies' efforts to obstruct our book. Howard greatly admired Sontag and saw no reason why she should not be the subject of a biography. When Gerry left W.W. Norton to accept a job heading Doubleday/Anchor books, we were disheartened. Authors are nearly always placed at a disadvantage when they lose their acquiring editors, since their books will be assigned to editors who already have other commitments. A book's second editor—even with the best will in the world—cannot recreate the initial enthusiasm for acquiring and conceiving a new book. If the writing of the book is well advanced—as ours was—then the next editor can only work at the margins, so to speak, making some helpful suggestions but always realizing that she or he has arrived at the party too late. Gerry himself seemed to be feeling a little guilty when he called to tell us about his move. He sounded nervous, even though he assured us that we would be in good hands with Alane Mason, a very capable editor.

Alane, in fact, was the best line editor we have ever worked with. It is hard to believe that there is an editor more meticulous when it comes to appraising a book sentence by sentence. She also has a superb sense of the architecture of a book. When we turned in our manuscript in the spring of 1999, she sent a detailed three-page letter. She was impressed with our research and seemed to take for granted that the book was well written. But our draft lacked one key ingredient: there was not enough cultural context. Too many times we described Sontag's actions as though they occurred in a vacuum. Without more social context, out subject's actions looked rather arbitrary. We also should look more carefully at Sontag's behavior. Did we always make it clear what her actions meant to her? In the interests of fairness, we owed it to our subject to think hard about the way she saw her behavior.

Alane's remarks coincided with those of our agent Elizabeth Frost-Knappman, who spotted in an even earlier draft too many judgments about Sontag's behavior. Describe, don't comment, and the readers can make up their own minds—this was essentially Elizabeth's advice, which Alane seconded. We took their point. We did have very strong feelings about the New York literary scene and about the way Sontag had manipulated it to her advantage, but it is self-defeating to begin with that thesis and not expect certain readers to rebel against it—if only to wonder what the contrary viewpoint might be. So in key passages we included much more cultural commentary and more balanced analysis of the implications of Sontag's career. The only problem with this approach is that some reviewers find it bland. I'm reminded of the reviewer of my Mailer biography who said it was too fair to be really interesting.

By the fall of 1999, we submitted another draft to Alane, which she thought "superb." We had responded to all of her major criticisms. She would continue to tinker with various passages, but we looked forward to the next major step: the legal reading and the dissemination of galleys. This was new territory for Alane: anticipating the reaction to a controversial biography. The first sign of trouble came when Alane sent us an email asking if we minded if Gerry took a look at our manuscript. With his commitment to the book and his considerable experience in New York literary matters (he had once been a PEN board member), he could be very helpful. Our initial reaction was wary, but we sent an email acceding to Alane's request. Yet almost immediately we had second thoughts: Gerry no longer worked for W. W. Norton, and we were uneasy about responding to two editors, especially since we had yet to receive the second half of our advance. We had no reason to distrust Gerry—quite the contrary— but it seemed unwise to let the manuscript move outside Norton at this sensitive stage. And then there was the contractual concern. Gerry had no standing in the contract, and yet we might be expected to make changes he suggested. We called Elizabeth, and her reaction was immediate: It was a very bad idea to involve Gerry. It had nothing to do with Gerry himself; Elizabeth regarded him as a fine editor to whom she would like to sell more books. There followed weeks and weeks of emails between us and Alane, and Alane and Elizabeth. Alane was astounded that we would not want Gerry's input. She implied that we did not care enough about the quality of our book. Gerry could save us a lot of grief, show us those passages where "you were leading with your chins." We wrote back that there was no way to fireproof an unauthorized biography. It was an illusion to think one could craft language that could short circuit criticism. Besides, Alane was adding another layer to the editorial process after she had deemed the book acceptable. Her emails became increasingly strident: she accused us of being "panicky authors"—a very strange charge to make given our track record and a proposal that clearly telegraphed how much trouble doing the biography would be. Alane dismissed with contempt Elizabeth's insistence on following the contract as well as her point that Alane was putting Gerry in an awkward position.

What made this exchange of emails particularly intense, on our side, was our worry that the manuscript or the galleys would be leaked to Sontag, who then might well seek an injunction to stop distribution of the book. If Norton could find a way to keep the book under wraps until it was on its way to bookstores, the likelihood of legal action diminished considerably, since the point of Sontag's efforts would be to kill the book, not to quarrel with it after it appeared. For us, just to collect the second half of our advance and to have the book published would be a major victory. What we feared most was tying up the book in further editing and ongoing legal readings, which is exactly what had happened to my Martha Gellhorn biography at Doubleday.

Alane never understood our concerns. She worked at Norton, a firm that prided itself on publishing books of integrity and treating authors respectfully. And we could not say, in so many words, what troubled us. What if Norton got cold feet? To say so was to express a doubt that would alienate the publisher. The book had already been deemed editorially acceptable, but Norton was holding back the advance until we responded to the legal reading. This gave them leverage, of course, although the contract made no distinction between legal and editorial acceptance and did not say that payment of the second half of the advance was contingent on the legal reading. So we continued through Elizabeth to press for our advance while assuring Norton that we would respond promptly to the legal reading as soon as we met with the firm's attorney.

Although we were confident we had a manuscript that should survive a legal reading without major changes, we could not be sure that Norton's attorney would see it that way. Publishers hire lawyers to keep them out of court. Consequently, these lawyers tend to make the most conservative readings of the law. A lawyer for St. Martin's Press had excised virtually all of my quotations and close paraphrases from Martha Gellhorn's unpublished papers and in the process destroyed the very concept of fair use. The process successfully eliminated any possibility of a copyright infringement suit but also killed some of the book's vitality.

Fortunately, Norton employed Renee Schwartz, a shrewd and sensible attorney. She saw no need to perform major surgery on a healthy literary manuscript. Her main concern seemed to be with our Notes and Comments section. She wanted to us to be more explicit about how we tied our narrative to documentary evidence such as letters and to the testimony we had gathered in interviews. She did not seem concerned with libel at all a propos of Sontag, evidently taking for granted that Sontag was a public figure and that what we had said about her was fair comment. Likewise, fair use was not a major issue, both because we had been sensible in restricting the amount of material we had quoted and because Schwartz honored the view of fair use we had worked out with Norton.

Schwartz's main concern, actually, was Annie Leibovitz. Without saying so, Schwartz apparently thought it was more likely that Sontag's companion rather than Sontag herself would make trouble for Norton. Leibovitz, in fact, had been very circumspect in her comments to the press about her relationship with Sontag, although they had very conspicuously been a couple for more than two decades—a fact we reported in our biography. Schwartz called for some fine-tuning and her caution may have been warranted given Sontag's next legal maneuver.

During our one meeting with Schwartz we readily acceded to nearly every suggestion she made. In many cases, her comments were more editorial than legal and resulted in a more accurate book. (After the meeting, she re-read parts of the manuscript and called for additional changes, relayed to us by Vic Schmalzer.) Before we left our meeting with her, however, we wanted one other issue resolved: Did Renee think it was advisable to include Gerry in editing of the manuscript? We were delighted to hear her say that "it might put Gerry in an awkward position." Even if he thought it was a good idea, he might very well regret it later. Alane responded that Norton had complete faith and trust in Gerry's judgment. Renee shrugged. Clearly it was not her place to adjudicate this controversy, and nothing more was said on that subject.

A few weeks later we were amazed to learn that Alane still planned to include Gerry in the final editorial process, and that she had interpreted Renee's remarks as confirming her decision to rely on Gerry. At this point, we turned the matter over to our agent. Elizabeth Frost-Knappman relayed our objection to taking the manuscript outside the house and outside the contract. Alane exploded. She sent us an email saying, okay, we had "won" and since Gerry would never get a chance to edit the book, we would never know how good the book could have been. To add to our punishment, she said in plain words that our recalcitrance meant, of course, that there would be less "push" for the book at Norton. She even went so far as to imply that other editors at the house had complained about certain passages that we had refused to change. Since we had a complete record of Alane's requests for changes and Renee's requests for changes, and since we had made virtually every alteration requested, we were baffled. We wrote to Alane, pointing out the discrepancy between the record and her accusatory remarks, and she responded not by denying we had made changes but by declaring that they were not enough.

After a few more weeks, Alane called us with still more corrections. She began by announcing that we had written a very good book and that her comments were in the spirit of making it even better. Her suggestions were excellent, and we agreed to all of them. Except for our continuing concern about how Norton would handle galleys (evidently no decision had been made yet), it looked as though we had finally reached an accommodation with Alane. Norton paid us the second half of our advance as soon as we completed the corrections mandated by the legal reading.

Then Elizabeth sent Alane an email telling her that I was about to publish a review of Sontag's new novel, *In America*, in *The New Criterion*. The journal had published several of my articles on Rebecca West. It had done more to promote West's reputation than any other American journal, and I had established a rapport with its literary editor, Roger Kimball and with the journal's founder, Hilton Kramer, whom I had interviewed for the Sontag biography. Kramer was hostile to Sontag, and the magazine's prominent Conservative stance has led to the erroneous assumption that anyone who writes for it is also Conservative. When my article "PEN's Iron Curtain" appeared in *The New Criterion*, a colleague of mine at New York University's Biography Seminar remarked that it was a "shame" that I had had to publish the piece in such a reactionary journal. Given my inability to interest liberals such as Navasky and Doctorow in the PEN controversy, however, I naturally took a different view.

At any rate, Alane called me in some agitation over *The New Criterion* review. She made no comment on the journal itself, but she asked what kind of review it was. "Well," I replied, "it's not a very good novel." Alane was concerned that a negative review would show bias that would be attributed to the biography (the novel is not criticized in the biography since Sontag had not quite finished it when we completed our book). I said I could not do anything about a book review that might be construed as showing animus against Sontag. She could always find something—if she were so inclined—to discredit the biography. Alane then asked if I would consider withdrawing the review. Too late, I said, the review was already in galleys. Alane declared that she was putting us "on notice" that she objected to the review. We reported this conversation immediately to Elizabeth, who was so concerned that she asked us to put a summary of it in writing to her. She then emailed Alane asking why she objected to a review she had not even read. Alane called us in a rage, denying that she had ever asked me to withdraw my review. She was only thinking of what was best for the book. In the course of our conversation she declared three times that Elizabeth was the stupidest agent she had ever dealt with. Couldn't we handle this problem by ourselves? Each time Alane made these remarks, we responded, "Alane, Elizabeth is our agent." Eventually Alane calmed down and apologized for what she called her "unprofessional behavior." We called Elizabeth, and with her agreement, we asked her to inform Norton that we no longer wanted any direct communication with Alane. Her call was the culmination of a series of abusive communications— mostly by email—that we felt had impugned our integrity and questioned our dedication to the project. From then on we heard from others at Norton, such as Vic Schmalzer and Alane's assistant, Stefanie Diaz.

We were, of course, never privy to the inner workings at Norton, but we do know that Sontag continued to put intense pressure on the publisher to send her the manuscript. In December 1999, Martin Garbus, a noted attorney specializing in First Amendment cases, called Norton requesting a copy of the manuscript. Vic Schmalzer declined to send it but promised Garbus that he would receive the galleys at the same time they were distributed to reviewers. This upset us, because it seemed that Garbus would have time to file a suit before the book reached bookstores.

Garbus next tried to obtain a copy of our manuscript from Elizabeth. Her husband and business partner, Edward Knappman, took Garbus's call and was told that Sontag was concerned that our book "violated the privacy rights of third parties"—a phrase Garbus would repeat in a letter to Elizabeth Frost-Knappman on December 17, 1999. During the phone call, Ed asked Garbus, "which third parties" might be involved and if Garbus represented them as well as Sontag. The lawyer declined to be specific. On December 20, Ed replied to Garbus, stating his remarks were "pure speculation" and adding,

> Apparently, the information you have is limited to the fact that Steve
> Wasserman of the Los Angeles Times received a request to sign a non-

disclosure and confidentiality agreement from our office in order to obtain a portion of the manuscript to consider for first serial rights. Mr. Wasserman had no legal right to pass this along to Roger Straus and violated the canon of ethics by doing so—an issue that will surely become public should there be any attempt to suppress or impede publication of the book by Drs. Rollyson and Paddock.

Was Annie Leibovitz one of those third parties? Was Sontag concerned about what we might say about her son David? We had heard a good deal of gossip about the private lives of Leibovitz, Sontag, and her son, but none of this made its way into the biography—not only for legal reasons, but also because we had chosen to write a book that focused on the development of Sontag's career and her status as icon.

Garbus apparently dropped out of the picture after receiving Edward Knappman's letter that accurately forecast that Garbus himself would become part of the story. On January 17, 2000, Elizabeth Manus's column in *The New York Observer* announced, "Susan Sontag Gets Jumpy":

> In case it's unclear, Susan Sontag really is against interpretation. Of her own life, that is. She has risen in protest again, this time of W. W. Norton's unauthorized biography of her.... The irony, of course, is that Ms. Sontag is a past president of PEN and a member of its board of trustees, making her a symbol of free speech worldwide.

Manus described how Steve Wasserman, a friend of Sontag's for over thirty years (he also had worked for Roger Straus) had faxed Sontag a copy of the confidentiality agreement concerning first serial rights for our biography. Then Roger Straus had written to Starling Lawrence that Elizabeth's pitch letter "leads us all to believe that W.W. Norton & Co. is about to publish a scandalous and shocking account of her [Ms. Sontag's] life." Straus added that it was "still hard for me to believe that a distinguished house such as W.W. Norton would be peddling the kind of biography that this confidentiality agreement and the covering letter suggests." What apparently set Straus off was Elizabeth's statement that we wrote about "Sontag's public persona and private passions, including her open love of women, the strategies behind her meteoric rise to fame, her political triumphs and missteps. Above all, they show how the life of Susan Sontag reveals the making of an icon." Elizabeth's words came directly from an early draft of catalogue copy written by Alane Mason. Indeed, it was Alane who convinced us and Norton that "the making of an icon" was a suitable title. Manus reported that she had learned from "publishing sources" that our book was actually "rather academic ... which is to say dry." Our comments to Manus focused on Sontag's unwillingness to have the machinery of her career exposed. "She doesn't want the hydraulics to show," Lisa said. "I think it's about being a powerhouse in New York City," I said.

The next week, Gerry Howard weighed in with a letter to the *Observer*. He identified himself as the biography's acquiring editor. He criticized Elizabeth for hyping the book in an attempt to market the serial rights (an agent's job, we thought) because her cover letter "misrepresents a seriously intended book." Sounding lofty, Gerry said, "My impression of recent developments surrounding its [the book's] embattled route to publication, as reported in your paper, is that almost everybody is behaving badly." But he saved his harshest words for Garbus, who he remembered as a "heroic defender of the right to publish" and who was now attempting to crush a book. Garbus, in fact, was attempting to exercise "prior restraint," which Gerry characterized as "two of the dirtiest words in constitutional law." Roger Straus, too, came off very badly. How did he dare to "take it upon himself to bullyrag another house out of publishing a book just because it may—probably will—ruffle his favorite author's tender feelings." Then there was Michael Scammell, Sontag's "hypocritical lap dog." Gerry ended his letter with a prediction:

> Look in the months to come for a concerted campaign by Ms. Sontag and company to prevent this biography from even being reviewed in the publications that matter for such a book. If a corporation of any size employed similar tactics to derail a book, a book it believed unfavorable, the howls of the literati would be justifiably loud. Tell me where the difference lies—I can't see any.

Perhaps it was Gerry Howard's letter, or more likely yet another article about the suppression of the biography published in *Content* magazine (May 2000), that began to show Sontag & Co. that they would pay a heavy price for their efforts to thwart our biography. Under the title "Agents of Influence: What Are Friends For?" Kaja Perinne observed that Steve Wasserman's behavior raised the "question of whether a book review editor's first obligation is to his newspaper or to his friends." She quoted Wasserman: "It seemed no breach of ethical practice whatsoever." But his colleagues disagreed. *Washington Post Book World* editor Marie Arana said that passing on a letter directed to her newspaper "would just be counter to our policy." Charles McGrath, editor of *The New York Times Book Review*, observed: "A book review and their staff need to strive for objectivity and stay out of the fray."

Perrine also provided some perspective on the controversy over how we handled Sontag's sex life: "One chapter is devoted to her [Sontag's] relationships with women as well as with men—a subject about which Sontag has shown herself to be particularly sensitive." In this short article, Perrine did not have space to point out that virtually all of our discussion of Sontag's sexuality was made in the context of criticism of her in the gay community and especially among gay and lesbian writers, who believed that Sontag's treatments of subjects like camp and AIDS would have been enhanced by some kind of discussion of her own sexual identity. In other words, we did not treat Sontag's "love of women" in isolation; we were attempting to explain the reasons why she remained silent on the subject.

Some of our interviewees raised the possibility that any discussion of Sontag's sexuality would provoke a lawsuit; others thought such a move improbable because it would be difficult for her to claim damage to her reputation or that she had been libeled simply because we "outed" her. In fact, we were not the first to out Sontag in print (we cited in the biography other occasions where her sexual relationships with women had been mentioned in print), although certainly we were the first writers to explore her sexuality and what it meant to her. That alone, some of our informants suggested, would bother her because we were complicating the heterosexual image she projected.

The story of Sontag's campaign to stop our book came to a head when Amanda Vaill, former Viking editor and herself a successful biographer, called us to say that *Vogue* had just assigned her to do an article about the whole controversy. She did an extensive interview with us and later reported that she had also spoken to Martin Garbus and other principals in the story. Yet *Vogue* never published the story. Exactly why, we never could find out, although an email from Amanda Vaill to me conveyed her impression that Annie Leibovitz had had a role in suppressing the interview.

Sontag's version of the genesis of the book and her reaction to it were delivered out of town, where she apparently felt free to lie. In the March 19, 2000, issue of *The Miami Herald*, Margaria Fichtner, a staff reporter who had written several flattering profiles of Sontag, quoted Sontag:

> "I've never met these people.... Obviously they're not friendly to me, and they never tried to get in touch with me. I'm told ... this has to do with some sort of settling of scores from the 60s.... She also denies that she tried to stop publication. "I'm not crazy. It's a free country. I can't possibly stop it, and I know that perfectly well. I was kind of hoping to get it vetted ... but they're playing hardball."

Then Sontag herself switched tactics. If the biography could not be suppressed, it would be belittled in a series of damning comments designed to seem off-hand but actually orchestrated by Sontag's writer friends and editors. She also began to release selectively material about her private life that would pre-empt what we said in our book. Sontag's campaign began in *Vanity Fair*, which had once considered running an article based on our book which was later shelved—perhaps because Annie Leibovitz is one of their primary photographers. In "Signature Sontag" (March 2000), Christopher Hitchens took time out from puffing Sontag's new novel and telling readers how she let him stroke her hair after her second bout with cancer to make this aside:

> Before we can go any further, however, there is a little bit of bother to be surmounted. With a slight frown she [Sontag] produced a catchpenny fax from some obscure literary agent in Connecticut, which touts for serialization a forthcoming "unauthorized first biography." In tones of wondrous and labored vulgarity, the handout speaks of "Sontag's public persona and private passions, including the open secret of her love of women; the strategies behind her meteoric rise to fame; her political triumphs and missteps." The subject of this sentence looks put out: "I don't think they can have talked to anyone who knew me in China or Vietnam or Bosnia. I know that my ex-husband won't have spoken to them, and certainly not David [her son]. They don't know my real friends. What do you think?" What I actually think is that this insecurity is rather charming.

The sentimentalizing of Sontag would continue in the profiles and reviews touting her novel. Her chief ally was *The New Yorker*, a magazine that used to publish frank profiles of powerful people. Although William Shawn has often been lionized as the magazine's genius editor, it was in fact Harold Ross who solicited and supported *The New Yorker*'s best journalism. Shawn came nowhere near matching, for example, Ross's staunch support for a profile that stripped powerful magazine tycoon Henry Luce of his pretensions. Luce put enormous pressure on Ross, who simply ignored him. Nowadays *The New Yorker* presents tea cozy lives. Thus it was no surprise that Joan Acocella, a Sontag friend, should tout Sontag's new novel in a profile titled "The Hunger Artist" (March 6, 2000). Once again, we were shrugged off with a carefully planted aside:

> This summer Norton will publish "Susan Sontag: The Making of an Icon," by Carl Rollyson, an English professor at Baruch College, and Lisa Paddock. According to their agent, the book will address the "open secret" of Sontag's "love of women," together with "the strategies behind her meteoric rise to fame." I don't know about the strategies, but as for Sontag's relationships with women, she says, "That I have had girlfriends as well as boyfriends is what? Is something I guess I never thought I was supposed to have to say, since it seems to me the most natural thing in the world."

Sontag's language made her sex life sound as if it was over by the time she graduated from high school. It might have been "natural" to have what she platonically calls boyfriends and girlfriends, but any number of witnesses to her career told us how concerned she and Roger Straus were not to have this subject aired in public. But one only has to go to the public record to read what has happened when any reporter dared ask Sontag about her love life. As our biography shows, Sontag has been consistently curt and evasive. But just before our biography was published, Sontag became positively garrulous on the subject of her sex life. Hence this item in the online *Guardian/Observer* (May 27, 2000):

> When you get older, 45 plus, men stop fancying you. Or put it another way, the men I fancy don't fancy me. I want a young man. I love beauty. So what's new? She says she has been in love seven times in her life, which seems quite a lot. "No, hang on," she says, "Actually, it's nine. Five women, four men."

She will talk about her bisexuality quite openly now. It's simple, she says. "As I've become less attractive to men, so I've found myself more with women. It's what happens. Ask any woman my age. More women come on to you than men. And women are fantastic. Around 40, women blossom. Women are a work-in-progress. Men burn out." To Sontag's biographers, her statement—like the one in *The New Yorker*—seems calculated to disarm, to make the subject of her sexuality sound banal. What is more, her statement does not square with our research which uncovered at least one sexual relationship with a woman before she married at the age of 17 and numerous other affairs with women thereafter. When our book was published, we received a letter from the wife of Phillip Rieff's brother. She complimented us on our accurate research and added that she was surprised about the ruckus over Sontag's sexuality. Everyone in the Rieff family knew Sontag had left Phillip because of her "love of women"—to use that much maligned phrase.

With Sontag suddenly sounding off about her sex life, it now seemed improbable that she would try to enjoin our biography. Norton never shared with us its strategy for heading off a lawsuit, but it apparently decided to shorten the usual time between distribution of galleys and distribution of the book, so that when the biography was published in July 2000, galleys had been out with reviewers for something less than three weeks.

If Sontag made any effort to suppress the appearance of reviews, we did not learn of it. The review ratio for our book was approximately one third positive, one third mixed, and one third negative. (It was predictable, though, that Steve Wasserman would find a reviewer to disparage our book in *The Los Angeles Times*.) This reception is not surprising or disturbing for an unauthorized biography of a living figure. Some reviewers begin with a bias against what they consider to be an invasion of privacy. This is especially true of those writing about biographies of literary figures that are revered or at least respected in ways that other public figures seldom are. Worshiping the author is a religious substitute for certain readers and reviewers who can be relied upon to regularly traduce literary biographies.

We were disappointed in most reviewers' unwillingness to engage with the biography's central concern: the making of an icon. Either reviewers saw no difference between Sontag and other writers, or they wanted more data. Just how powerful was Susan Sontag? We had thought the point was about the perception of power, not how many divisions Sontag could actually put into the field. But most critical reviewers did not deal with the book's main idea at all. Instead, they said we did not get inside of Sontag; because we could not say what she felt, the book was hollow. It was the classic case of reviewers demanding a book that the authors had not intended to produce. Our biography provides a view of Sontag from the outside; it describes how she had built her career— not how she felt about that career. Indeed, there is every indication that Sontag was in denial that she had a career. She never deigned to use the word and cut off interviewers who attempted to question her about her image.

The rest of the criticism was routine—the sort every literary biographer confronts. We were too hard on our subject; we were too soft. We did not discuss her work enough. Walter Goodman, in "Publishing Declares Open Season on Famous Figures" (*The New York Times*, November 23, 2000), lumped us in with a new wave of debunking biographies. How a critic who has written so much about the arts scene and about publishing and politics could presume, as Goodman did, that we had written the book intending it to be a best seller is beyond us. If he had made one call to the publisher, he would discovered that the initial print run was 10,000 copies and that there had been a small second printing of 2,500 copies. Norton had no advertising budget for our book and there was no author tour and no plan to publish a paperback edition. That Norton thought it was publishing a serious book did not even occur to Goodman.

Sontag's response to our biography after it was published appeared in Simon Houpt's article, "Goodbye Essays, Hello Fiction, Says Sontag" (*Toronto Globe and Mail*, October 23, 2000):

"I haven't read it and I've never seen it," Sontag says, perhaps a little briskly, when the subject comes up. "I know it was conceived as a very hostile enterprise" … Sontag says the book's authors "have connections" to the conservative periodical *The New Criterion*.

Shortly after our book was published we received this report: one of Sontag's former lovers called her up to commiserate about the biography. Sontag wanted to know if her ex had read the whole book. No, she had not. "Well, read all of it," Sontag said. To what end, I cannot say.

A few reviews continued to trickle in, but the life of a literary biography (and of most books) rarely lasts more than six months—at least as far as the bookstores and media are concerned. W. W. Norton in London decided not to publish the book and other British houses "chickened out"—to use James Bone's words in an article about our biography in the London *Times* (November 11, 2000). Bone reported that the issue of Sontag's sexuality seemed to be a stumbling block with British publishers who have to deal with libel laws that are not biographer-friendly. Bone quoted from an interview with us: "We did not call her lesbian. We did not call her bisexual.… We talk about the relationships and why she, like many, did not want to be labeled." He noted that the passages on Annie Leibovitz were a particular sore point, though he quoted our statement, "It's not a secret, it was just never written about." What is explosive about this book is the fact that it was written. When we started the book, people thought we were hitting the beaches on D-Day.

Postscript

Sontag died on December 28, 2004, just shy of her 72nd birthday, succumbing to her third cancer. Almost immediately a controversy erupted as the result of a writer in *The Los Angeles Times* who decried what he saw as an attempt to suppress acknowledgment of Sontag's sexual identity. Most obituaries mentioned only that she had been married and had a son. A spokesman for *The New York Times* explained that the newspaper of record could not verify the exact nature of Sontag's relationship with Annie Leibovitz, and that neither Leibovitz nor David Rieff would comment. So much for investigative journalism. The newspaper had actively collaborated in the presentation of Sontag, the alluring heterosexual icon with a Sunday magazine piece designed to promote the appearance of her novel *The Volcano Lover* (1992). Her marriage and son were mentioned but nothing else about her private life, even though other profiles in the magazine—such as one on Rebecca West—had gone into considerable detail about her personal life. Only Erik Homberger, writing in a British newspaper, directly addressed what he called Sontag's "gay sensibility." But my obituary in *The New York Sun* did—if only in passing—state as a fact that she had male and female lovers.

In 2006, Annie Leibovitz published *A Photographer's Life* and announced in her introduction: "I don't have two lives. This is one life, and the personal pictures and the assignment work are all part of it." Her new work was "the closest thing to who I am that I've ever done." Not only did she include intimate family photographs and her celebrated personality portraits of public figures ranging from Colin Powell to Demi Moore, she also, for the first time, published engaging and disquieting photographs of her "friend," Susan Sontag. These shots show, for example, the writer lounging on a paper-strewn bed with a typewriter on a table nearby; the writer in a hospital bed enduring the agony of chemotherapy; and, finally, the writer lying dead, bruised and bloated after her last bout with cancer.

This is not a book I ever expected Leibovitz to produce. Even more reticent than Sontag, Leibovitz had been downright hostile when questioned about her sexuality and her relationship with Sontag. That scare quotes still need to be wrapped around "friend" to refer to the Sontag/Leibovitz liaison exposes the inadequacy of Leibovitz's book. If life and work are one, what are connections between family, work, and friendship—not to mention the role love plays in Leibovitz's biography and photography?

Both Leibovitz's text and her photographs compartmentalize. If Sontag ever met Leibovitz's family, the photographs do not show it, and Leibovitz's words do not acknowledge any such encounters. If Sontag, a celebrity herself, had any dealings with Leibovitz's assigned subjects (Sontag certainly knew some of them), again the photographs and text do not say. As seemingly candid as this book is, the Sontag of *On Photography* would have cast a skeptical eye on it, noting that photographs conceal as much as they reveal.

A Photographer's Life does not hang together any more than Leibovitz's account of her own life does. And this is a shame. She told the *Guardian* that if Sontag were standing behind her, "She would be championing this work." How could this be, when Leibovitz also says Sontag would not have wanted the photographs published while she was alive? Caught in contradictions within contradictions, Leibovitz only made matters worse when she concluded the *Guardian* interview by saying: "Susan always said she felt that art really had to rise above the personal." This assertion is immediately followed by the last words of the article: "Leibovitz disagrees."

Beginning with Leibovitz's book, then David Rieff's memoir of his mother, and also other memoirs and books about Sontag, I began to consider the possibility of writing an updated and revised edition of the biography, especially when Sontag's papers, including extensive correspondence were sold to the University of California, Los Angeles and made available to scholars. Of special interest, of course, was my discovery that Sontag had a file on Rollyson and Paddock. Now I'm able to reveal what went on behind the scenes in correspondence over the three years that led up to the publication of our biography in June 2000.

To poet John Hollander Sontag confided: "They've even written twice to a nice young man who used to clean my apartment (ten years ago!), who read me their second letter over the phone." For my biography of Rebecca West, I had interviewed her hairdresser, and I believe in speaking with anyone who has had interactions with my subjects. To Andrew Wylie, Sontag deplored the work of any biographer who did not seek her approval— precisely what no self-respecting independent biographer would want to do. But to Sontag, we were "rogue biographers ... who specialized in doing unauthorized biographies (everybody from Marilyn Monroe and Mohammed [sic] Ali to lots of writers)." Although Ali had not been one of our subjects, she repeated this information to Chip Delany, a highly respected writer of science fiction who had interviewed her. He had described an encounter with me, and Sontag responded, "You thought he was nice. Maybe he is, or was (to you)." Unlike her other friends, Delany did not immediately acquiesce to her anathema, repeating his impression that I was "a highly intelligent man, well spoken and quite sincere," who had made a careful study of Sontag's work. In fact, Delany and I met several times and engaged in an extensive correspondence, disagreeing about some aspects of biography. But there was no room for nuance in Sontag's outrage

The Sontag circle closed ranks, with Stephen Koch assuring Sontag that my previous work was "worthless." Christopher Hitchens had his fun about the letter from "Rollyson and Paddock, which turns out not to be a firm of Dickensian solicitors." With her permission, he was willing to talk about certain matters—like Sarajevo—but, he added, "I would, naturally, have kept quiet about 'the Circle.'" Sontag replied, urging Hitchens to read about us in Janny Scott's *New York Times* article on unauthorized biographers of living figures: "Do read to the end. I see a divorce in this couple's future. Or am I just being (as always) romantic?" Why Sontag wrongly predicted a divorce is not clear, except that I expressed no concern about anyone writing about my life, and Lisa said she would not like it. Later Christopher Hitchens wrote to test out what he could say in a biographical profile of Sontag, adding, "As you see, I am not Rollyson nor was meant to be."

A contest seemed to develop over who could write the most reassuring letter, while also vilifying Sontag's biographers:

> I trust it goes without saying that I would never have anything to do with those *pepenadores* (garbage-pickers) proposing to write a "biography" of you [Ted Mooney].

> I told him [me] that I had known you intermittently since we both were teenagers but that I couldn't talk with him about this unless I had your permission—and boy was he pissed off! It suggested to me he did not intend to even try getting your cooperation and just wanted to dig up dirt [Ned Polsky].

> These awful people implied that they would give me a great review if I collaborated with them [John Richardson].

Of course no professional biographer would behave as Polsky reported, and Richardson, Picasso's biographer, knew better than to suppose that such a promise could be kept, let alone offered.

Of all the commentary on our book, we thought only one piece actually probed the issues we were trying to raise. Carlin Romano, a reviewer for the *Philadelphia Inquirer* who had interviewed Sontag several times, did not endorse our viewpoint and did not express an opinion on our book per se, but he did recognize its significance. In "Public Intellectuals' Private Lives: Who's In or Who's Out?" (June 16, 2000), a piece on publishing that appeared in *The Chronicle of Higher Education*, he compared our biography to Saul Bellow's novel *Ravelstein*, which is based on the life of academic Allan Bloom. Romano recapitulated the harsh criticism both books had received for exposing the lives of thinkers, noting in particular that Sontag had challenged our qualifications, and that Bellow had been attacked for hiding behind the mask of fiction even when his descriptions of Bloom seemed virtually photographic to many of Bloom's friends. Romano then concluded:

> The Sontag spat suggests that some mulling of tentative conclusions from the *Ravelstein* brouhaha is in order. Would a Saul Bellow novel about Sontag solve that little qualification problem? (He is after all, a somebody). Would a biography of Bloom by Rollyson and Paddock, lacking personal familiarity with Bloom, do more for the culture than Bellow's take?

Romano further noted that there had been fierce debate about how much the public needs to know about the private lives of politicians, but that "no remotely comparable debate has taken place in regard to such matters as outing public intellectuals." After considering the reviews of our biography, we continue to be astounded that most reviewers could not even *see* the issue clearly enough to argue about it.

Two weeks before the publication of our biography, Romano outlined an approach the reviewers of our biography might have deemed worth considering:

> Do the details of Bloom's "Athenian" homosexuality and pronounced materialism force us to reevaluate *The Closing of the American Mind*? If so, some may soon argue that we should read Sontag differently—as Edmund White implied we might read Proust differently if we factored in his sexuality—because the Rollyson-Paddock book, whatever the ultimate judgment on its quality, shines light in places its subject preferred to keep in shadows.

Alas, Romano's indication went unheeded. No one took up his suggestion that the "*Ravelstein* debate—and the likely fracas to come over the Sontag biography—will radiate more light if it spurs critics to confront such puzzles." Will the revised and updated edition of *Susan Sontag: The Making of an Icon* receive a different hearing? Stay tuned.

8

Becoming Jill Craigie's Deauthorized Biographer and Michael Foot's Boswell

The Quest

I was looking for a new subject. And there she was: "British Filmmaker and Socialist, Dies at 85," *The New York Times* announced on December 18, 1999. The obituary called Jill Craigie a feminist and observed that her "half-century marriage to Labor Party Leader Michael Foot put her at the heart of the country's leftist politics." The obituary presented Craigie's life in overlapping phases. After years in boarding schools that resembled those places of confinement in Charlotte Brontë's novels, Craigie emerged in World War II London as a pioneering documentary filmmaker—the first woman director to attract national attention. She combined an outspoken socialism and a concern for the aesthetics of modern life with a determination to tell the story of the modern women's movement.

From other obituaries and feature articles I gradually pieced together her story, discovering the pivotal moment in her life: In 1944, Craigie encountered the survivors of the suffragette generation who had gathered at the statue of their great leader, Emmeline Pankhurst. Craigie befriended and interviewed these women, then sought funding for a film that ultimately could not be made in wartime London. Instead, she produced *Out of Chaos* (1944), one of the first documentaries about modern art—featuring Henry Moore, Graham Sutherland, Stanley Spencer, and Paul Nash. Craigie put Kenneth Clark on camera for the first time, directing him in a style that he would later perfect for *Civilization*, his groundbreaking television series about art.

In 1945, Craigie met Michael Foot, then conducting his first campaign for Parliament. In her film *The Way We Live* (1946), Foot's speech to the people of Plymouth epitomizes the spirit of the British Labour Party in the historic election that would determine how postwar Britain was to be rebuilt. Craigie and Foot would become a political team. In *Diaries of a Cabinet Minister* (1975), Richard Crossman wrote that Craigie fought for her husband like a tiger; she was not merely interested in politics; she was a politician herself. A forceful presence in the debate about Britain's quality of life and its place in the world, she engaged in the campaign for unilateral nuclear disarmament. She also wrote screenplays, articles, and her crowning achievement, *Daughters of Dissent*, a magisterial history of the drive for women's rights unfortunately incomplete at the time of her death. *Daughters of Dissent*, along with *Two Hours from London* (1994), Craigie's searing documentary on the siege of Dubrovnik, constitute the legacy of a writer, filmmaker, and political activist who kept enlarging the scope of what it means to be a twentieth-century woman.

Craigie's six decades of involvement with women's issues provides a virtual barometer of changes in social and political attitudes both in Great Britain and in the world at large. She tried to integrate her feminism into every aspect of her life. Even as she was involved in the air raid alert system in wartime London (making sure people got to shelters during the bombing), she was trying to get financing for her film on the suffragettes. When she could not obtain funding for her film, she turned instead to a radio documentary on the suffragettes, broadcast in 1950 as "The Woman's Rebellion." In 1951, she directed a film documentary, *To Be a Woman* (1951), a forceful feminist plea for equal pay for equal work. In the 1950s she protested the threat of nuclear war in public speeches that included an impassioned protest against the dangers of radiation. Citing such risks as birth defects, she spoke as a mother and feminist, making the issue of nuclear proliferation a woman's issue. At the same time, of course, she campaigned fiercely within the Labour Party for a whole range of issues— including public housing, which she thought should be organically tied to human communities so that the classes intermingled in a setting reminiscent of the traditional village green. She had an aesthetic aspiration to make people's lives vivid and rewarding. Inspired by her friend, Lewis Mumford, and her mentor, the great Labour Party Leader Aneurin Bevan (another Mumford admirer), Craigie portrayed the need for town planning in her documentary *The Way We Live*, which featured the "Plymouth Plan," designed to rebuild the city and to draw all classes of the community together. Craigie was part of a generation of political women—including Michael Foot's close friend and Labour party colleague, Barbara Castle, who called themselves "William Morris Socialists." Like the Victorian domestic polymath, they appreciated such matters as the need to craft pattern and color into the forms and structures of everyday life. It was precisely this impulse that prompted Craigie to direct the television documentary *Who Are the Vandals?* (1967), an excoriation of housing developers who had ruined a good deal of the English landscape.

In the 1970s, energized by the women's movement Craigie began her epic book about the drive for female enfranchisement, beginning in the middle of the 19th century and climaxing with the great suffragette agitation directly preceding World War I. Her impressively documented study relies on a deep reading of secondary sources as well as on the copious primary evidence she had begun collecting in the 1940s with her interviews with suffragettes. Craigie's book is also a disguised autobiography: *Daughters of Dissent* explores the complex interaction of women's issues, the demands of the Labour movement, and the development of modern political parties and their constituencies from the perspective of a woman who had access to cabinet ministers and prime ministers and campaigned alongside her husband in his quest for high office. In 1975, through the intervention of her husband, then a cabinet secretary in the Harold Wilson government, Craigie obtained new records about the treatment of suffragettes in British prisons, records previously sequestered under the Official Secrets Act.

Also in the 1970s, Craigie became actively involved in the founding of Virago Press. Indeed, Craigie, who brought back into print a good deal of the texts now important to the discipline of women's studies, first suggested many of this feminist publisher's titles. Countless scholars in the field can testify to Craigie's encouragement of their work as well as to her critical, demanding judgment that women's studies must produce new data and give due credit both to militants such as Emmeline Pankhurst and to gradualists or more reform-minded figures such as Millicent Fawcett. *Daughters of Dissent* explores the conflicting but also complementary roles of these two great figures and their families. The stories of the Pankhursts and the Fawcetts form the spine of Craigie's book. And the same dramatic contrast between these feminist dynasties also forms the basis of a musical comedy and a film script that Craigie left in her papers.

In the 1980s and 1990s, Craigie became increasingly involved in a study of Yugoslavia. For the last fifteen years of her life, she traveled to Dubrovnik at least once each year with her husband, who had formed a close relationship with dissident Milovan Djilas (who stayed in London with Foot and Craigie when Tito allowed him to travel). Inspired by her friendship with Rebecca West, the author of the *Black Lamb and Grey Falcon*—still the greatest book ever written about Yugoslavia and the fate of Central Europe—Craigie, in her 80s, resumed her career as documentary film-maker, completing *Two Hours from London* (1994), a stinging indictment of the West's failure to intervene in the wars in Yugoslavia.

The Backstory

Seven years before Jill's death, I had interviewed Jill and Michael for my biography of Rebecca West. Jill had been instrumental in convincing Virago Press to reprint several of West's books. Jill had sought out Rebecca and became her friend. West—such a formidable presence on the British literary scene—often seemed an intimidating *grande dame* in her fortress-like Kingston House flat. Victoria Glenndinning, who wanted to do West's biography, told me she worried she would put a foot wrong, praise some-one who had become West's enemy, or venture an opinion Dame Rebecca would scorn. Even Stanley Olson, a West crony, seemed nervous, working hard to perform up to Dame Rebecca's standards, according to Elizabeth Leyshon, West's secretary in the late 1970s. She told me that Jill Craigie seemed the only visitor entirely at ease with West. Jill herself said she loved Rebecca. And Rebecca, grateful for Jill's efforts on her behalf, gave her a treasured scrapbook of her feminist writings, which Jill showed me in the living room of her enchanting Pilgrim's Lane house in Hampstead.

Michael often sent Rebecca charming notes, courting her with unabashed enthusiasm, an endearing characteristic of a man who loved to celebrate his heroes and heroines. Like Jill, who wrote an affecting obit-uary of West, Michael wrote a rousing piece praising the patriotic great-ness of her masterpiece, *Black Lamb and Grey Falcon*. Rebecca reciprocated his affection and admiration, sending him encouraging notes and attend-ing a few entertaining dinners at Pilgrim's Lane. Michael, sitting at Rebecca's feet, would quote from Byron, and she would relish their good-natured arguments about a poet she had often disparaged.

I learned all this in 1992 and 1993 dining with Jill and Michael and visiting them at Pilgrims Lane. Michael had just retired from Parliament, and the couple were selling their cottage in Tredegar now that he would no longer be representing a constituency in Wales. Over dinner Jill asked me if I knew anyone who might like to buy it. "A good place for a writer," she added, smiling at me. Her "big eyes," which both her daughter and an ex-lover, William MacQuitty, extolled, seemed to swallow me up. I wanted to buy the place on the spot, such was her charm—and Michael's. They displayed not just the good humor biographers experience during interviews that go well, but also extended an affection that amounted to a blessing.

Jill mentioned that she was working on a film about Yugoslavia, but then I had no idea that she had retired much earlier from a career as a director and screenwriter. We talked about my other biographical subjects. Jill was keen to learn how I felt about Lillian Hellman. I mentioned that she had put me to much trouble trying to determine the facts of her biography. For instance, she had lied about her age. Jill perked up, saying almost with asperity, "I hope you don't hold that against her." Jill discussed how hard it was for women to hold their own in a man's world and why a woman might resort to lying about her age. Later, I realized she was speaking about herself. In the early 1940s, in wartime London, she had shaved three years off her age, making her debut as a young filmmaker seem all that more sensational. All her obituaries got her birthdate wrong. It was 1911, not 1914. Not even her husband knew the truth—or rather Michael stubbornly refused to ratify the records I found: passports, birth certificate, death certificate all giving 1911 as her birthdate. There was some "mistake," he was sure. His refusal to recognize reality—which is the burden my memoir, *A Private Life of Michael Foot*—reminds me of the old joke about the husband who catches his wife in an act of adultery. She says to him, "This proves you don't trust me. You prefer to believe the evidence of your own eyes rather than what I tell you."

Jill wrote to me before my Rebecca West biography appeared in 1995, emphasizing she was pleased with my work because I was the first biographer to do justice to West's feminism.

Michael, then writing about H. G. Wells, not only liked how I handled the Wells–West liaison, he also extolled my book in his Wells biography.

Hooked

In 1996, my wife and I began work on *Susan Sontag: The Making of an Icon*. I had no contact with Jill and Michael during the three years remaining in Jill's life. Yet after she died, Michael sent me a notice of her memorial service, which I received too late because I had moved. I was touched that he had taken the trouble to contact me, and I began to wonder how he might react to my desire to write a biography of his wife.

Doing a biography of Jill Craigie would be quite a departure for an unauthorized biographer. I had always shied away from seeking the approval of my subjects and their estates, although in the end I earned the trust of West's family, friends, and agents. I could hardly write about Jill Craigie without Michael's cooperation. I *knew* Michael. He had helped me. Jill's papers were at Pilgrim's Lane. I could not hope to document her life without access to this material. Unlike a Susan Sontag or Norman Mailer, with a large body of work and correspondence I could find in the collections of others, much of Jill Craigie's work was unpublished and even how much of it existed was a mystery. Jill had built up an aura about her private collection of papers documenting the suffragist movement. She had published articles and interviews, but how much she had actually written of her legendary study, *Daughters of Dissent*, no one really knew. Scholars had visited her and used the collection, but no one had seen all of it or assessed the quality of Jill's unfinished manuscript.

I was operating on a hunch: No matter how much or how little I would discover, the story of Jill Craigie's life and her marriage to Michael Foot, would be fascinating. I knew Jill and Michael were unique, with lives that crossed the boundaries of the literary and political worlds of modern Britain. But how to approach Michael?

By the end of December, I had contacted Gloria Ferris and Rivers Scott, my literary agents in London. They had first given me Michael Foot's address and phone number when I wanted to interview him and Jill for my Rebecca West biography. Rivers and Gloria had a client, Mervyn Jones, who was writing a biography of Michael while I was working on West. I asked Rivers and Gloria what they thought of my doing Jill's biography. Gloria cautioned me that Jill would not be as "big" a subject as Rebecca West or Martha Gellhorn and therefore I should not expect as much support from a publisher as my previous work had attracted. In other words, the advance was likely to be smaller. But if I wanted to pursue the project, Gloria said she would contact Mervyn Jones and ask him how Michael was likely to react to my proposal to write his wife's life.

After conferring with Mervyn, Gloria advised me to write Michael a letter expressing my interest. And so I did, saying that perhaps it was premature to propose a biography of Jill, but I wanted him to know that I felt her loss and would be honored to be considered if Michael should want her life written. About two weeks later he called me at home. I was living in the country (Cape May County, New Jersey), and it seemed some sort of miracle hearing his cheery voice coming over the line from London. He seemed over the moon with joy. I was the one to do it! He assured me. This is what Jill would have wanted. Having spent nearly twenty years as an outlaw biographer, I can assure you his welcoming words were astonishing and gratifying. He reiterated how much he and Jill had liked my Rebecca West biography. When could I come to London so that we could discuss how to proceed with the biography? he wanted to know. His tone sounded urgent. Whatever lingering doubts I had about attracting a publisher and finding enough material for a biography vanished. I was hooked.

Becoming Boswell

By March of 2000 I was on Michael Foot's doorstep ringing his bell. When Michael greeted me at the entrance to their home just three months after Jill's death, his pallid complexion shocked me. I thought that I had arrived at death's door. He had aged more than a decade. I remembered that he sometimes stumbled, even with a cane, but now he was all wobble. Yet his voice was as strong as ever and just as engaging as always.

Michael wasted no time promising me every sort of assistance. He provided unfettered access to Jill's study. I was to live with him whenever I was in London. I was to go about the house as if it were my own. I could rifle through every drawer, cupboard, room and receptacle. I slept on a sofa bed in Michael's library. Each night before retiring, I would go through a shelf or pile of books (his only filing system) filled with letters and reviews and notes. Every night brought a new revelation. A few letters from Mary Welsh, Hemingway's fourth wife, whom Michael had known in the war, were tucked into Hemingway books. In a debunking biography of Michael's hero, Aneurin Bevan, I read Michael's comment on the flyleaf, which began "Read with rising anger...."

I often thought of Boswell and Johnson during my stays with Michael Foot. In Michael's company, I was very much a Boswell, keen to get the great man to talk. I recorded everything, compiling a hundred hours of Michael reminiscing and nearly another hundred of others commenting on him. Scholars estimate that Boswell spent something like four hundred days in Samuel Johnson's company. Over a period of three years and ten trips to England, I lived for something like one hundred days with Michael. Boswell knew Johnson much longer (more than twenty years), but he did not live with his subject and see him throughout the entire course of a day and night. I was with Michael from breakfast to lunch to drinks and dinner and usually more talk right up until bedtime. I observed the cycle of Michael's days and became a part of them, sometimes locking up the house at night or taking messages when he was away for part of a day—

and once having to rush down the stairs of his Hampstead house and into the street to pick up him where he tripped and fell.

Michael was a gallant man who rarely let down his guard. But with me, perhaps because I was American and because we spent so many continuous hours together, he would sometimes reveal himself. He was profoundly angry the night I had to pick him up in the street. Sitting at the kitchen table he nearly sobbed and said, "You don't know what it is like to grow old. You don't know." His humiliation was palpable.

Our conversations—like most conversations—were circular. Michael would keep coming back to the same topics, digress, then lose his place— "I was just ... [un-huh] ... I was just...." A soundtrack accompanied his conversations. He could not walk without making noise, groaning in different octaves and punctuating many expressions with a "Whee!"

Michael wanted my biography of Jill to do what she could not do for herself: write the whole story of what it means to be a woman. Like the subjects of *Daughters of Dissent*, her never completed epic about the struggle for female suffrage, Jill saw herself as a dissident fighting for recognition.

My March meeting with Michael lasted for nearly two hours. Toward the end of the interview, I brought up his relationship with Julie, Jill's daughter by her first marriage. Mervyn had told me Julie had not liked the idea of her mother marrying Michael. Michael acknowledged a difficult period of adjustment for both of them but urged me to discuss the matter with Julie. Michael was never one to discuss relationships in depth. I would have to press him again and again—usually in response to what others said—to get him to open up. His pauses were blanks I had to fill in by talking to others. Michael was not openly recalcitrant, but he would often cut off discussion by reverting to the sort of encouragement that became a refrain in our relationship: "Anyhow, Carl, I'm very glad that you're doing it. And I'm going to have a sleep now."

Even as Michael was heading off for his nap, and I was backing out of Jill's study, where our first conversation about my biography of her took place. I stopped and said, "I've just got to take a quick peek in here [a drawer]. I want to see if it contains more manuscript." As I fingered photocopies and note cards, Michael said, "There's nothing to be hidden." I took him at his word.

"Michael's life is one long love affair. It is a love affair with the Labour party, a love affair with Hazlitt, Swift, H. G. Wells, and my mother," Julie told me over drinks in a pub the next day.

Julie first caught sight of Michael right at the end of the war, shortly after her mother had made her film *The Way We Live*, shot in bombed-out Plymouth and featuring a cameo performance by Michael Foot who was campaigning for a parliamentary seat during what became the Labour landslide of 1945. Jill, a beauty, had her pick of men and was then involved with a handsome suitor, her producer William MacQuitty, while at the same time conducting an affair with a good looking painter, Dennis Matthews. She was also still married to her second husband, Jeffrey Dell.

Yet to Julie's amazement, Jill set out to captivate Michael early on. "He was the most revolting specimen of a man I'd ever seen," Julie recalled. "He had asthma and eczema. How could my mother touch him, let alone get in bed with him?" This shy, myopic man appealed to Jill because unlike so many of her other lovers, he talked of building a better world and took her entirely on her own terms, barely inquiring about her past. What he did know only made him prouder of his conquest. He would later brag to me about how Jill had led on so many men. He spoke of winning her. During the early days of their courtship, she had shown up at a miner's gala event in Durham with another man, "but," he chortled, "she came home with me."

Michael's brothers, by his own account, were astounded when he won Jill. Brought up as a strict Methodist, Michael never had the easygoing attitude toward sex that seemed second nature to Jill. With Jill, Julie could talk about sex freely, sharing the most intimate details of her relationships. Sex, in Michael's Plymouth home, had been unmentionable: "Don't put your hands under the covers, young man!" his mother admonished him.

Michael's trusting nature, his absolute faith in Jill, irritated Julie. The director Ronnie Neame, who employed Jill in the 1950s to write screenplays for *The Million Pound Note* and *Windom's Way*, was, Julie recalled, "always round the house." The teenaged Julie became suspicious. As soon as Michael came home, she would say, "Ronnie's just left." Michael, never one to become jealous, would laugh and call Julie Iago. There was something wrong with a man, in Michael's view, if he wasn't in love with Jill. He scoffed at the idea of Ronnie as Jill's lover when I raised the subject with him later, and Julie did the same, even though she admitted, "Michael was a loving man but no sexual athlete, and my mother was a sexy woman." Jill once confessed to Julie that Michael had "many wonderful attributes, but after five years their sex life was virtually over." Michael would make the most of his romantic revivals with Jill during their many trips abroad, especially to Venice, but Jill's own journal reveals how terribly disappointed she was by his flagging sexual appetite.

"Was Jill jealous of Michael?" I asked Julie. "You can't publish this if Michael is still alive," she replied, her voice dropping. "She had cause to." I mentioned Jill's comment in a published interview that if Michael had an affair she did not want to know about it. "She knew about it," Julie said, "and it devastated her." Julie then began to tell me in capsule form the story of Michael's affair with Lamia (not her real name). "It isn't publishable," she repeated. I agreed, although in the end, I published part of the story in *To Be a Woman: The Life of Jill Craigie* after a struggle with Michael and those close to him about what was really central to the story of the Foot–Craigie marriage.

Jill stuck by Michael, "out of love," Julie believed, "but also out of a sense that he was making a contribution to society. She was the most subservient feminist ever. Intellectually, she was a feminist, but in her behavior she was not." Recalling the marriage's dynamics in the 1970s and thereafter, Julie noted that if Michael wanted a cup of coffee and Jill was writing her book, he got his cup of coffee. She was always complaining about these interruptions. "Why not go away for six weeks and finish your book?" Julie would ask her. "But who would take care of Michael?" Jill replied. No one—not Julie, not anyone—could take care of Michael as Jill did. To Jill, Michael was "special." And then Julie added, "Excuse my language, but fuck that! He was just a man. I took issue there, *strongly*. I think my mother had quite a tough time with Michael. He adored her in a cerebral way, but she had to do all the dog work." He was attentive. He brought Jill flowers and gifts, often consulting with Julie about what Jill might like best. But to Julie, Michael never put Jill first. "He did on a certain level. He only wanted to hear praise of her after she died. But that tells me that he realized he had not worshipped her as he should have done."

After listening to Julie over the course of three years, I did begin to wonder why Michael never gave Jill the space or time she gave him. I could never formulate the question in a way that would not seem accusatory, especially to a man who was still grieving. But in retrospect, I wish I had asked: "Michael, did you ever—especially after you retired from public office—just say to Jill, 'Why don't you go off and finish your book. I'll get on.'" All sorts of friends and family—as I discovered—were quite willing to coddle him. Other than complaining to others—as Jane Carlyle did about her mate—Jill never made an issue of her husband's selfishness. And perhaps, for all sorts of reasons, she did not really want to finish her book, but the nagging question is why he did not do more to encourage her. He was interested in her work. He read it and made editorial suggestions (which he did not want me to mention in her biography for fear this would somehow diminish her achievement), but as far as making some significant alteration in a life built around him, he seemed incapable of proposing a plan for her book that would free her to confront the formidable task of telling the story of women's struggle for equality.

Michael was the male partner in a dance, but he did not know how to lead. Or rather, he led by default, since Jill did not challenge his authority. He simply filled a vacuum. As a political man, he would have the same problem: He had a solid group of adherents, but he could not use that base to assert his authority. He was a sort of effigy of a great man. And he seems to have known it, since he became leader of the Labour party only after considerable prodding from Jill and others. It would have looked cowardly not to accept the leadership. But Michael was a sort of hollow man, as he acknowledged with self-deprecating humor during his 1983 campaign against Margaret Thatcher: "I'm here to impersonate the leader of the Labour party. What have I been doing the rest of the week? You might well ask."

The Rape

The next day Mervyn Jones listened to me expatiate on my enthusiasm for doing Jill's biography. He paused and then said there were problems. Jill was not the feminist Michael made her out to be. And Mervyn seemed to regret that his obituary of Jill had repeated Michael's high opinion of her. I assured Mervyn that after writing about Lillian Hellman, Martha Gellhorn, Rebecca West, and Susan Sontag, I was prepared for difficulties. Jill did not get on well with women, Mervyn alleged. And he did not see how I could present a true picture of Jill without contradicting Michael's idealized image.

Jill had given Mervyn a rough time over Michael's biography, which she thought neglected her own role in Michael's life, mischaracterized her experience as a mother, and failed to capture Michael's domestic side and the comforts of their home in Pilgrim's Lane. To Mervyn, Jill seemed rather high handed. "When Jill said we're having dinner, it was a royal command. If you were doing something else, she would say, 'Drop it.'" This aspect of Jill did get short shrift in my biography. Michael objected to Mervyn's remarks, which I included in a draft without using Mervyn's name, and I could see that unless I identified my source, neither Michael nor the reader would take the criticism seriously. Mervyn warned me that Michael would not be able to see—or admit?—that Jill had an overbearing quality.

I asked Mervyn what he knew about Arthur Koestler's rape of Jill, a story that Michael himself first revealed in a review of a book about Koestler. Michael caused an uproar in the press and among Jill's and Michael's friends. Frederic Raphael wrote a piece questioning Jill's account, suggesting she had exaggerated or perhaps had even led Koestler on. And there were other skeptics, although another woman came forward, writing a letter to the press that described Koestler's assault on her (she managed to escape being raped). Then it was revealed that Koestler had also raped one of Dick Crossman's wives.

Jill had kept the rape secret for more than forty years—supposedly not even telling Michael—but had blurted it out late one night at a small party with her friends, many of whom I interviewed on subsequent trips to England. Mervyn was skeptical about the story, although he believed Koestler quite capable of rape. Mervyn had asked Jill, "Did you tell Michael?" She hesitated, and said, "Michael saw the scratches on my arm. He said, 'What's this?' And I didn't tell Michael I was fully raped but that I was assaulted and that it was Arthur." It all seemed a strange story to Mervyn, especially when Jill said Michael's response was, "Well, you have to admit he's a very good writer." Mervyn thought this was an unbelievably "crass thing to say. A man has raped your wife—I couldn't believe Michael had said this."

As I pieced together the story of Jill's rape for my biography of her, I realized there was a missing element: exactly what Michael knew and what he did about it. I spoke with him many times about the rape but never came close to comprehending what, in the end, was the truth. But I also held back certain testimony, which led me to believe that Mervyn's assessment of Jill and his belief in Michael was misguided. The Koestler rape became just one of many instances when Michael did not stand by Jill. To do so, would have meant an ugly confrontation with his wife's rapist, a writer Michael would continue to rhapsodize over in our conversations.

In spite of Michael's assurances that it was "my book" and he would interfere in no way, my agents encouraged me to get a commitment from him in writing. From my hotel, at the end of my first trip to Pilgrim's Lane, I sent him the following letter:

Dear Michael,
    I thank you again for the wonderful meal and all the encouragement for my proposed biography of Jill. I shall now begin to write a synopsis my agents will show publishers.
    It would be good to have in hand two items when I submit the synop-

sis: 1. A letter from you stating that I have permission to examine Jill's private papers and that I have your confidence and cooperation. 2. A list of people you think I should interview. This list could be attached to your letter. It would demonstrate your enthusiasm for the project and confirm my access to those who should figure in the biography.

I am sorry to put you to so much trouble, but I know from past experience that publishers are demanding an increasing amount of evidence proving the biographer will be able to write a persuasive book.

Jill is not well known in America, yet I would very much like her name, her work, and her life to be known there. So I think these supporting statements (your letter and list) will prove vital.

I will write or call you when I have the exact dates of my return to London in June—around the 21st I believe. And I do hope that I will be able to stay with you and that it is not an inconvenience for you.

Do let me know about Dubrovnik. I will make every effort to attend the event.

As ever,

Carl

Michael had invited me to join him in Dubrovnik for a commemoration of Jill's life amidst her friends there, and this was just the first of several signs that he meant what he said about full access to everything I needed for my biography. But I never received a response to this letter, although we kept in touch by phone, and I detected no lull in his enthusiasm for my doing Jill's biography.

I had to make a decision. Should I press him for a commitment in writing? Biographers such as Martin Duberman and A. Scott Berg have insisted on formal agreements with their subjects' estates, specifying that the biographer has permission to quote from documents, writings, and other papers. In addition, the agreements stipulate that no one in the family or any literary executor has the legal authority to request alterations in the biographer's manuscript. I decided not to press for a written agreement, believing it might spoil the amicable relationship I had with Michael. Because he was a journalist and understood the writer's need to be independent, I never dreamed he would try to censor my work. On the contrary, he was wooing me and making it abundantly clear that he was grateful for my treating Jill with the respect I had accorded subjects far better known and accomplished than his wife.

My letter to Michael became a moot concern a few months later when my American agent informed me she saw no hope of a sale in the U.S. Furthermore, early on it became clear that Aurum Press, publisher of my Gellhorn biography, would make an offer to buy the Craigie biography. So I did not press Michael for a written agreement or statement of support.

In the event, Aurum did buy the book and was content with my verbal assurances that I had Michael's solid backing. That I was staying with him during my London visits and that he had invited me to join him in Dubrovnik for a celebration of Jill's time there provided convincing proof enough that I had in hand the material for a biography.

Buffering the Biography

In June 2000, on my next stay at Pilgrim's Lane I began to investigate Jill's life before she met Michael in 1945. I would continue to be surprised at how little Michael knew about her apart from what she herself had told him. She had been able, in fact, to fashion an image of herself for him that he could not bring himself to contest, even when I began to present him with evidence that Jill had sometimes misrepresented her life.

When I mentioned that Jill had a brief career as an actress, Michael responded, "I didn't know that. She never told that to me." In 1937, she appeared in a film, *Makeup*, written by her second husband, Jeffrey Dell. They had also collaborated on a successful stage play. "I see," Michael said, seeming to muse over this new information. "I never met Jeffrey Dell. Jill said he was very clever." That seemed to sum up all Michael knew about the man—or cared to know. Michael was not the kind of spouse to concern himself with his wife's former life. "Jill didn't talk much about Jeffrey Dell." Michael never wanted to examine Jill's life critically. I recalled that Michael Bessie, a friend of Michael's since the 1940s, remarked, "I wonder what kind of a source on Jill Michael is. He is so kindly a person."

In June 2000, I had settled into a cozy stay at Pilgrim's Lane. Only later would I begin to see that by providing me with so much access and comfort, Michael was buffering the biography. I don't mean that he made some sort of calculation that I would be indebted because of his generosity. It was simply in Michael's nature, I believe, to extend his liberality, which easily segued into his thinking I would produce a biography in the same spirit of amity that characterized our jolly talks together. I did not realize then that I could not count on Michael to be his own man. He had a minder, Jenny Stringer. I met her during the course of my June 2000 stay at Pilgrim's Lane. Although she promised me an interview, it would be quite some time before she would sit for one. Julie, on the other hand, served as a kind of foil to Michael and Jenny. She was very observant and outspoken. Julie loved private, domestic life, and she had little patience for the sacrifices Jill and other women made to Michael's status as a public man. Michael would eventually sour on me because I gave Julie so much of a voice in my biography of her mother.

Michael's praise for Jill seemed extravagant to nearly everyone I spoke with about her. She was a filmmaker, a journalist, and finally a kind of historian, but she did not make history. Michael wanted to make an epic out of her life and regarded my biography as a way to recover from the defeat of her death. It seemed odd to me, however, that Jill's book *Daughters of Dissent*, which I came to regard as her unfinished masterpiece, provoked so much uneasiness in Michael. He proved resistant to my proposal that it should be published with a foreword and afterword explaining Jill's intentions and how she planned to complete her work. She left eighteen substantial chapters (well over 250,000 words). When Mike Bessie said the book needed considerable editing and shortening to be published, that pretty much shelved the project in Michael's mind.

Lamia

In September 2000, I joined Michael for a week in Dubrovnik. Although I came at my own expense, he had invited (and paid for) several friends and family members to journey there as a kind of celebration of the many holidays he and Jill had enjoyed in this charming, compact, and historical city. Rebecca West had called it a "city on a coin."

In this festive atmosphere it was difficult to raise critical questions about Michael's relationship with Jill and how she viewed her marriage to Michael. She had, in effect, given up pursuing a film career in the 1950s to concentrate—as she told many friends and interviewers—on family life. As usual, only Julie seemed willing to talk about this period, explaining that her mother had sold a Renoir painting rather than ask Michael for money. He never gave her enough to run the house, but Jill had her pride and dreaded confronting him about money, and that only made Julie angrier. She remembered how humiliated her mother had been when Lady Beaverbrook bought her a dress for a social occasion at the Beaverbrook estate.

Julie told me that during the first week of Michael's Dubrovnik stay (I arrived at the beginning of their second week there) several of his London friends had flown over as part of his commemoration of Jill in the city she loved. The wife of Bob Edwards (an intimate of Michael's who edited *Tribune* after Michael left the job) told Julie that Michael was one of the most selfish men she had ever met. It seemed a shocking statement to me at the time; Michael was so affable and so obviously engaged with other people. He did not strike me as a monomaniac who would hold forth only about himself. But in effect, in Jill, he found a collaborator—as Carlyle had done with Jane—who might complain from time to time, but who never seriously challenged his own vision of himself or of the world he had a right to rule.

By making no demands (for example, "You must give up your career"), by seeming not to interfere in crucial decisions (should she abort the child she had conceived by him before they were married?) he effectively placed the burden of decision on her. She was the one who had to choose—over and over again. Michael could just be himself. This is the free ride men so often enjoy in their marriages.

At this early stage, however, I did not realize that one truly sensitive issue for Michael was how I treated his marriage. My main concern then was how Michael would react when I brought up the subject of his adultery. Mike Bessie had advised me to write up the story and then show it, in person, to Michael, saying that I would take it out if he strongly objected to placing it in the biography. But that option bothered me. I had told Michael I was my own man, and I could not now envision holding my book hostage to his judgment. So I had to decide when I would discuss the issue with him.

Jenny, I was sure, knew about Lamia, and so I decided to test her reactions. She was wary and said she would speak to me about Lamia after I had discussed the affair with Michael. Jenny became more recalcitrant when she realized how much of the Lamia affair I already knew from Julie. In retrospect, I can see what was at stake: Who had power and authority over this story? It alarmed Jenny, I'm sure, that Julie had made herself such an important source. Julie was the wild card Jenny could not control, except by trying to mitigate what Julie said. I understood as much, but only now do I see how worried Jenny was that the indiscreet Julie would challenge the control Jenny wished to exercise.

A dismayed Jenny attempted to contradict or dilute Julie's acerbic asides. But what about Jenny's bias? She was the caretaker, the damage control operative—more sensible in some respects than Julie but also a politico palliating vexing situations. Julie was direct, Jenny oblique. Julie exaggerated, Jenny temporized. Jenny spoke of "scenarios," implying that Julie had a tendency to fictionalize. Everything had to go "according to her plot." Jenny spoke so low I wondered if my recorder could pick up her voice (it did just barely). She spoke, it seemed to me, as though she were trying to fly under the radar.

On our return to London, I found it hard to have Michael entirely to myself. At home there was always a housekeeper (Emma), many calls, and visitors. So I was delighted when Emma went out shopping. I started out in as disarming a fashion as possible describing my reactions to Jill's book. I read Michael a passage where Jill expressed her regret that biographers had so little to say about their subjects' private lives: "Consequently, we are left with the impression that the Fawcetts were rare specimens who knew nothing of personal tests and fluctuating emotions. Clearly, much more was happening beneath this artificial surface." I read to Michael several statements about adultery in one of Jill's diaries. Michael sensed where I was going and admitted there had been tensions in his marriage. I pressed on, noting the need to tell the full story of their life together. Michael spoke haltingly, promising me that he would tell me what I wanted to know, but perhaps not just then. It seemed necessary now to name what I was after, so I told him that based on what Jill had written, I had to assume there had been some adultery in their marriage. For a good four minutes Michael said nothing. Then slowly, with great hesitation, he told me about three women, only one of whom, Lamia, had disturbed his marriage. The details were sketchy, and he promised to say more later on. It was a start, I said to myself, as Emma returned from her shopping.

Michael's account of his involvement with Lamia did not square with Julie's version or jibe with Jill's account of it in her letters. I was never able to determine whether he was holding back details or really had forgotten or reshaped the story—a common enough tendency in reminiscences. Dinner with Julie and Paul Foot, Michael's nephew, brought me no nearer the Lamia story, although Paul knew all about it because she had shown up at his *Private Eye* office seeking, it seemed, to blackmail Michael. After Paul departed, Julie said, "He wishes that nobody knew about Lamia." I told Julie I had gathered that. "You'll find him very, very reticent," Julie added. "That why I said I had talked to Michael," I told her, adding, "He [Paul] thinks the personal life should remain the personal life and not part of a biography."

Authorized Biography

Michael's enthusiasm for my biography of Jill seemed to suffer no diminution even as I queried him about his affair with Lamia. He took a sympathetic interest in my discussion of the difficulties I had had working on other biographies and the efforts made by Martha Gellhorn, Susan Sontag and others to prevent publication. "We don't believe in authorized biographies," Michael concluded. "All authorized biographies are hereby condemned."

The first troubling sign that he did not understand my view of biography arose in our discussion of Elizabeth Frank's biography of Indira Gandhi. Michael had heard the biographer discussed her subject's love life, and that had soured him on the book. I suggested he might be overreacting to the controversy that ensued when the Gandhi family objected to Frank's version of events. Surely Michael could see that his friendship with Indira and her family could not, in itself, weigh against the researches of a serious biographer. I later read the book and saw no reason to dispute Frank's account, which, after all, was a report, not a flat statement of fact. But to Michael and his ilk any suggestion that Indira, his friend, who had spent the war years in London quite happily, would even have considered a life apart from India was anathema.

Ronnie and the Rape

I was eager to leave Pilgrim's Lane for a dinner with two of Michael's friends, Peter and Celine, who had befriended Jill's housekeeper/confidant Kathy Seary. I needed another perspective. Celine had been Ronnie Neame's lover for many years. When the couple broke up, she found herself without the home Ronnie promised her. Even though Jill had worked closely with Ronnie on several films, she helped Celine mount a successful legal case that restored the house to Celine. Peter had come along a little later, introduced to Celine by Jill. So Celine had reason to be doubly grateful to Jill. Yet at the same time, she could be critical of Jill and Michael, and though she was at odds with Julie, the two women often corroborated one another's stories. However, on one sore point regarding the Foot/Craigie marriage what Celine had to say caused considerable consternation, provoking Michael and Julie to join in an unusual alliance against her.

"Do you think Jill was ever unfaithful to Michael?" Julie asked me the previous day, adding, "I'm quite sure Ronnie was in love with my mother." Celine, I told Julie, seemed to be hinting as much and perhaps more. Julie was adamant in her belief that her mother had never been unfaithful to Michael. That conviction I resolved to test in due course this very night at dinner. What I learned I would not be able to discuss with Michael or

Julie until my next trip. And Celine, who had thrown a sort of blot on my picture of Jill, would feel the repercussions, for she had told me that Jill in fact had had a long-standing affair with Ronnie Neame. Celine startled us all by exclaiming, "Jill was no saint." This was no attack on Jill but simply Celine's belief that she was doing justice, balancing my realistic view of Michael against what she perhaps supposed was my idealistic view of Jill. This piece of intelligence meant that at different times Jill and Celine had had the same lover. Celine had vowed that this was so after I had noted that I could find no evidence whatsoever that Jill had been unfaithful to Michael. How Julie and Michael would react to Celine's revelation was to color the rest of my work on Jill's life and prove, in the end, a conundrum I could not quite crack, but one that belongs in this book because it says so much about how the biographer has to hazard certain choices and take the consequences.

Celine seemed to sense that I was headed for trouble: "I always thought he would be a bit worried about your interviewing the three of us." I paused, hoping Celine would say something more. When she did not, I said: "Well, if he is, he hasn't said." She seemed to have in mind her very critical remarks about Julie and how badly she served Jill during Jill's last illness. I said, "He has to know by the questions I've asked him—that I want to know everything. When I began the book my agent said, 'Well, you know you may not be able to publish this [Jill's biography] until Michael is gone. There may be things he won't want to talk about.' I said, 'I really don't want to do a book like that. I'd rather hash it out with him.'" Peter said, "He doesn't seem anxious, does he?" I didn't think so, but that was not to say that I could not write something that would hurt Michael, I told Peter. Celine said she did not think Michael cared that much what I said about him, but rather that he might object to anything unflattering I might write about Jill. How right Celine was.

My first encounter on returning to England was with Julie. Eager to tell her what
I had learned from Celine, I said:

> It was bothering me that I knew about Michael [his adultery] and nothing about Jill. Maybe there was nothing to know.
> [JH] Which is what I always thought.
> [CR] But I couldn't take that for granted. I remembered your saying Ronnie was around a lot.
> [JH] All the time.
> [CR] And she confided in Ronnie about the rape. So far as I know he was the only man she confided in.

After considerable roundabout discussion of my impressions of Ronnie, I noted that Ronnie did not even hint at any sort of intimate or sexual relationship with Jill. "I don't think they did, myself," Julie said. So I came out with it:

> [CR] Well ...
> [JH] You think they did?
> [CR] According to the person who told me, they did. And Ronnie told this person.
> [JH] Ah, well, that's a different matter, isn't it? Men tend to ... men tend to ... he was still with his wife then.
> [CR] Yes, but remember your mother's advice to you.
> [JH] Never go with a married man.
> [CR] Well, you told me that one story about having an affair with a married man because it would be safer.
> [JH] Oh, yeah, that one.
> [CR] Anyway, Ronnie said he had had a 14-year affair [with Jill], and it stopped with the accident in 1963.
> [JH] I don't believe it. [Julie laughed] I really don't believe it. Not because I think my mother was above having an affair ... because—I was around a lot—
> [CR] This came out at the time of Lamia, actually. Jill was so upset about Lamia that this friend of hers [who knew Jill had had an affair with Ronnie] said to Jill, "Well, you're no saint either."
> [JH] Who's this friend?
> [CR] Who could it be?

I did not mean to be coy. I wanted to see what Julie would say and if there was someone I had overlooked who might corroborate Celine. "Celine?" Julie asked. I nodded, and Julie immediately said, "Then it's not credible, absolutely not credible. She doesn't know. She was ditched by Ronnie." I knew that story. And later after Julie got in touch with him, Ronnie denied Celine's story and implied she was a fantasist. "She has a vivid imagination," Julie added.

I pressed on. Julie conceded her mother was a tremendous flirt, but she still could not bring herself to believe it had amounted to more than that.

> [CR] But you think Ronnie might have said something like this [that he was having an affair with Jill] or implied it. Celine must have a very vivid imagination. She was very specific.
> [JH] Ronnie and she [Jill] had a very close friendship for many years, and I thought Ronnie was in love with her. But she was so newly married to Michael that I don't think for a moment she'd have gone to bed ... because in those days Michael certainly had not been unfaithful.

But according to Celine via Ronnie, Jill's affair had begun in 1951, six years after she had first become involved with Michael. And Michael himself was just about to become involved with Elizabeth Thomas. But did Jill know about Elizabeth Thomas? Julie asked. She certainly had her suspicions, I said. Would Celine go so far as to make up such a story? She may have been motivated by hard feelings against Ronnie, although I never heard her say anything against him, except to assert that he was wrong to deny her the house he had promised. The most Julie would concede was a one-night stand with Ronnie. But a fourteen-year affair? Never! "She and Michael were good together then," Julie insisted, and "they were trying to have a baby. She wouldn't have risked sleeping with someone else. I had many criticisms of my mother, but that's not one of them."

Does all this matter? It did to me because it would have a bearing on what kind of man Michael was, what he knew, and what he chose to know. The alleged affair with Ronnie remained in play for me, and would always do so, because I could not rule it out.

When I saw Celine again, I had some explaining to do. She was put out with me because I had told Julie about Celine's claim that Jill and Ronnie had been lovers. Before I could tell Celine that I had told Julie, Julie had told Michael, and then both Michael and Julie were upset that Celine should say such a thing, which they deemed preposterous. My only excuse, really, was that Celine had told me about this affair right at the end of my previous trip and there had not been time to have a sitdown with Michael or Julie before I left England. That was true enough, but I also think it had all been too cozy, the way I had been cosseted during the research for this book, and it seemed to me I needed to explore Jill's sex life in the same way I had done Michael's. But until Celine had opened up, I had no avenue of inquiry.

So in conversation I told Celine that I was going to bring up the subject of Jill and Ronnie but had not done so yet. I had pressed Michael at various times about whether he thought Jill had been unfaithful. "Because he is a gentleman he would never say," Celine said. "If she did," Michael had told me, "it would not matter." Michael had read his Bertrand Russell and accepted his counsel that jealousy was an emotion not worth indulging in.

"I don't know if you asked Ronnie about it," Celine inquired. "I wrote Ronnie, I interviewed Ronnie twice. I thought and thought about what I should do about this. I couldn't write him a letter and say, 'I know you had an affair with Jill.'" "He won't tell you unless you tell him what you know,"

Celine advised me. "Well, I sent him an email. I didn't mention you. I said that when I first interviewed him I was just beginning on the book. I knew very little, but I've learned a great deal now, and Michael wants this to be a candid biography, and I know you had a very close relationship with Jill, and it might be easier if I come to see you in California." He never answered this message.

"He won't come out with the information unless you tell him you know about it," Celine repeated. "You see, Michael and Ronnie are from a different age. They have a certain sensibility." "How are you so sure?" I asked Celine. "How do you know?" She had lived with Ronnie for five years (1982–1987). Celine said: "Michael used to make jokes about it [Ronnie's affair with Jill]. I'm a very sensitive woman, and Ronnie was very straight with me. And Jill? "Did she sort of acknowledge it without acknowledging it?" I asked. "Yes," Celine said. Jill confided in Celine about Michael's affair with Lamia. Celine continued,

> "And I said to her, you must have been quite understanding." Jill replied: "Absolutely not. I threatened him." She laughed. I said, "That's a bit unfair of you." She laughed. Come on, the two of us had a proper woman's relationship. It was understood.

I pressed Celine on this point: "But Jill never said it in so many words." Celine countered: "She said to Ronnie, 'Did you ever tell Celine we had an affair.' And he said, 'No, but Celine's very sensitive, and I think she probably knows.'" All four—Ronnie, Celine, Jill, and Michael—supposedly shared this understanding. Celine said to Ronnie, "Michael is an admirable man. The way he behaves with you." The two men loved each other, Celine insisted: "That's why Julie was a cow, the way she approached him [Michael]." Celine claimed there had been other people in the room when Julie asked Michael about Ronnie and Jill. Celine's words also made it sound as though to admit an affair was a betrayal of Ronnie as well, of the sort of gentleman's agreement Michael had with him. Julie had just come in one day and confronted him with what I had told her about Ronnie and Jill. Celine implied that Michael had no choice but to deny it. "Do you think Julie was really shocked?" I asked. "No," Celine said. "You should have known that she would do that," Celine said. "Yes, I should have. It was a mistake," I agreed. But Peter really said what I couldn't: "I don't think it was a mistake because you had to ignite some kind of reaction. You've got a limited amount of time...." Celine interrupted: "But the reaction was to Michael, not to you," Celine said to me. "But there was nowhere else for the reaction to go," Peter observed.

My problem, of course, is that I had only Celine as a source. Ronnie never did respond to my queries, and Julie only made it worse by emailing him and asking him, in effect, to deny it. Peter believed Celine, but then Peter was her lover. Ronnie would say in his email to Jill that Celine was a fantasist. But it nagged at me—it always will—because I thought the affair entirely possible, even though I could not prove it. What I did know is that Ronnie was indeed very fond of Michael and very protective of Jill. His comments to me were very guarded even before the issue of an affair arose. I continued to press Celine for details. The affair had lasted 14 years—from 1949 to 1963. So they had stopped being lovers after the terrible car crash? I asked. I was thinking about how the accident had been Jill's fault. "Did she feel guilty?" "No," Celine said, "He [Ronnie] did. Because Michael was being so kind to her." Jill was very depressed. So Michael phoned Ronnie and urged him to see Jill in hospital. Ronnie told Celine, "I didn't want to see her in the hospital because of our relationship. But Michael said, "Ronnie, Jill misses you desperately. Please." Ronnie was so moved he could not continue the affair. "He loved Michael," Celine said.

"Did Jill give you any sense of why she needed this affair?" I asked Celine. "Michael was very busy, day and night." What to think? Julie had told me that Jill had said many times that Michael was not a very good sex partner. The first few years had been fine but afterwards ... "Jill was very forthright about sex. She talked about it with me all the time," Celine said. This corroborated Julie's testimony and that of Julie's friends. Jill certainly had no sentimental compunctions about being unfaithful. None of this *proved*, of course, that Celine was telling the truth. "Given the way Michael handles this story he preserves his deniability," I said. "That's right," Peter spoke up, "good phrase."

"Michael loved *The End of the Affair*," Celine said. "Loved it. It was a reminder. It was about a woman having an affair. I loaned it to Michael." Celine thought Michael understood that he could not satisfy Jill's needs. And as long as Jill was discreet, he did not mind. This was, in fact, an arrangement that Michael had described between Olivia Manning, her husband Reggie, and Jerry Slattery (their doctor). "He was working. He had no choice. Jill was miserable waiting for him to come back home."

Celine made it clear to me that she thought my biography would be imbalanced if I did not see the marriage between Michael and Jill as one of equals, which meant (so far as Celine was concerned) that Jill, like Michael, had needs outside of marriage. "If Michael had not opened his mouth about his indiscretions, I would not have opened my mouth about hers," Celine insisted. "I had to redress an injustice.... Jill was going to get what she wanted. What upset Julie and Jenny was that I knew something that they did not." I told Celine that I thought Jenny regarded Celine and Peter as competitors. "Guardians of the ark," Peter added. I suggested that until Celine spoke up, Julie had control over the story.

Michael, too, seemed now just a bit withdrawn to me. I had told him about Kathy Seary's account of how Lamia had knocked on the door at Pilgrim's Lane and Jill had answered with "Fuck off! Fuck off! Fuck off!" and then slammed the door. Michael's only comment, "I see." I predicted, rightly enough, that I would learn no more about Lamia from Michael. I did not fully realize, though, that by starting to go off the reservation, so to speak, by doing interviews with Milton Shulman and Anne Robinson, I had begun to take possession of the story in ways that made Michael uneasy. I'm not sure he realized it quite then, either. It would take my reporting in the biography an even more sensitive matter that would ignite Michael's anger and realization that I would indeed produce a biography not entirely in harmony with his *amour propre*.

I was about to leave Pilgrim's Lane for a day at the British Film Institute. On the way out I mentioned to Michael that I wanted to speak with him about Celine.

[MF] About Ronnie?
[CR] Yes.
[MF] I don't think she ever had.... She may have done ... had an affair with Ronnie. You mean that?
[CR] She [Celine] told me that that was what Ronnie told her. It went on for some time. According to Ronnie, it ended with the accident in 1963. I don't understand why Celine would make this up. So that would mean Ronnie would have to make it up. He doesn't strike me that way. I don't think he would make it up. I don't think it takes away.... I was reading Paul's book on Shelley. There is this wonderful line in Shelley. Paul thinks Shelley is in love with Mary Godwin and he's also very attracted to Clare—one of the lines in one of his poems about how his love is not divided, although he loves these two women.
[MF] That's right. Ah, well.
[CR] You understand that. We talked about that.
[MF] Yes. So I don't think even if Celine is right, and I really don't think—she was pretty close to Jill at one time. She said that Jill shared confidences with her. I don't see Celine lying about that. She says that Jill said it to her?
[CR] She doesn't say that Jill actually said it to her in so many words. But she said that they joked around and shared confidences.
[MF] Now, that's different.
[CR] Yes, it is different. But she says that Ronnie was quite open about that [the affair with Jill].

Throughout this conversation, Michael seemed skeptical, although not as adamant as Julie. "I don't think I can get Ronnie to talk about it," I told Michael. "Given that you're alive and it's going to hurt you." Michael said, "It's not going to hurt me one way or the other. So you ought to see what he says. I still don't believe it. But there you are." Michael thought there were several other men Jill admired more and was fond of. They were more likely candidates. "Whatever happened, I haven't the slightest grievance against Jill. I bloody well shouldn't have. I'm quite interested, of course, to know what happened in such cases, but I must say from my recollections of it I don't think Ronnie was one of the ones who attracted her." That settled it for Michael.

I had another go with Julie: She adamantly rejected the idea that Jill and Ronnie Neame had had an affair. "He wasn't her type," Julie insisted. She had asked her mother many times if she had had an affair with Ronnie, and Jill had always said no. "Ronnie wasn't all that attractive," Julie added. Julie had never seen Ronnie at the hospital after the 1963 accident. By then Ronnie was in America, Julie said. "He never even sent flowers. He was not in Jill's life then." And Michael could not have phoned Ronnie because he was on life support machines. But did it matter where Ronnie lived? And would Michael have not have been able to use a phone at some point in his recovery? So why would Celine want to make up such a story? I asked Julie. Celine wanted to believe she was contributing to the biography, Julie suggested, and it made Celine feel powerful to have this knowledge. But even so, in the world of mixed motivations Celine might be right.

Was I going to contact Ronnie again? Julie wanted to know. I intended to, but I wasn't sure how to judge the result even if he did talk. "If he says no [he did not have an affair], it would not prove anything, and if he says yes it doesn't prove it either." I felt I had reached an impasse. Short of finding a third party who might have evidence to confirm or dispute Celine's story, I saw no way to make a definitive judgment. Julie and Michael never asked me if I was going to put Celine's comments about Ronnie and Jill in the biography. I still wasn't sure what to do. Which is why, in the end, I decided to excise any mention of a Jill/Ronnie affair.

Julie built up Celine as the villain of the piece as much as Celine did the same for Julie, although Julie conceded that Celine had a kind heart. Celine talked too much, Julie said, and so much of it was rubbish, but Celine meant well—until that is, she brought up the Ronnie/Jill affair. That was disgusting, in Julie's opinion. "Celine is adamant," is all I would say. The clinching point with Julie is how strongly Jill felt about not having affairs with married men. She would not make love to Henry Moore because he had a wife whom Jill liked. And there were other instances of the same kind. Jill knew Ronnie's wife and son. She simply wouldn't engage in such an affair. Julie and Michael agreed.

My next trip to London in July 2001 coincided with the publication of *Beautiful Exile: The Life of Martha Gellhorn*. My biography received excellent reviews, with a few negative ones, including a personal attack on me by one of Gellhorn's friends, the journalist John Pilger. Michael wanted to know why. "Well, he said I wrote a salacious book," I told Michael. Of course, it was nothing of the kind. Michael's response was, "Dirty sod. I tell you, I've got very strong feelings about him. The way he's behaved over the breakup of Yugoslavia. It's absolutely outrageous. Pilger bilge, I call it. But we have to be careful about it because Paul is a close friend of Pilger." I said, "Paul may not have a good opinion of me anymore if he's been talking to Pilger." Michael dismissed the idea.

Pilgrimage to Plymouth

One of the highlights of this trip was a visit to Plymouth, Michael's homeground—our first stop a stay at Michael's niece's home. Ally was very welcoming, although her husband Owen seemed startled when I took out my tape recorder. I explained my working methods. He asked what would happen if Michael did not like my biography of Jill. I laughed and said that might mean we wouldn't be friends anymore and he'd kick me out of his house. Owen look bemused.

Later that day Julie and I got into a conversation about authorized biography after I told her about Owen. "It [authorized biography] verges on autobiography," she said. "Yes, it does," I agreed. "You're not going to be able to put in the shit," she declared. But she fully understood my position. "There have been a number of cases," I pointed out, in which biographers had signed agreements with estates stipulating they could not interfere "because the biographer is afraid that as in a romance, when the family falls out of love with you, then you're stuck. But I just think that changes the atmosphere, to face Michael with a contract and say, 'Sign this.' I couldn't do it." Julie agreed, "I don't think that would work with Michael. He would put his back up."

Back in Pilgrim's Lane we got onto the subject of Barbara Castle again. She was Michael's longtime Labour party ally, although she thought he had tempered his leftism as soon as he joined Harold Wilson's cabinet and then worked closely with Wilson's successor, James Callaghan, who fired Barbara—much to her dismay when Michael refused to resign in support of her. Michael was determined to stay in her good graces, especially since he had angered her by expressing considerable skepticism about her published diaries. He had turned down the request of an unauthorized biographer for an interview about Barbara, knowing that Barbara would not like him to cooperate with anyone she had not authorized.

I understood his loyalty to friends, but I put it to him that there was another argument: Wasn't Barbara, in effect, asking Michael to censor himself. After all, half of what he had to say to a biographer constituted his experience, not Barbara's. Michael conceded my point, but I could tell he would bow to Barbara's wishes anyway.

Tom Hancock, an architect inspired by Jill's writings on town planning, came to lunch at Pilgrim's Lane. He asked Michael directly about the extraordinary fact that Michael had included me in his household. It really was a remarkable thing to do. Yet all Michael said was the house had been designed for others to enjoy. So many members of Michael's family had stayed at Pilgrim's Lane. Paul Foot wrote a book there. All of Julie's children had lived with Michael and Jill at various points in their youth. And so many others—like me—had enjoyed extended stays, basking in the Craigie/Foot hospitality.

But my residence at Pilgrim's Lane was different, Tom understood. I was a writer, and my material was Jill and Michael, and I had become part of his daily routine. What Michael offered me went well beyond what Tom called "generous spirited." He was staking a claim on me, even though I emphasized to Michael that I had to maintain my independence as a biographer. No matter how many times I had reiterated that position, no matter how many times Michael acceded to it, my place in his entourage certainly gave every appearance of *dependence*. I was like that biographer in Clint Eastwood's *The Unforgiven*, a part of my subject's retinue, the very definition of biographer as follower.

After Tom left, Michael mentioned that a good friend, Francis Wheen, had expressed an interest in doing Michael's biography. Michael began this conversation gingerly. He clearly thought I might be upset about Wheen because Michael had given me such encouragement. I really wasn't upset. I had never troubled myself about doing subjects other biographers were already working on and could not see how I could object to someone doing the same to me. Michael's talk with me about Wheen did, however, strengthen my desire to write about him. I felt I had a unique and privileged point of view, and my pride as a writer was aroused. I'm not speaking of a competitive instinct. I was simply in possession of material that I knew I would one day develop. It really didn't matter whether Wheen—and later, another historian—would make appeals to Michael that he found attractive.

A Two-Column Biography

"I wonder if you'll recognize her [Jill] from Carl's book?" Julie asked Michael. I laughed again. "It will be really interesting," Julie remarked slyly. Michael did not reply. I thought then—and am even surer now—that Julie had a much better grasp of the dynamics of Jill's biography than Michael did. He could not see outside of his relationship with Jill. "Anyhow, don't you have any of that nonsense that Jill wouldn't like a book done [a biography of her]," Michael told me. "I could live with that," I replied. To Michael it was very important to believe that Jill had given her blessing to my biography. But how could he speak for Jill? Julie told me that Jill had great reservations about such a book when it had been proposed to her. "It wouldn't make any difference, anyway," Julie argued. She understood that I would have gone ahead anyway, regardless of what I might think of Jill's reaction to my efforts. "It would make a difference if she thought that, Julie," Michael insisted. "Susan Sontag didn't want hers done. Martha Gellhorn didn't want it done. A good book came out of that," Julie noted. Michael countered: "That's something quite different. You were saying Jill didn't want a book written about her. That's balls, absolute balls." Julie told him straight up:

> You're deceiving yourself. We spent a whole evening, a whole dinner, talking her into it.
> [MF] Sally [Vincent]?
> [JH] She liked Sally, so it wasn't because of Sally. She said, "My life's not interesting. I don't like talking about myself," she kept saying.

This scene had taken place at Pilgrim's Lane during Jill's last illness shortly after Sally had done a very fine profile of Michael and Jill.

The relentless Julie brought Michael up short again: "You and my mother were not in accord on the subject of books. You are romanticizing her. She was very worried about having the library floor strengthened." Michael had to concede: "She was right about that." I said to Michael: "Now you tell me." I suddenly pictured myself crashing through the floor one night, buried among the piles of books that made up the columns surrounding my bedside. Then Michael relapsed, saying Jill "had exactly the same ideas about books as I had. Partly learned from my father."

After listening to the back and forth between Julie and Michael, I said: "I now realize how I'm going to write this biography. It will be in two columns: one for you and one for Julie. It's going to be a two-column biography." Julie laughed and Michael said, "That's quite a good idea." Indicating Julie, Michael said, "Sometimes she's got good ideas, but ..." Julie filled in the gap: "Only when they agree with you." Michael ignored her and said to me: "Sometimes she's absolutely cracked. You know that, don't you?" Then Julie asked him: "And are you ever cracked?" "Yes," he responded. "As long as we agree," Julie laughed. Michael said he would be cracked if he did not accept Julie's point.

Sex Is Boring

During an interview with Tony Benn, a Labour MP who had taken positions to the left of Michael when Michael was leader in the early 1980s, I was surprised to hear Benn say, "Biographies that expose sexual activities are a bit boring. I'm not very much in favor of destroying people retrospectively because of their sexual exploits. For all I know Michael may have had other dalliances, though I never thought so." I said there had been some. I saw no point in not saying so, since my biography would deal with them. "It's the story of a wonderful marriage. It had its ups and down." Boring? Surely Benn meant dealing with the sexual life of politicians was distasteful to him.

Bedfellows in Biography

The highlight of my March 2002 trip to England was a tour of Michael's constituency in Wales. Michael's friends, Alan and Meaghan Fox, were putting us up. "So the book now is going to be devoted entirely to Jill?" Meghan asked. "Yes," I assured her, "and he [I nodded toward Michael] only comes into it when it is relevant." Everyone had a good laugh. "I'm finding lots of things I didn't know about her," Michael said. I don't think I had ever heard him actually say that before. "There have been some surprises," I agreed.

Alan asked him if he wanted anything. "A whiskey," Michael replied. Actually, this was the second time he had worked the request into conversation. "I don't drink anymore," Alan said. "Whish," Michael said, using one of his favorite expressions. It seemed to express a faint air of astonishment. Actually, Alan did still drink wine. "You posh lot," Michael said. "I've given up wine now—not quite, but almost. I don't mind whiskey." Meghan asked me: "Would you want a whiskey?" I said, "I'm going to join him because he will be upset if I don't. Everyone scoffed. A little later Meghan asked: "Do you want some more whiskey, Michael?" He said, "A touch." She looked at him and said, "I can see you looking at the bottom of your glass." We laughed. "If I have another half, I promise you I will stagger upstairs," Michael said. "Are you having one?" Michael asked me. "You see," I said to the Foxes, "He keeps track. I have to match him." Michael suddenly sallied: "Look how she [Meghan] gets me drunk." He loved this sort of mock outrage that was patently unfair to its targets. "I'm just going to finish this whiskey. You'll still have some tomorrow?" Michael asked. Meghan assured him of a supply for the next two days. "Thanks to you all," Michael said. "What bed is he in?" Michael asked pointing at me. "Not the same as mine?" I said to Michael: "That's what happens when you have a biographer. Same bed." With our sleeping arrangements, sorted out Michael and I went off to our respective rooms.

There were many times when I considered my arrangement with Michael as too cozy. I tried to maintain my independence by reminding him and others of my view of the biographer as an independent agent. When Michael invited Elizabeth Rushdie, Salman Rushdie's second wife to dinner, I did not expect that she would feel free to speak her mind. Although I thought the wary Elizabeth would leave shortly after Michael retired for the evening, she gradually opened up after I told her more about my research. Elizabeth knew about Jill's true age, having heard about it from an Indian friend who also knew Jill and Michael and had had a glimpse at Jill's passport. Elizabeth thought Michael did know Jill's true age, but that he was perfectly capable of backing her up even when the facts stated the contrary. The gallant Michael would do anything to protect Jill's version of her own life.

When I told Elizabeth that Ronnie Neame was amazed that Michael claimed not to have known about the Koestler rape until Jill blurted it out at a dinner party decades later, Elizabeth said that Jill was furious that Michael refused to break off relations with Koestler. The implication was that Michael knew all along. I had to wonder, because a footnote in David Cesarini's biography of Koestler mentions Jill's bruises, which Michael had asked her about after the rape. Jill had also told Mervyn Jones about them. But in Cesarini Jill is supposed to have dissembled, not wishing to tell Michael the truth because it would prove an awkward secret for a public man to bear. Later Julie told me that Elizabeth was concerned that perhaps she had been indiscreet. It seemed to me that Michael enjoyed male bonding. He had overlooked his hero Nye Bevan's passes at Jill; he did not confront Koestler; he told Elizabeth he wanted to continue seeing her estranged husband. Was it plausible, for example, that Jill would have told the story of the rape to a dinner party if Michael did not already know it? And what did it reveal about his feelings for Jill if he could not then resist leaking her story in a review of a book about Koestler?

Over dinner the following evening Jenny Stringer told me she disapproved of my including the Lamia story in my biography of Jill. The press would sensationalize it. I understood that this would happen, but that did not mean I should not write the whole life. I did not press my case; clearly, she had drawn a line.

The next day Michael went off to Plymouth, and I returned home. Although I would make two more trips to Pilgrim's Lane, it was time to start writing Jill's biography.

Sex Is Not So Boring

I returned to London eager to get Michael's reaction to Tony Benn's obituary of Barbara Castle. I said to him:

> You know the last time I was here I spoke with Tony Benn. I told him I was dealing with all aspects of Jill's life, and I was describing to him the kind of biography I was writing. He said he really wasn't in favor of saying that much about the private lives of public figures, that he didn't like gossip in biography. I told him I thought it all had its place—the whole story. People really wanted to know what that person was like, and Jill in her own book had said she wished she knew more about the personalities of some of the women she was writing about. He said, "No, I don't believe you need to know all that much," and he was quite adamant. So then I was reading these obituaries of Barbara Castle, and he wrote

one.... He mentions you, and at the end of the obituary he just throws in a sentence about how you and Barbara were lovers. I was stunned. I was astonished because it seemed gratuitous. I couldn't see why he had put that in after he had given me this lecture. How can you just throw it into an obituary?

"First time I've heard of it, actually," Michael said. "I'll send you a copy," I said. Benn had coupled a comment about how Michael had not supported Barbara on a particular issue with the fact that they had been lovers. Michael simply would not engage in a discussion of Benn on this point.

At breakfast, Michael told me about "a rather anguished letter," he had recently received. He had written an obituary of Barbara Castle in which he referred to an affair she had with William Mellor, *Tribune*'s first editor. "My first job was also with him, and so that's when we'd known each other." Michael described the Castle/Mellor liaison as lasting a decade, until he died in 1943. One of Mellor's sons had written to Michael to say, "We're rather surprised because we thought the affair was less lengthy." Apparently the son saw Michael's view of it as an insult to his mother. To me, Michael's comment only illustrated how impossible it is to write any sort of honest biography without offending someone. Michael's response was merely to reply to the chap that they must meet sometime and talk about it.

We then had one of our periodic discussions about the nature of biography. I had been reading Montaigne. I told him how struck I was by this passage: "I have a singular curiosity to pry into the souls and the natural and true opinions of the authors with whom I converse." Montaigne, I added, would much rather learn about what Brutus said in his tent the night before a battle than about the speech the hero delivered the next day for public consumption. Montaigne enjoyed reading about the private lives, the failings, the little quirks of great men. This relish for intimacy appealed to me, I said, because "contemporary critics of biography are so often suggesting that when you write about what seem to be trivial or minor incidents there is no point to that, when in fact they often do reveal personality. Montaigne understood that much better than critics do today." Michael agreed: "Yes, you bet. You'd have to knock out a lot of Montaigne if he couldn't do that. Perfectly true, Carl. People say you musn't put any of this stuff [the "minute particulars" Johnson insisted on]. You must use your own judgment."

We were coming to the end of what Michael could tell me. I returned home to make calls to a few more sources. I sent Michael chapters on Jill's early life, to which he responded favorably. The trouble did not begin until April 2003, during my final stay at Pilgrim's Lane.

Trouble

"Now, I'll go and ring Jennie to see, maybe, if she could do tomorrow. There are some things I'd like to...." Sure, I agreed. Michael now had seen the entire first draft of my biography. He was upset, although he hardly showed it:

> The early parts of it [Jill's book] I read very carefully ... and ... you know ... in a kind of way I was more in favor of it than anybody else. I don't like the idea that I really partly held her up. I think what held her up at the end was the conclusion. She'd got up to 1911 or whatever it was [actually 1906–1907] ... where she stopped was the whole great climax of the ... and so I think that the thought of her having to write the whole of that was a kind of inhibition. She had a kind of block on it.

My biography contained several explanations of why Jill could not finish her book: She was intimidated by new scholarship that drove her constantly to revise what she had already written; she was concerned about the growing ranks of feminist scholars and other historians who would review her work; she was a one-book author who treated the suffragist history as her baby; she was as committed to Michael and her marriage, to her home and family, as she was to her book. Then there was her involvement in making *Two Hours from London*.

The one obstacle Michael could not accept was himself. Jill complained about him to Julie, to Jill's friends Celine and Moni, to Anne Foot, wife of his brother John, and to many other friends, family, and acquaintances. Jill wanted him out of the house because he kept interrupting her writing. He believed in her project, no doubt, but he never was able to grasp what even those who were fond of him could see: He was selfish, perhaps unconsciously so as he was bred by a mother who always put her boys first. Like Carlyle, Michael (albeit in a less peremptory manner) expected his wife's constant attendance. Of course, Jill used Michael as an excuse, and it can always be said that writers tend to blame their blockages on others, rather than face their own inability to get on with their projects. I did not make Michael the main source of Jill's problem, but rather portrayed him as part of a complex of factors that inhibited her. Also, I presented Jill's point of view as filtered through Julie and others. And my insistence on that approach enraged him, although at this juncture he still managed to control his temper.

Michael sputtered as he summoned his defense. I listened for a long while. The thought occurred to me later that he never seriously considered what kind of conditions might have spurred Jill on. Writing came easily to Michael. What Jill needed was for Michael to say, "Look here, you have two chapters left. Why don't you go off to wherever you like and get them done?" Jill might well have objected that she could not cart her archive somewhere else. "Well, then," he could have said, "I propose to go off for a month to Jamaica to visit my nephew Oliver." But he did not like to leave home. When Jill told him, during the Lamia affair, that he should leave Pilgrim's Lane, Michael's first thought was for his books. How could he live without them? Jill had reported as much in a letter to Julie. Michael wanted all the comforts of home, and as many people close to him noted, it was Jill who made the sacrifices. That was Jill's choice, to be sure, but Michael could nonetheless have pushed Jill out of her rut by breaking the pattern of a domestic life that suited him but got in the way of her book. Jill still might not have taken Michael up on such a proposal, but it interested me that he never made the offer. It never occurred to him to do so. I know as much because this is a subject we spoke about many, many times. It shocked Michael that I could not simply present his point of view. All other perspectives, especially Julie's, were not only wrong, they had no place in the biography.

When I first met Jill in 1994, she told me she had only two chapters left to write. She said she was stuck. "So how do we go about unsticking you?" Michael could have asked. That was the crucial year. Michael had been retired for two years. Surely it was Jill's turn? I never put this case so baldly in Jill's biography, and in the first draft I was not as clear as I should have been concerning Michael's general encouragement of her book project. That aspect I amended, but my amendment was not enough to appease Michael. He believed I had betrayed him.

Michael now was going round and round repeating his apologia, "I never had a quarrel with Jill about money, you know," he said, touching on another sore point. "Your story there that she's very hard pressed for money. All that comes from Julie, I'm afraid. But I know a damn sight more about the money she had than Julie." I began to reply, but he overrode me: "We never had a quarrel about money." My biography never said they did, since Jill avoided the subject with Michael. He continued: "I don't mean to say that she never felt hard up in any way, and of course she did sell the two pictures—maybe more—the Henry Moore and the Renoir she had from Malcolm Macdonald, and another...." But this had been Julie's point: Jill would rather sell her own things than ask Michael for money.

He never seemed to consider why that was so, why a wife would not discuss such matters with her husband.

Michael pointed to all the money he had put into the house that had been Jill's to design. He paid for their holidays. "There are several references you make to the money, and I don't like that at all. I don't think it's correct. I think you've got them from Julie." I finally broke in and said: "Well, actually, they are from Jill's letters to Julie," as I made clear in the notes and the text. "Well, of course the ones in the letters are right for you to quote," Michael demurred. But what Jill said in the letters corroborated what Julie said to me in interviews. "Even if you quote the letters, it's not a fair picture of what happened to this house," Michael then added. But I was keenly interested in how Jill felt about money. He recoiled from the portrait I had drawn from Jill's letters and interviews with Julie that exposed his everyday pettiness about household expenses and money. He did not want this portrait in the biography. But Michael's meanness about money (a word, by the way, that Jenny Stringer half-jokingly used to taunt him with) showed how in some respects he was a little man, a little man like Carlyle had been when confronted with his wife's domestic concerns. Michael was a penny wise-pound foolish sort of man. He could pay for everyone's dinner and fail to give Jill enough money to run the house, get groceries, and so on. Jill had found it impossible to engage him on this issue. And I was a Boswellian biographer of minute particulars. That money was a form of control Michael exercised was evident to me from comments like Anne Robinson's. During her walks with Jill in Hampstead, Robinson marveled that her friend did not even know how much Michael made as a member of Parliament.

My stomach churns as I recall Jenny Stringer's visit to Pilgrim's Lane the next day. I had authored six biographies and was used to criticism. I have always offered my interviewees the opportunity to review their remarks and suggest corrections, although I have never surrendered control over a biographical narrative to any of my sources. Sensing that Jenny came armed, I began to turn on my tape recorder. She objected. I pointed out that I wanted a precise a record of our meeting. Michael had never expressed the slightest qualm about my tape recordings, and after I made my point, Jenny relented. Having won that concession, I decided to compromise where I had to in order to preserve the larger truths of the book. I saw no value—not then anyway—in being confrontational. Later, I would have to change my tactics, when I realized that any ground I gave would result in more demands for changes. Jenny objected to a passage in which

Celine described Jill during her last illness "having Michael going up and down stairs supplying her needs: water, milk, a pillow etc., Celine remembers." Jenny commented: "Well, that's not very nice." Jenny continued: "Celine thought Jill was angry because she was the one dying. He [Michael] looked dead tired." Jenny commented:

> Now this is not fair because Michael wanted to do this.
> [CR] Well, this is just Celine's impression.
> [JS] He never left her side.
> [CR] I have no problem taking that out if it doesn't jibe with the general situation.
> [JS] It suggests Jill was ordering him about.

I did take the passage out, primarily to appease. Without her interference, I would have presented a fuller picture even if witnesses contradicted each other. The truth is that Jill did order Michael about—not only when she was dying, but many times in the house as well. This I learned from a range of witnesses, many of whom did not know one another.

> [JS] Then Celine says [to Jill], "You can't do this to Michael. He's an old man. He needs his sleep." Well, she wasn't doing it to Michael. Michael was wanting to do it himself. I think that's right, isn't it Michael?
> [MF] You bet. I thought she was still going to stay [survive].

My narrative never questioned Michael's devotion to Jill during her final illness. But Celine was one of the few frank witnesses who explained the toll Jill's last days took on Michael.

What infuriated me about this sit-down with Jenny is that I had been asking her for three years to give me her version of what happened during Jill's final days. Jenny always found a reason to put me off. Now she was doing the fine turning to ensure that Michael emerged as a saint. Jill's own conflicting emotions, her anger at Michael for never putting her first came out as she was dying. Her anger did not mean she no longer loved this great man; on the contrary, her anger resulted from disappointment that such a great and generous man had such a flaw. As she lay dying, he was certainly putting her first, but for Jill his effort came too late. This bitter truth was hard to bear. I don't think Michael ever confronted it, and I confess I did not have the courage to do what he could not. In retrospect, I feel rather like James Anthony Froude, who held back the knowledge of Carlyle's impotence and let the world know only in the posthumous publication of *My Relations with Carlyle*. A close reader of Froude's biography can detect a passage where he hints at Carlyle's impotence, and a perceptive reader of *To Be a Woman* could, I believe, sense my feeling that for all their loving companionship Michael failed Jill in a fundamental way. But to have been as explicit as I am here would have brought the house of Foot down upon me I am sure. Michael did not believe in censorship, so I have no right to suggest he would have suppressed my biography, but I also have no doubt that a campaign would have been waged against me by his surrogates. And I did not want to end like Froude, who spent a good deal of his remaining life defending himself against the charges of Carlyle's family and friends.

My book then included a scene with Julie at her mother's death bed. As her mother died, Julie said, "I'm free." Julie told me this, but then asked me to remove the quotation when she saw my text. The comment expressed how much of a burden her mother's judgment had always placed upon her. "That's got to go," Jenny said. "Julie wants it out," I answered. I began to notice how, in the course of this meeting and a subsequent one, even the pretense of giving me suggestions was abandoned. I was now the hired hand doing Michael's bidding. I resolved, right then, that I would have to draw the line.

Michael and Jenny were trying to be helpful, if controlling, and Jenny ended this session with a compliment about how I had included some of the tributes to Jill in the letters sent to Michael after her death. But she continued: "'He feels guilty for not having been with her.' I think Celine must have said that. I don't know what it means." I said it would take more explanation or should be cut, so I would cut it. Both Celine and Julie, in fact, had come to similar conclusions even though they did not like one another.

Then there was the touchy matter of taking equity out of the house so that Julie could buy her flat. I described how Jenny, Moni and Denis Forman, as well as Anne Robinson and her husband helped Michael and Jill with their financial plan.

> [JS] Then you say, "In the process Michael realized that their helpmates had become critical of Julie. They believed she wanted the house signed over to her." Well, that's not true.
> [MF] Never.

Julie had objected to this passage as well, I told them. So where had I got this impression? From Celine and Anne Robinson—the latter, in particular, expressed her suspicions of Julie's motivations. Anne, at this point, was not in Michael's inner circle and could speak with a freedom others could not. Celine never seemed to care if what she said got her into trouble.

Jenny objected to a passage in which I quoted Esther (Julie's daughter) saying that Jill was angry with Michael for "not letting her go." Jenny asked

Michael, "Is that right." He said, "No. I can't remember." I replied, "Right or wrong, this is what Esther said." Jenny countered, "I don't think she was angry. Anyway, you don't have to put it in." I did not reply. "You're going to think about it?" Jenny asked. I laughed and said, "Yes. I'll check with Esther." "Don't do that," Jenny said quickly. "Leave it, leave it." Her tactics were clear: As much as possible confine discussion of the biography to Pilgrim's Lane; when the biography left the house, so to speak, it would be subject to other points of view. "I just want to get it right," I said alluding to my wish to speak with Esther again. "I'll just email Esther." Jenny conceded: "It's difficult to piece it altogether, actually." Indeed, and she had contributed to the difficulty. "Don't say I … I don't want to cause a dispute," Jenny said.

That concluded our first session. I would have another with Jenny alone at her house, when she tried to get me to cut out the Lamia story. She would not have done so in Michael's hearing, because he had already praised my handling of the episode. I did not ask to record her because I knew she would not stand for it. What I learned from her did not change the biography. We spent a good deal of time arguing about my vision of biography and why I believed Jenny was wrong to censor the story of the marriage.

Jenny then objected that I had emphasized the mother/daughter relationship too much and to Jill's detriment. "Don't you think," I said, "that readers will see that this is a daughter's point of view? Are they going to take everything Julie says as objective, historical fact? Aren't these her feelings about her mother? How can you be so certain about how people are going to read this biography?" Julie did not play by Michael's and Jenny's political rules, and her lack of discretion infuriated them. Our meeting was not acrimonious, but I did not give any ground. And of course Jenny made no concessions. Then she took me to a bad Chinese restaurant.

The Aftermath

I did not tape the last face-to-face meeting about the biography. Going in I knew how fraught it would be, and I thought the tape recorder would add to the tension. Instead, as soon as I arrived at Philadelphia airport, I asked my wife, Lisa Paddock, to drive home so that I could recount into my tape recorder how I had seen Michael unravel. Reflecting on the scene, I said:

Julie was getting back from Italy and she called: "Should I come and get you to go over photographs?" I said, "Well, I can't do that because Jenny is coming over and we're going to talk about the book." She said, "Maybe I should be there." I said, "I think it's in my interest and yours that you are." I didn't say this to Michael. I wanted to avoid sitting down with him and Jenny and then having to go to Julie and have to explain it all again. "This is what they don't like." I thought, "I'll be damned if I'm going to run back and forth between contending parties. Just let them have it all out around the table." So Julie came, and Michael started reading this one passage where Julie says to me, "Have you even seen Michael's anger? It can be really frightening. Jill was frightened of his anger." That's when he went ballistic. "This is outrageous. Leave the house!" Julie just sat there, kept her composure. She said quietly, "I just said she was...." "SHE WASN'T AFRAID OF MY ANGER. WE NEVER HAD ANY QUARREL!" He went on and on in a rage. Jenny kept saying, "Maybe I should go. Maybe I should go." I just sat there, and then I said, "Michael, Ursula Owen described how frightening your anger could be." Well, that was somehow a different matter, he indicated. The thing that really offended me was that at one point he was in such a rage he said, "THIS IS COMING OUT!" I wanted to say to him, "Michael, I thought this was my book." Well, it is coming out because Julie said to Michael, "Well, if you feel that strongly about it, take it out." She didn't take back what she said. I didn't see why she should. It took him about two days to calm down.

I told Lisa about my meeting with Jenny and her efforts to get me to cut out the Lamia story. Jenny would work on Michael, I predicted, and in a few months I expected to hear from him that he wanted the Lamia chapter out of the biography. I told Lisa how Jenny muttered that what I wrote was "fiction," yet in the end she only demanded about a half dozen corrections. A further assault would come via the mails. Jenny wanted references to Barbara Castle cut because they might hurt her family. At one point, Michael demanded I send back my tape recordings. I did not even reply to that request. I made further cosmetic changes, but stood firm on the rest. All of my recordings are available in my archive at McFarlin Library, the University of Tulsa. The archive also includes the full, unedited version of *A Private Life of Michael Foot* (close to 200,000 words, as well as several revised drafts).

"We were sitting in the garden," I told Lisa about my last afternoon with Michael at Pilgrim's Lane, "and he said, 'Well, Ken Morgan's doing my biography. That cuts you out.'" It was that quick and that curt. No preamble and nothing afterwards. "I think he's angry with you," Lisa said, "I do." I was certainly angry with him, I admitted.

[LP] Didn't you sort of know it would go like this?
[CR] How could it not? He's a politician. He wants to control everything.

I told Lisa Michael was angry about the house money–allowance issue. "He's angry about that? How small," she said. Jenny had objected to my writing that Jill had re-invented herself before she met Michael. "She just wanted to move on," Jenny said. How could Jenny know? I was writing about a period 30 years before the two women had met. "Oh man," Lisa said.

On my last night at Pilgrim's Lane, Michael asked me to call him when I got home. He had no particular purpose in mind other than to be sure I got home safely, but he had never before made such a request. I think it was his effort to smooth things over. I didn't call him, but he phoned me, and we had a short, awkward conversation about nothing much that I can recall.

On April 29, 2003, I received a letter from Paul Foot. I cannot quote it without getting permission from his estate, which I have no inclination to obtain. But I will quote his last sentence, which refers to the Lamia story, and what he expected me to do with it: "If you leave it out, I will be truly grateful. If you leave it in, I certainly won't want to see you or correspond with you again." My May 13, 2003, email to Piers Burnett, my Aurum Press editor, provides a good idea of what I was confronting:

> I will be faxing you shortly a letter from Paul Foot. He asks me to cut out the chapter called Obsession. He says the parts quoting him are inaccurate. In fact, all such quotations come directly from Jill's letters written shortly after seeing Paul. I don't think he realizes where I got my quotations from, although the context is clear in the chapter, I believe. The quotations he objects to reflect Jill's state of mind and her understanding of what Paul said. I have no inclination to change a word. I would trust what she says in the letters sooner than his reconstruction of what he said over 30 years ago, and he won't reconstruct what he said anyway.
>
> I seem to recall that I sent you an email about the Obsession chapter some time ago, saying that I knew through Julie that Paul was opposed to it. I sent him the whole book because I hoped he might relent and speak with me about the Obsession chapter. I also sent him the book because I did not want him to be approached by the press without having read what I wrote.
>
> I should also say that I have received two phone calls from Michael's close friends who plead with me to omit the chapter. Michael, on the other hand, told Paul that he thought I had done a good job on the chapter and that Michael did not see how he could ask me to remove the chapter from the book. Nevertheless Paul urged Michael to tell me to take the chapter out of the book. I suspect that Michael's friends and Paul are still working on him in the hope that he will call and ask that

the chapter be taken out. If Michael or anyone else calls, I will refuse to eliminate the chapter.

Pauls acts as if I have pulled a fast one. But I was very firm with Michael and everyone concerned with the biography that I would not have myself put in the position of the keeper of the secrets. I would tell what I felt needed telling. Anyone who knows anything about my other books should know I'm not going to back down—EVER.

Paul's assertion that Jill would not have wanted the Obsession chapter is beside the point. Who can say she would have wanted any biography? What I can say is that her own book *Daughters of Dissent* takes a very dim view of biographers who are asked to do what Paul & Co are asking me to do: SANITIZE a life. I won't do it.

I've decided not to reply to Paul. He would see my rationale as self-serving, and it is clear he distrusts my motives.

I tell you all this just to keep you informed. You asked me if Michael would help publicize the book. I still think so. But we have to be prepared for some coolness from him if the circle around him succeeds in convincing him that somehow the biography—or at least the Obsession chapter—is some kind of betrayal on my part. I don't expect Paul or anyone else close to Michael to make the issue public. They would be very foolish to do so and only give publicity to what they are trying to suppress.

I'm faxing a copy of this email to Rivers and Gloria so that they are aware of developments.

I'm not terribly surprised at this turn of events. It seems to come with the territory I have always explored as a biographer.

On June 4, I wrote to Julie reiterating what I had told Piers. She was hoping that I could come over to London and smooth over matters with Michael. I explained:

I haven't spoken with him about Moni or Paul because I don't want to raise a ruckus. I don't want to upset him. I don't want him to think I want him to do something about it. There is nothing that has to be done since I have no intention of omitting the [Obsession] chapter. When I said I wouldn't stay with Michael, I did not mean to imply that I had any hard feelings about him. Rather, I was suggesting that Moni, Paul, and Jenny have created an atmosphere that has made it impossible for me to behave as I did before. Their attitude won't affect the book and won't affect my attitude toward Michael. They believe they are protecting him. But given what they have said, I just can't go on as usual and then have it said once again that somehow I took advantage of Michael.

The tone of Michael's letters, beginning in August 2003, speak for themselves:

It is absurd to say that I am trying to dictate an authorised biography. No one who has seen the facilities to which I put at your disposal would come to that conclusion. All the changes or deletions I have proposed are designed to ensure that you paint the truest picture of Jill and my relations with her.

But Michael was not correcting statements of fact. He was objecting to my interpretations and expecting me to accept his. And how did providing "facilities" demonstrate I was not an authorized biographer? Quite the contrary. Because Michael had been so accommodating some of those close to him assumed I was the authorized biographer—notwithstanding my protests to the contrary.

Michael wanted me to take out any reference to Paul in the Obsession chapter. But Paul was an integral part of the story—as Jill demonstrated in her own letters. Michael even objected to my mentioning that Jill was reading Gore Vidal's memoir *Palimpsest* on her final visit to Dubrovnik. Julie had told me the story about how she had enjoyed the sex scenes. But Michael contended that if I were to "publish the paragraph referring to Gore Vidal, I think it would give an absolutely false picture of Jill's last visit to Dubrovnik." Why? The Vidal story was only a few sentences amid much else I discussed about her final days in Dubrovnik. Michael's letters seem so petty and sounded so obviously like Jenny Stringer who supervised the drafting of these letters and sent me advance email copies of them. Michael's letter closed with this fusillade:

> I note you say on the cover blurb that the book was written "with the full cooperation of Michael Foot." You are now receiving further cooperation and I trust you will be translating it into action. When you have carried out all the changes I have asked for I think you will have had a truer picture of my relationship with Jill and indeed will have produced a better book. So please, no more nonsense about authorised biographies. When the book is finally published I think that most of your readers will marvel at the facilities that have been at your disposal.

Thus he equated his cooperation with my doing his bidding.

I responded to Michael's letter via email the same day and received a reply on August 4, which began:

> I must say I am shocked, as I think any normal reader would be, by your statement that you do not understand my objection to the so-called Gore Vidal reference. What the quotation suggests is that Jill—on her last visit to her beloved Dubrovnik, mind you—was concerned about the absence of sexual relations, some three years after my prostate operation as it happens.

But the passage had nothing to do with Michael. I never mentioned his prostate operation, and the point of my few sentences on her reading of Vidal had to do with her still taking a lively interest in sex and stories about sex.

And this time he was demanding I take out all references to Kathy Seary, Jill's housekeeper who he had urged me to interview. What had all this to do with the book he said was my own? On August 3, I wrote Michael:

> Did I misunderstand your position on authorized biographers? When I received your comments, there were in the form of commands, not suggestions. And I did not understand why you thought the book would be held up by your demands for changes. Most of your demands are simply deletions. Nothing is easier than to cut a book to bits.

To Michael's complaint that I had him making statements that were libelous (he did not deny making them, for after all they had been recorded), I replied:

> Would Tony Benn or Harriet Harmon suc Michael Foot? Michael Foot? An icon of the Labour Party who just celebrated his 90th birthday at 10 Downing Street? Not bloody likely.

Here is how he ended his August 4 letter:

> My views on authorised biographies should not be interpreted to mean that a biographer is at liberty to make distortions that give an untrue account of his or her subject. So please, no further nonsense about that. I suggest you at once show the whole of this correspondence to your publisher.

I replied the same day, telling him I had already sent copies of his letters to my publisher, and why he should think otherwise mystified me. He treated me as though I was a neophyte—and a rather dim one at that. Did he really suppose my publisher would set me straight? Here is what I wrote my publisher:

> Dear Piers,
>   Here is the latest letter from Michael Foot. I think he has lost all perspective, reading into passages implications that are just not there.
>   Gloria [my agent] has in hand everything I have sent you. Michael seems to think I've done something my publisher would disapprove of. I will be sending you my reply to him in a separate email.

None of Michael's objections, needless to say, caused the publisher any concern.

I did, however, send Michael a letter saying that I would seriously consider his objections. I did so because I was willing to make a few changes just to cool him off and because I saw no point in prolonging a correspondence in which I affirmed my independence while he emphasized my

indebtedness to his "facilities." His letter of August lowered the temper-
ature. He expressed his relief that I would indeed "treat seriously" all his
proposals for changes.

On August 7, I emailed my editor:

Dear Piers,
    I just faxed Michael's latest letter and my reply to Gloria and
Rivers.
    I suspect Michael will still be upset when he sees that in the copy-
edited ms I have not made all the corrections he deems essential.
When you send him the copyedited ms with my changes, he may try
to delay publication as he comes up with yet more changes. At least
that is my hunch. I've known too many cases in which the author concedes a point and then is expected to concede again and again and
again. So as he soon as Michael wins a point, he'll want to win a few
more. What I suggest, then, is that you give him a fairly short time to
read the copyedited ms.—no longer than you or anyone else would
have as you are preparing to go to galley stage. I would point out that
he has now seen the ms. twice and the copyedited ms. will be his third
go. If he objects to changes I have not made, or if he finds new changes
to be made, then he has to be firmly told NO MORE. He has been given
his "serious consideration." I certainly will have no trouble telling him
that. And it will be at that point, perhaps, that Michael Bessie should
be contacted, and, if he is willing, he might tell Michael, "Look, you've
had your say. Anything more really would look like you are trying to
control the process. And Carl is going to go ahead, and you can only
make things worse by attempting to stop or delay him"—something
like that.
    By the way, Michael has not acknowledged in any letter that I made
several changes in response to his first reading of the ms.

On August 20, Julie sent me a sympathetic email acknowledging my
difficulties. She suggested that Michael was genuinely shocked that Jill
was short of money and that was because Jill could never bear to bring
up the subject with him. This was a side of Jill he simply was not prepared
to accept. As she concluded, "he cannot bear to have the picture of Jill he
carries in his head and heart in anyway tarnished I guess." Julie said
Michael thought Jenny had been too hard on me. Perhaps so, but Michael
never suggested as much to me.

At any rate, the furor of letters had subsided. In the end, my publisher
waited almost a year to publish the book. I was never quite sure why. I
was told it was because another publisher was in the process of buying
Aurum Press, and some projects just had to wait until the business was
concluded. Whatever the reason, when Michael finally did see the galleys,

he surprised me by asking for only a few more changes, which the publisher gratefully made with my approval. Paul Foot's sudden death on July 18, 2004, apparently made it possible for Michael to return to his earlier approval of my account of his adultery. My biography was published in May 2005 to generally good reviews and very poor sales.

Michael and I spoke only one other time after my last visit to him in April 2003, when he called in the spring of 2005 to say he was upset about a *Daily Mail* serialization of my biography. He hated the tabloid, calling it "The Forger's Gazette." I told Michael I had no authority to stop the serialization, and I would not profit a penny from its publication. I had told the publisher that Michael would be upset, but the publisher could not resist the £10,000 payment the *Mail* offered. I was square with Michael: I did not object to the publisher's decision. We never spoke again.

Examples of Material Deleted at Michael Foot's Request from *To Be a Woman: The Life of Jill Craigie*

Chapter 10: Recently Michael Foot discovered in his library a letter (dated March 24, 1953) from Harley Street doctor reporting the result of a semen test: "your semen is of sufficient quality to fertilise your wife. The poor quantity means that it will be necessary for you to deposit this amount approximately in the neighbourhood of the entrance to the womb; you have not sufficient to spare to be lost in the vagina." The doctor gave explicit instructions as to how a pregnancy might be achieved, but in spite of their best efforts Jill could not conceive a child.

Chapter 11: Julie took greater offense at she watched politicians stick their tongues half way down Jill's throat. She hectored Michael about it. He would reply that of course men accosted Jill.

Chapter 20: Is every man a victim of his penis?—Jill Craigie, "Odd Reflections"

Chapter 21: Did Michael do enough to help Jill? Julie thought not. What had Michael ever really given up for Jill? Jill took the point, yet she did not press Michael for more.

Chapter 26: Binh, a Vietnamese restaurateur, catered a dinner once. Her food was delicious, but Jill thought Binh just a little too familiar with Michael, and Binh never catered another dinner.

Another friend of Michael's remembers Jill calling with an invitation to dinner: "It was always a royal command. If you were doing something else, she'd say drop it." She often antagonized women by adopting this tone, he reports.

At one point, Jill proposed to Julie that she take a lover, a married man who did not want to leave his wife. That way neither marriage would break up and no one would get hurt.

Jenny Stringer argued with Jill about her choices—too much impatiens and bursts of color to the point of vulgarity. Jenny preferred more design, classical lines, and interesting foliage. Jill called Jenny a snob. So it was just as well that Jenny did not like going early to market.

Chapter 27: Yet in Julie's view, he himself did not worship her enough. For all his kind heartedness and love, Michael was viewed by some observers as essentially a selfish man.

Chapter 30: Julie recalls that during one of their earlier conversations about sex, Jill (then at least 80) said, "Oh my God, I long to feel a man inside me." Julie emphasizes, "She meant it."

Postscript

A Private Life of Michael Foot was conceived on that day in 2003 when Michael announced to me he had a biographer, Kenneth Morgan, and "that cuts you out." Well, it didn't. I decided to use the material I already had, as I explained in my preface:

> This is not a conventional biography. I rely not on documents but almost exclusively on recorded interviews and memories of Michael Foot constituting a raw record of conversations not smoothed over by a biographical narrative. This is a book about process. I show how I went about obtaining my story, which ostensibly concerned Jill Craigie, the subject of *To Be a Woman: The Life of Jill Craigie*. But Michael, who entered Jill's life in 1945, was such an important source that inevitably I learned as much about him as about her.
>
> Readers come to biographies to learn about the subject, not the biographer. And yet the biographer is, in a sense, half the story. Or as Paul Murray Kendall put it in *The Art of Biography*, every biography is an autobiography. So this book is an effort to show how a biographer struggles to tell his own story even as family and friends cherish differing narratives about that same subject. My wish is to highlight these clashes of perception rather than reconcile their discrepancies.
>
> There is value, too, in showing the rough edges of biography, the stops and starts, in an unapologetic fashion. I have to wonder, as well, if there has ever been a biography that has treated a British political and literary figure in quite so revealing a fashion.

My London agent was certain she could sell the book to a British trade house. After trying them all she gave up, and the book remained unsold. Michael died in 2010, and the verdict held that Michael Foot, a failed leader, was largely forgotten. There simply wasn't a big enough market to justify an advance for a trade biography.

I contemplated self-publishing *A Private Life of Michael Foot*, but I realized the book would have difficulty attracting attention and probably would not get the reviews or feature articles that an established publisher might be able to attract. Then an English friend suggested I submit the book to University of Plymouth Press. The university has a Jill Craigie theater, and her film about the rebuilding of the city is often shown, and, of course, it is where Michael grew up. The Press was interested but could not offer me an advance and would do the book as print-on-demand, which meant it would not get into bookstores because a p.o.d. book is not returnable for credit at the publisher. Even so, the book would be competitively priced in paperback, hardback, and ebook, and it would appear on online sites. It was the best deal I could get, and I was pleased with the production, especially when I realized lawyers would not vet the book. Although my editor asked me some searching questions about the book, making sure in his own mind that no libel issues were at stake, I was surprised that my own assurances sufficed. At a trade publisher I am certain that some passages in the book, although not libelous, would nevertheless have been removed by lawyers trying to make absolutely sure that their clients (the publishers were not sued).

The book has engendered interest because of Jeremy Corbyn's ascent to the Labour party leadership. The press has pointed out how similar some of his policies are to Michael Foot's, although, as I have been tweeting, there are significant differences as well. I worried, as did trade publishers who turned down the book, that it might be attacked. But so far the book has not received negative attention, although a reporter from *Camden New Journal* asked me on twitter why I didn't confront Michael with Julie's "claim" that he made a pass at her. I didn't answer him directly. I just said I decided not to use the story in the Craigie biography but did use it in *A Private Life of Michael Foot*. I also said Julie did not make a big deal about it, although a *Telegraph* headline said Foot tried to seduce her. Of course I never put it that way. Nor did Julie. The whole story—hardly a story even—takes up less than a page. I never intended to show Michael anything in *A Private Life of Michael Foot*, which was finished in 2007. I didn't want to publish the book until after he died. The one time I asked him about making a pass at a friend's wife, he said, "Depends on what you mean by a pass." A very Bill Clintonesque answer that is in my book. I never saw the value of questioning Michael since I didn't see the incident as looming large in Jill's biography. And afterwards I had no contact with Michael and so wasn't going to resume contact just to ask him if he made a pass at Julie. But how to explain all that to a reporter?

One response to *A Private Life of Michael Foot* crystallized why, after 2003, I did not contact Michael: "reading what other people said about him including Kenneth Morgan, made me realise how Michael had such a particular view of the world, which other people had to fit into, and that included Jill." I agreed and replied: "I think I could have patched it up with him, but I think I would have paid a price in my own estimation of myself."

9

Intermission: From Picking a Victim to Pontificating on Subjects

In the spring of 2003, I decided to take a respite. Between 1986 and 2003, I had produced biographies of Marilyn Monroe, Lillian Hellman, Martha Gellhorn, Norman Mailer, Rebecca West, Susan Sontag, and Jill Craigie (not published until 2005). I was worn out—not with biography per se, but with the traveling and the enormous expense of it all. Archival work, interviews, and mainly uncomprehending reviews had not daunted my enthusiasm for the genre but chastened me as to what it had done for my own reputation, which had not advanced much if measured by critical attention and the size of my book advances. I was just part of a middling generation of biographers. No reviewer ever started by sizing up my oeuvre. No one seemed to perceive the connections between one biography and another. I should not have expected more. Reviewers simply don't have the time and are not paid enough to do other than examine the work at hand, although I hoped to rectify that—at least in my work for *The New York Sun,* which provided me with the space to do for biographers what I wanted done for my work: discuss their books week after week in the light of the genre itself and of the work of other biographers.

The review/column in the *Sun* also had the result of calling attention to myself in ways that my biographies had not. Suddenly I saw my name attached to publisher's ads in blurbs that extolled their authors' work, and in blogs that also disseminated some of my less flattering remarks. Now I got emails from grateful authors. Surprisingly, I never got messages from those who received negative reviews. I expected more complaints, but other than an occasional letter addressed to the *Sun,* no one wanted to start an argument with me. I had the illusion—and some of my biographer-friends seemed to share it—that I actually had some sort of power.

I reviewed a phenomenal range of subjects: literary figures, politicians, scientists, and all kinds of public figures. It was an education. I would not have read all of those books if I had not been paid to do so, and I couldn't refuse to do so in my guise as Dr. Biography. I also learned that not all biographers are in love with the genre itself. I can't tell you how many biographies I've read and wanted to say to the biographer: Don't you have any sense of affection for your genre and those who practice it? Why do you pretend that other biographies of your subject do not exist? Why do you tuck them away in the bibliography and bury them deep in your notes when I know damn well they have had more of an impact on you than you care to acknowledge?

Which is why, in the end, I turned to pontification, to writing about biography as well writing biography. James Panero's *New Criterion* review of *Reading Biography,* my collection of *New York Sun* reviews, evokes better than anything else what a peculiar dude I became: "Carl Rollyson reads biographies. He writes biographies. He writes about reading biographies. He writes about writing biographies. Writers are the subject of many of the biographies he reads and writes. Whew!"

After about three years my writing in *The New York Sun* had run its course, and after several changes of editors, I decided to call it quits. I looked for an online outlet that might give me even more latitude not just to review biographies but also to delve into their backstories, showing how biographical narratives are produced. I found my opportunity by writing a column every two weeks for bibliobuffet.com, which, alas, is no longer publishing new work. Every two weeks I had the freedom to address any topic I wished in a column I titled "Biographology," stealing the word from an editor's email.

One of my bugbears was what I called "proprietary biography," the institution by which subjects and their estates attempt to corral all the resources required to control whoever dares to write a biography. As an example, I took a figure close to hand: "I suppose one owns the facts of one's own life," Ted Hughes once said, complaining about the biographers who had appropriated his. My answer would be: "You started it." No one put a gun to Hughes's head and said, "You must appear on BBC radio with your wife Sylvia Plath and explain what your marriage and creative partnership means to you." But that is what he did, and in the process he projected an idea of himself, his wife, and his marriage that was a myth. I don't mean this myth was a falsehood. It was, rather, a story that appealed to him, a story that Sylvia partially believed in—and then set out to dismantle as soon as he left her. As she did so, she began writing letters and poems that recast the narrative of their lives. Whatever her motivations, the result was an appeal to the world that the world has happily acknowledged in biographies and dozens of other books that set out to understand what happened.

Ted Hughes took the position that biographers have no right to muck about with his life and that he knew better anyway since he was *there* when it all happened. Tell that to the judge, Mr. Hughes, the judge who knows that eyewitness testimony is not always reliable, and that those who arrive on the scene after the event and begin collecting forensic evidence often have a better perspective than do the parties who participated in the event. Of course, biography is not a science, and biographers, like scientists, make mistakes. But to suppose that there is a somehow an absolute truth, an infallible standard by which biographers can be judged, is preposterous.

Over the course of his post–Sylvia Plath life, Hughes himself changed his mind about many things, including the reasons for her suicide, as I documented in *American Isis: The Life and Art of Sylvia Plath*. Hughes was abetted by those librarians, archivists, and other custodians of literary papers otherwise known as toadies. If you go to the Sylvia Plath collection at the Lilly Library in Indiana, you can read through her papers and those of others connected to her. But you may not photocopy without express permission from the Plath estate, which may very well deny your request— especially if you are a biographer. Head down to Atlanta to the Ted Hughes Papers and you receive the same welcome. And pretty much the same is true at the British Library, which has the papers of Olwyn Hughes. Until recently she has repelled the brood of biographers on the trail of the sister-in-law Olwyn hated.

Certain libraries collude with literary estates that seek to define literary history on their own terms. You would think a librarian who is supposed to disseminate knowledge would feel some compunction about slavering after the papers of the renowned. But instead, many of them have heeded the siren call of the late Howard Gotlieb, the entrepreneurial head of special collections at Boston University's Mugar Memorial Library. He promised writers like Martha Gellhorn that he would lock away her papers and exhibit them only to a select few—otherwise known as authorized biographers. The poor man used to get hectoring calls from not so poor Martha, who would berate him with oaths about that rogue Rollyson who had not sought and did not wish her blessing.

The literary papers of canonized writers are like the gold in Fort Knox. The papers are there to establish the full faith and credit of the archive.

The papers accrue in value to the extent that no one gets to see them. Thus proprietary biography is born. And the authorized biographer becomes part of a franchise.

Not all research collections are so administered, I am relieved to say. And so I can go to Smith College, enter the Mortimer Rare Book Room, and see *everything* in the Plath collection, have it photocopied, even take pictures of it with my iphone. And this means that not only Plath scholars, but generations of undergraduates at Smith have been able to examine firsthand Plath's writings as she first set them down on the page. They can read her mother's letters and much else. I was able to read Aurelia Plath's annotations to a scholarly study of her daughter's poetry, something Ted Hughes never saw and would never permit access to if he had his way.

Hughes sent a trunk to Emory University that is sealed until 2023. Who knows what is in it? Whatever revelations it may contain will probably be attached to yet another permission form, holding back history, bludgeoning biography into submission, in a futile effort to own, rather to own up to, what he has done.

Postscript: Excerpts from a London Diary

Wednesday, January 11, 2011

This morning I arrived at the British Library at 9:25. A long queue had formed awaiting the building's opening. I remarked to a friendly looking chap that if we had been in front of the New York Public Library waiting for it to open, everyone would have been crowded around the entrance in no discernible order. He laughed and said, yes, he had been to New York City. How orderly of the British, I said. In New York it is a free for all, with taxis stopping to pick up fares even if it means holding up traffic and incurring the wrath of drivers quick to get on the horn.

I've been thinking about what it was like for Sylvia Plath to settle in London in 1959 and die there four years later. It was a different country, then, in some respects. It was still recovering from the war—as I could see when I first visited London in the summer of 1963, about six months after Plath's death, although I had not heard of Plath then. Indeed, most Americans had not heard of her and would not until the early 1970s when Al Alvarez, more than anyone else, made her known through his memoir of her in *The Savage God*. Alvarez had championed her work even earlier when as poetry editor of *The Observer* he printed poems that almost no one else would touch—certainly not *The New Yorker*, her favored venue.

Even British literary lights like Karl Miller deemed her work "too extreme" when in his capacity as an editor at *The New Statesman* he had rejected poems like "Daddy" and "Lady Lazarus." This Alvarez learned from a chance meeting with Miller on a London street.

Plath was the poet Alvarez had dreamed of, since she fulfilled his call for poetry written in Britain to jettison its all-too-genteel gloss and get down to the ground, so to speak. Plath had jumped the queue, and broke the way the poetic line should flow on to the page. This was especially apparent to Alvarez because she read the poems aloud as performances. She had done so for herself while composing her last, great works. I wonder, if in fact, she needed that stately, if shabby, old world propriety to stage her breakout. Perhaps not, but the cold English climate certainly stimulated her to generate her own heat.

Yet not only Alvarez but also a British publishing house, Heinemann, had been quicker to accept Plath's first book than any American press, although Knopf eventually followed suit. There had to be, in other words, rude awakenings at work in the mother country—as indeed there were, although they were called the "angry young men." The angry young women would show up a decade later, although they were not called as such. When women started "bitching," as Marion Meade put it in her book with that single word as her salvo, and wrote chapters about the fascism of family life that made women merely the props and the servants of the male ego, they discovered the prophetic Plath of "Daddy, whose every woman adores a fascist."

Plath arrived in London as Mrs. Hughes, since he was the first one of this couple to win major literary prizes and fellowships. The city held out some kind of stimulation that Sylvia could not obtain back home. This train of thought led me to look for ways in which the English do jump queues—or at least define places where order and high courtesy do not prevail. I've always been struck while walking in London that as a pedestrian approaches a side street vehicles do not yield but rush right past. You would think someone in command of a couple thousand pounds of steel would be wary of knocking down a human obstacle. But it is customary, not offensive, for vehicles to command the right of way in these instances. Perhaps this is because there are so many marked cross walks where vehicles must defer to pedestrians. Any street crossing not so marked is virtually a signal to go ahead without braking. What looks like aggressive driving to me is just customary behavior to the Brit who has his or her own way of remaining on the go. In other words, each culture, however different, has its own dynamic and idea of what constitutes good behavior and its insulting opposite. The trouble is we (that is, both sides of the transatlantic cultural coin) don't always appreciate how our respective cultures encourage as well as retard our initiative.

Ted Hughes's friends—almost to a man and woman—disliked Sylvia Plath, the pushy, spoiled, self-absorbed American, as they saw her. And she had that side to her, no doubt. She was a go-ahead American, and when Ted married her, that is what he wanted. He didn't have a clue how to make a life, or a living, as a poet, and Sylvia did. Ted's friends could not believe how oblivious Sylvia could be of what they considered common courtesy. I know how Sylvia felt, having lived in a British home and spent something like an entire year in the country in over forty trips since 1963. You would think after that much exposure I would know how to comport myself. And yet like her I can entirely forget my place (as the British might call it) and defy the decorum of the occasion or the venue. So there I was on my first day fresh (well not so fresh) off the plane, checking into my hotel, and then rushing to the British Library acutely aware—as Sylvia always was—that time is a wasting. I didn't stop to eat but decided in my bleary-eyed state to subsist on eyedrops and gum until closing time. Fiercely focusing on the file in front of me and heading toward the counter to pick up yet another folder, I was suddenly taken aback by the librarian's BIG FROWN. As I opened my mouth to make my request, she interrupted: "No chewing in the reading room." I thought she was going to ask me to stand in the corner (one of my habitual haunts in kindergarten). I can just imagine the countless ways Sylvia had the same impact on the inhabitants of Albion. In fact, I don't have to imagine how Sylvia offended. All I have to do is read Dido Merwin's rant against Plath in an appendix to Anne Stevenson's biography.

If Al Alvarez became Sylvia's steadfast friend toward the end of her life it is because he is so thoroughly English and yet so utterly comfortable with America and Americans. Unlike Ted Hughes, who disliked what he called cellophane-wrapped America when he arrived in 1957, Alvarez reveled in his American interludes, and he greeted me with extraordinary warmth and a feeling of instant camaraderie—exactly the sort of openness that Ted Hughes scorned in the Americans he met since he could not believe it was anything more than a habit of superficial agreeability. I imagine Sylvia found it restful to be in Alvarez's company. He was such a receptive listener and an astute critic. I can't tell the whole story here, but by the end of my three hours with him, he was reading to me from his diary, which recounted a shocking event that will has it place in the last chapter of my Plath biography.

Thursday, January 12

9:15: Off for another day at the British Library. No gum this time. I rather feel like my daughter when she was about six or seven, visiting me after her mother and I had divorced. Amelia had to adjust to the new regime, so to speak. Her Daddy had a new wife quite different from Mom. This was, I seem to recall, my daughter's second trip to Detroit, where I was living then. She had flown from New Jersey, escorted by a flight attendant down the ramp to my awaiting arms. When we arrived at my apartment, Amelia looked around and sat down on the couch. How was she feeling? I asked. "Fine," she said. She always said "fine" when I asked her that question. But this time, she sighed happily and said, "And I know all the rules." I laughed and didn't inquire further. This is rather a long-winded of saying, as I finish this sentence, and actually depart from my hotel, that I feel like announcing to the librarian of the BIG FROWN, "I know all the rules."

10:05: "You haven't tied it properly." So says you know who. I give her a look (use your imagination). She gives me a look (ditto). Silently she re-ties the collection of files (drafts of Ted Hughes self-exculpatory "Birthday Letters"). And I carry back to my desk the next folder, which must be placed inside a large box (maybe two feet by eighteen inches). It would be more convenient if I could put it all flat next to my iPod touch and keyboard. "BUT NO!!!!!!!!!!!!!" as John Belushi used to say.

3:00: I've run out of my quota of requests for the day. No more file folders for me! No one told me I could make only ten requests. That may seem a lot but sometimes I'm fishing—that is I can't tell from the catalogue description whether the folder I request will have anything pertaining to my concerns. So some folders I dispatch in a minute; others need a half hour or more. And to request a folder is a nightmare entailing a multi-step process with nearly every step requiring me to re-enter my library pass number. And since I can only request four items at a time, I'm at the mercy of the librarians who don't always remember to enter in the system that I've already returned a folder. So I keep getting messages that I have reached the limit of my requests even when I've returned several folders.

Just went to the desk to see if I was really out of requests and learned that I could apply to get one more precious folder. The librarian asks me to write down the catalog number on a slip he hands me. Now, mind you, I have NO documents on my desk, and I write the number on the slip he gives me. When I turn it in, he scrutinizes the slip and then says, "Is that a pen?" At first, I don't take in what he's asking. I think he means I've left

something out in the arcane number codes. BUT NO!!!!!!!!!!!!!!!!!!!!!!!!!!!!!!!!!
He's telling me that only pencils can be used in the Reading Room. Okay,
I know that, but I'm not using the pen to take notes. I just absentmindedly
used what was available. Blimey. I want to tell him to bugger off. But I
hold my tongue.

One more folder and then I'm going to get a drink! At least the last
folder is a find: Sylvia's description of the folk around her Devon home,
Court Green. She took more of an interest in the locals than Ted did. She
describes the birth of her son, a big boy weighing almost ten pounds. Giving birth to him had made her feel like her insides were being torn out,
and yet the midwife announced that Plath had not suffered a scratch.

The free wifi is nice, except that anytime I put my ipod to sleep, I
have to log back in and promise not to do anything obscene. How did they
know I had been tempted to cock a snook at the staff?

Here's a nice little bit I read in one of Sylvia's descriptions of a Devon
home interior: "The typical British wallpaper—a pale beige embossed with
faintly sheened white roses, the effect of cream scum patterns on weak
tea." Thus is your habitat immortalized Rose and Percy Key!

4:45: I can't take it anymore. I'm out of here.

5:30: Spent the evening with an old friend complaining about the
British Library. She is an American working for a banking firm in London.
She supplied me with many more examples of the overcomplicated British
way of doing things. It's built into the language, I observe: "Why say pressured when you can say pressurized?" I tell her, picking a word I've often
heard on British newscasts. And have you ever noticed the way British
historians use the passive voice? Deadly.

And yet Sylvia Plath chose London over New York or Boston or any
other American homeground. And I've come here often for holidays but
also to research the lives of Martha Gellhorn, Rebecca West, Jill Craigie,
and now Sylvia Plath. What is it that attracted them—and me?

Friday, January 13

11:15: I'm in Hampstead, in a Starbucks, enjoying the free wifi. I've
just returned an article I borrowed from Al Alvarez and I'm writing this
diary, and also waiting for Keats House to open. Amy Lowell, one of my
long term biographical projects, wrote a biography of Keats and was
instrumental in making sure his Hampstead house remained a national
treasure, using not only her wealth for its refurbishment but also enlisting
a legion of American contributors to do so as well. Call it a literary foreign
aid program.

1:00: On the way to Keats's house, I walk down Pilgrim's Lane and stop at #66, which used to be Michael Foot's home. Sold up after he died a few years ago, it is being rehabbed, gutted, which does not surprise me since during my three years of visiting Michael (2000–2003) I saw the home deteriorating. Michael did not see the disrepair. He was in his mid–90s and just happy to remain in the home that his wife, Jill Craigie, picked out in 1963 and refurbished. Jill had a wonderful sense of decor and design, but Michael did not have her eye or her interests.

Keats House is just a few streets down. It looks more imposing than it was in Keats's day. A later owner put an addition on the house, but inside the scale of the rooms, the furnishings, are pretty close to what Keats had known. Although the brochure mentions the house was redone in the 1920s, I'm aggrieved to see that Lowell is not mentioned. Without her funds and her magnificent organizing efforts the house might well have been lost to posterity.

Saturday, January 14

At the train station on the way to Cornwall. I notice the sign saying that if you are drunk and disorderly, you can enjoy the walk home. In other words, the rail management reserves the right to refuse rowdy passengers. I recall my friend last night noting how much her British fellow employees drink just as soon as the workday is over.

12:30: A splendid time in Cornwall with Elizabeth Sigmund, one of Sylvia's friends, who has wonderful memories and papers to share. One startling moment: Her recollection of Ted's reaction to Sylvia's death about a month later when Elizabeth visited him: "It's not given to every man to murder a genius." "You didn't murder her," Elizabeth replied. "I might as well have done," he concluded.

5:30: Elizabeth's husband drives me to the Weary Friar Inn, near the small village of Pillaton.

6:30: Down from my cozy top floor room for dinner I enter the pub-like dining room, order a Guinness and scrutinize the menu. The locals give me a friendly, curious look, and I decide to do a Sylvia Plath—that is, take part in the badinage in the vicinity of my table. As the waitress approaches I am primed, waiting to take the pitch. "It says here," I speak up as though I am about to express a community concern about the dinner menu, "you have award-winning local sausages. But I'm partial to the liver and bacon. However it does not appear to have won any awards." Debate at the bar ensues—one patron advancing the motion that the links may be too sweet. But he fails to attract a second, and after a respectful silence

I announce my vote for the porkers. Tactful smiles all round—in deference to the one dissenter. For the nonce, I'm included in the conversation, and though I don't have much to say, everyone is pleased by the way I polish off my sausages, capping off the meal with local blackberry ice cream.

Sunday, January 15

A breakfast of perfectly prepared poached eggs on toast. I memorialize the event in the Inn's guestbook. Then a marvelous morning walk overlooking beautiful felt-green valleys. Returning to the Inn I notice a wall that notes this building dates back to the 12th century. It's the kind of historic site that excited Sylvia. She had a tumulus on her Devon property and loved to think of it as a Roman remnant.

12:30: Actually it has been recently discovered that the mound is a Norman site, Elizabeth tells me during another afternoon of talk. When I compliment her husband William on his fine onion tart that I am devouring, Elizabeth reminds me that Sylvia was a lusty eater. Then she recalls eating a meal with Sylvia balancing her baby boy Nicholas on her lap. "Watch his eyes," she told Elizabeth. "See that greedy look? He's making sure he gets his share."

7:00: On the train back to London, the conductor is asking for tickets. I produce mine with alacrity and am rewarded with the good word "Smashing." Yes indeed, the pilgrimage to Pillaton has been … well, smashing. It's rather wonderful the way the British brighten up mundane transactions. Martha Gellhorn once explained why she loved riding London buses, recalling the time the ticket taker accepted her offering with a cheerful sally, "Thank you, my blossom."

Monday, January 6: An uneventful return to Philadelphia airport. Customs man asks me what I've been doing abroad. "Researching a writer," I reply. And to my surprise he launches into how much he loves the writing of Somerset Maugham.

Go figure.

Reviews

If you judged me only by the reviews of, say, my Hellman, Gellhorn, and Sontag biographies, you might think, "a pretty pedestrian biographer." If you looked, instead, at the reviews of my Marilyn Monroe, Rebecca West, and Jill Craigie biographies—let's just say you might have a higher opinion, although even with those books I took some knocks. The reviewer in the *Financial Times* called my Rebecca West biography "unreadable." Which raises the question: How could the same person have provoked such varying responses? A complex of factors filter into reviews. I can't speak for other authors, but here is what I have learned:

1. Sometimes my subjects get reviewed, not me. A reviewer hates Lillian Hellman and so hates my book too.
2. The reviewer either has nothing to say about my book, or does not know how to say it, and so gives a book report—meaning he or she merely repeats what's in my book, writing, in effect, not a review but a profile of my subject.
3. The review is really about the reviewer. That is, the reviewer asserts authority by distilling the biographer's work, presenting it as the reviewer's own expertise, and then rendering a judgment, positive or negative, on the biography.
4. The reviewer has in mind what a biography of the subject should look like. The biography does not conform to the reviewer's vision. Instead of reviewing the book at hand, the reviewer complains that the biography is disappointing or worse.
5. The reviewer is mainly interested in just one aspect of the subject— let's say the subject's politics. If the biographer's politics do not match the reviewer's, the biographer will not get a good review.
6. The reviewer does not like biography, period, and will make snide remarks about biographers as second-raters or even worse.
7. In very rare cases, a reviewer and a biographer seem to share the same wave-length. This usually happens because an astute assigning editor actually picks someone who can write about both the subject of the biography and the biographer's approach. The result is not necessarily a positive review of the book, but in most cases the outcome is likely to please the biographer.

10

Another Sylvia Plath Biography?

In 2004, Jillian Becker published a memoir of Sylvia Plath, and in 2007, Yehuda Koren and Eilat Negev published a biography of Assia Wevill, Ted Hughes's lover who also committed suicide, taking the life of her daughter as well. I wrote about these books in *The New York Sun,* expressing my conviction that a new biography of Plath was needed, and that I was the one to write it. Normally, the next step would be to convince my agent, but I had parted company with her, and at the moment was without representation.

Then at a party for the *Sun,* I broached the idea to a literary agent. She said, as I feared, that there were too many biographies already. She shook her head. Couldn't sell a Plath biography in such a crowded field no matter how fresh my approach. I took that agent's no to be representative of what her colleagues would tell me. Later, a good friend of mine, a well-seasoned biographer, also seemed quite skeptical. My Plath articles in the *Sun* attracted no notice. No one answered my call.

Even with plenty of projects and commissioned pieces to do, I could not put aside my Plath obsession. I had already interrupted work on a biography of Amy Lowell to plunge into one of Dana Andrews when his daughter came calling for someone to write the biography of her father, and now I was going to put a second biography on hold to write a proposal for yet a third subject? I plead temporary insanity, although I had the presence of mind to realize that to go ahead without an agent would be folly. Even very accomplished writers nowadays do not get editors to answer their email inquiries. Agents have become the gatekeepers.

I recovered from my lunacy, I thought, until I noticed that the first annual meeting of the Biographers International Organization (BIO) in May 2010 would include speed dating appointments with agents. I decided to have a go. I had no proposal to show but brought along my two *New York Sun* articles and the pitch for my Plath biography that I would make in these ten-minute dates. Because I've published more than 30 books— many of them for trade houses—I did not tout myself but just launched into my Plath patter. It was a high-energy performance. The agent had to believe in me as much as I wanted to believe in the agent if I was going to drop everything and do a Plath biography.

Agent #1, a male, said, "My guess is that publishers will want a woman to write such a book." I was stunned, since he knew I had already published several biographies of women. Although he unenthusiastically offered to read my proposal when it was ready, I had already crossed him off the list. Frankly, I wanted an over-the-top reaction: "Oh, yes, you're the one to do it!"

Agent #2, another male, listened rather stonily as I explained my angle, and then he asked, "Have you had a breakout book?" He wanted to know about my numbers. I've had respectable sales for some of my biographies, but certainly no best sellers. He was noncommittal and asked me to think about whether I really wanted to put in the time and energy required to sell the book to a trade house. I felt like I was a book salesman watching a bookstore buyer go to his computer to see how my last biography sold: "Rollyson's last one sold five copies, I'll take three copies this time."

Agent #3, a female, showed real curiosity as I came close to perfecting my argument that previous biographers had not served Plath well and that no one else in the world could possibly write a better Plath biography. But doubts arose when I said I had yet to write the proposal. She certainly wanted to see it, but we were already in the cooling off period.

Agent #4, another female and my last best hope on earth, seemed to glow throughout my pitch, which now seemed pitch-perfect. When could she see the proposal? she asked. I told her I would get on it as soon as I returned home. She expressed no doubt she could sell the book. Some writers might have been wary of her optimism. How could an agent in today's grim market be so confident? But she was exactly what I needed— a voice that said, in effect, "What are you waiting for?"

Six weeks later I delivered the proposal. My new agent loved it and requested minor revisions. But I would also have to write a sample chapter, she insisted. I groaned, realizing now virtually the whole summer had been taken up with what might be a fruitless venture. But at this point I couldn't help myself. I was too heavily invested, and I had a backer.

In mid–September, the proposal went out and received, as expected, several rejections in the first round. Most editors praised my approach but said it was a crowded field. While we were waiting for what I feared would be the remaining rebuffs, my agent—still as bullish as ever—prepared for a second round of submissions. It did not prove necessary after an enthusiastic editor at St. Martin's Press contacted me, requested a few more bullet points, secured the requisite support from her colleagues, and bought the proposal for a decent advance.

It still seems like a fairy tale to me, and I am no wiser about the formula for success. Pick a subject that no one has heard of, and you will be told, "We can't buy the book because no one has heard of her." Or, "We can't buy the book because everyone has heard of him and the market for X biographies is saturated." Or, "We can't buy the book because you don't have a track record." Or, "We can't buy the book because you have too much of a track record." All I can say is that even in a dire market that drives writers to put up with less than ideal representation, finding the right agent may require rejecting the wrong one.

A successful proposal, in my experience, has been rejected many times until the right agent and the right publisher comes along. Sooner or later I have to hope I have a pitch that *someone* will buy. They have to buy something, after all, even if, afterwards, they suffer buyers' remorse. Thanks to my wife, Lisa Paddock, I came up with a nifty title, "American Isis: The Life and Death of Sylvia Plath." Later my editor urged me to change the subtitle to "The Life and Art of Sylvia Plath," saying, "Death is such a downer." I thought his comment absurd, since everyone is curious about why Plath took her life, but I conceded the point to make him happy.

Before letting rip in my proposal, I began with this epigraph, from Apuleius's *The Golden Ass*:

> I am nature, the universal Mother, mistress of all the elements, primordial child of time, sovereign of all things spiritual, queen of the dead, queen of the ocean, queen also of the immortals, the single manifestation of all gods and goddesses that are, my nod governs the shining heights of Heavens, the wholesome sea breezes. Though I am worshipped in many aspects, known by countless names ... some know me as Juno, some as Bellona ... the Egyptians who excel in ancient learning and worship call me by my true name.... Queen Isis.

Then I launched headlong into my pitch, presented here just as I put it in the proposal: Sylvia Plath is the Marilyn Monroe of modern literature. Plath occupies a place no other writer can supplant. Sister poet Anne Sexton recognized as much when she called Plath's suicide a "good career move." That crass comment reveals a stratospheric ambition Plath and

Sexton shared. They wanted to be more than great writers; they wanted nothing less than to become central to the mythology of modern consciousness. Plath has superseded Sexton because—as Marilyn Monroe said, speaking of herself—Plath was dreaming the hardest. At the age of eight Plath was already writing herself into the public eye, later winning prizes and exhibiting herself as the epitome of the modern woman who wanted it all and, in having it all, would make herself and what she wrote both threatening and alluring, deadly and life-affirming.

Biographers have puzzled over what Ted Hughes meant when he said, "It was either her or me." This much is clear: He did not want to play Osiris to her Isis. Although he began their marriage thinking she needed him to complete herself, he gradually realized his role was to act as a consort in her mythology.

Biographers have misconstrued Plath, becoming fixated on her psychological problems, on what Ted Hughes did to her, and on one another—with Janet Malcolm heading up the forensic team of those who suppose that it is somehow unseemly to rake up the life of a "silent woman" who cannot speak for herself when, in truth, Plath wanted to be wholly known. Hughes was astonished to learn that his wife had entrusted his love letters to her mother, but Aurelia Plath was not surprised, having raised nothing less than a primordial child of time, a woman who wrote for the ages, unconcerned about her husband's petty notions of privacy.

Plath needs a new biography, one that recognizes her overwhelming desire to be a cynosure, a guiding force and focal point for modern women and men. The pressures on a woman who sees herself in such megalomaniacal terms are enormous, and understanding such pressures and her responses to them will yield a fresh and startling biography that makes Plath's writing, her marriage, and her suicide essential reading for anyone wishing to fathom the workings of the modern mentality, the way we live now.

Unlike other writers of her generation, Plath realized that the worlds of high art and popular culture were converging. As a young child she was as attracted to best selling novels as she was to high art. Before she graduated from high school she had read *Gone with the Wind* three times. Before entering college, she published a story in *Seventeen* magazine, and she soon became a protégé of Olive Higgins Prouty, author of *Stella Dallas* and *Now, Voyager*. Ted Hughes was baffled by Plath's desire to write popular prose because like most "serious" writers of his generation he drew a line separating vulgar from fine art. His friends did not like Plath—indeed they saw her as an American vulgarian—but she persisted in her multitasking approach to literature. Although much emphasis has been placed on her last brief but brilliant period as a poet, in fact during this time she was also planning and writing two new novels and contemplating a career beyond poetry.

Susan Sontag is often treated as a master of melding highbrow and pop that occurred in the 1960s, but in fact Sontag abhorred mass entertainment and retreated to Parnassus as soon as she saw the consequences of converging mainstream and minority (elitist) audiences. Indeed, in an interview, Sontag explicitly rejected Plath's need for popular approval. Sontag could not conceive of an artist who performed on all levels of culture at once. Plath, much bolder than Sontag and a much greater artist, took on everything her society had on offer. Witness, for example, Plath's journal entry for October 4, 1959:

> Marilyn Monroe appeared to me last night in a dream as a kind of fairy godmother. An occasion of "chatting" with audience much as the occasion with Eliot will turn out, I suppose. I spoke, almost in tears, of how much she and Arthur Miller meant to us, although they could, of course, not know us at all. She gave me an expert manicure. I had not washed my hair, and asked her about hairdressers, saying no matter where I went, they always imposed a horrid cut on me. She invited me to visit during the Christmas holidays, promising a new, flowering life.

No passage in Plath's writings better displays her unique sensibility. And yet her biographers have ignored or misconceived this crucial evidence. In *Rough Magic: A Biography of Sylvia Plath*, Paul Alexander calls the dream "strange." Ronald Hayman in *The Death and Life of Sylvia Plath* calls the audience with Monroe one of Plath's "less disturbing" dreams. These inept characterizations are typical of the kind of misdirected narratives that plague Plath's legacy.

Plath imagines Marilyn Monroe as a healer and source of inspiration at a time when most women and men regarded the actress as little more than a sex symbol, the embodiment of a male fantasy. "What a doll!" the apartment superintendent keeps declaring in *The Seven Year Itch*. And yet, in the same film Monroe functions as a soothing and supportive figure for the clumsy Tom Ewell, telling him he is "just elegant." And she does so in exactly the kind of maternal, fairy godmother way that makes Plath's dream not strange but familiar. Marilyn Monroe "chats" with Sylvia Plath. The sex goddess girl-talks Sylvia. This concatenation of high and low segues into the reference to T. S. Eliot, whom Plath and Hughes were going to meet shortly. Plath was anticipating an Eliot who might be a great poet, but who was also someone she could chat up. The "audience" becomes, in Plath's dream, a very American talk.

Who in 1959 thought of the marriage of Marilyn Monroe and Arthur Miller as a role model? Only Sylvia Plath, who regarded Hughes as her hero, as Monroe looked up to Miller. The Plath–Hughes and Monroe–Miller marriages both occurred in June of 1956. Like Miller, Hughes wanted his work to be critically praised and also broadly accepted. Both men glommed onto wives who would extend their range by expanding their audience. And just as Miller wrote for Monroe's movies, Hughes dreamed of selling his children's fables to Walt Disney. He saw his wife Sylvia as a symbol of America and a conduit to success—even though he understood next to nothing about her native land or her motivations. Their marriage broke down, in part, because Hughes, like Miller, failed to comprehend his wife's ambition. Indeed, both men shrank from their wives' all-consuming aspirations.

That Monroe could give Plath an "expert manicure" seems strange only to a biographer who does not understand that Monroe's gift is to appear as available and anodyne. Plath, always meticulous about personal hygiene, conceived of a domesticated Monroe, now ensconced in a happy union with a great writer—the same fate Plath imagined for herself, avoiding the "horrid cut" her culture imposed even on women of achievement. Marilyn Monroe was all promise for Sylvia Plath.

My biography will be about what happened to that promise and why, ultimately, figures like Ted Hughes could be of no help to Sylvia Plath. He wanted a private world that went against the very grain of the persona Plath was in the process of building. He let her down in ways far more disturbing than his infidelity.

In *Her Husband*, Diane Middlebrook has written persuasively about how Hughes perceived Plath as an incarnation of Robert Graves's white goddess. But Plath saw herself quite differently. She resembles, it seems to me, an American Isis. She wanted to be an ideal mother and wife—but with her power, her magic, intact. Isis, especially in her earliest Egyptian incarnation (before the imposition of the Osiris myth), seems a perfect metaphor for Plath, since the mythology includes the goddess's association with all levels of society, rich and poor. Hughes mistakenly thought Plath wealthy because she went to the best colleges and dressed well, although in fact these privileges were the hard won effort by Plath and her mother, who worked long hours to ensure her daughter's place in society. Hughes—biographers have failed to notice—was a naïf compared to Plath, who worked a hard eight hours per day as a field hand the summer before she entered Smith so that she would have enough money to afford the clothes and books her scholarship did not provide.

Small wonder Plath has become such a revered figure. This was a domestic goddess who loved to cook and clean—not as diversions from writing, as Hughes and Plath biographers have supposed, but because she appreciated the joys of everyday life that were part of being a whole woman. Ted Hughes did not know how to balance a checkbook. Sylvia Plath did. He never washed his clothes. Sylvia Plath did. He did not know how to compete in a quickly changing literary world. Sylvia Plath did. He drew back from her satire of friends and family in *The Bell Jar,* completely misconceiving her art, which deliberately transgressed the lines between art and autobiography.

Plath is a genre breaker and a cross-cultural heroine. She bridges cultures like the Isis who eventually became a beloved object of worship throughout the Greco-Roman world. Plath has become the object of a cult-like following, her grave a pilgrimage site—like the sanctuaries erected in honor of Isis. The defacing of Plath's grave markers, so that "Sylvia Plath Hughes" reads "Sylvia Plath," is more than just retribution against Ted Hughes—it is an assertion that his very name is an affront to the mythology of Sylvia Plath.

The Isis—like Plath encompasses characteristics that would seem at odds. Plath's suicide—particularly her poems that flirt with death—have become part of the eros and thanatos of her biography. And it is precisely this sort of tension between conflicting elements that transforms Plath into a modern icon, one that will continue to enchant and bedevil biographers. "Another biography of Sylvia Plath?" a publisher will ask. The same question was put to me about my biography of Marilyn Monroe, which first appeared in 1986 and is still in print despite twenty or more books about Monroe that have followed. The time to define the Plath myth for a new cohort of readers and writers is now.

11

Biography, My Father, Dana Andrews and Me

In the summer of 2011, I sat day after day, beginning usually by 6:00 a.m. and quitting between 11:00 and noon, writing my biography of Dana Andrews (1909–1992), best known for playing the detective in *Laura* (1944), the picture (he always said picture) that made him a star. I expected to finish a draft by July, so that I could get on with my biography of Sylvia Plath. Not that I was rushing it. Dana Andrews was no less important to me than Sylvia Plath, and in some ways he is more important to me than she is (more on this later). I'm just explaining the way I work. I often describe my writing as exercising a mental muscle, which has grown stronger, I believe, by my diurnal, matter of fact method of getting to work. Rare is the day I fail to produce a thousand words unless it is a teaching day. I rarely get sick. I don't deviate much from this regimen, which fills me with joy and fullness like nothing else does. After noon I eat, play with my Scotties, ride a bike, garden, go to the gym or, if I can summon the energy, read (now usually on my Kindle, iPhone, or iPad). If I can find what I want as an audio or a text-to-speech Kindle book, I am overjoyed to have someone read to me, even in a computer generated voice, while I cook and clean and get on with what Martha Gellhorn called the kitchen of life. At night, I watch movies or television series—usually online. I can't do much else, I guess, because of who I am and because I find biography an all-consuming enterprise. Except for the writing part, I do not do this alone. I also have a low maintenance wife, Lisa Paddock, who edits much of what I write— which is fortunate for you, dear reader—who watches movies with me and has to put up with my palaver about what I've just written. A writer herself (a better one than I), she understands what a self-absorbed biography drone I have become. It can't be easy for her. I'm afraid to ask.

Biographers don't usually get so personal, since readers come to their books wanting to know about the subject, not the biographer. And yet, as Paul Murray Kendall asserts in *The Art of Biography*, every biography is an autobiography. That statement may not hold true for every biographer, of course. I know a Pulitzer Prize–winning biographer who scoffs at the idea, saying it is the subject that interests him, not some personal connection he believes exists. For him, I suspect, the psychology of the biographer is a bore, not to mention a diversion from the main event.

As long as I can remember, I have been obsessed with *Laura*. I can't remember when this obsession started, but I have a vivid memory of showing the film to my former agent one summer in the mid–1990s. It was late at night, and after watching it on a fairly small screen in VHS format, she turned to me perplexed. The plot seemed improbable; the film was dated. I could hardly contain my outrage. She did not respond to it as a stylized piece of romanticism—a film noir as the French so appositely started calling it in the 1950s—but rather as a piece of failed realism. I should have known then what I realized only years later: I should junk that agent! Just recently, when I told an old professor of mine about my Dana Andrews biography, he said condescendingly, "What a wonderful piece of shlock *Laura* is." He did not seem to see the steam coming out of my ears. And let me record one more insult before I rev up my motor about *Laura*: "Isn't Dana Andrews a rather small subject?" This from a member of the NYU biography seminar I attend. I held my tongue and smoldered. As Billy Crystal says, "Don't get me started!"

You get it, I'm sure. To speak slightingly of *Laura* or Dana Andrews is to strike at the heart of what I do, what I am, and where I come from. When I watch *Laura* and Dana Andrews, I am watching myself, my father, and what I do as a biographer. By the time I was thirteen, my father was dead, and I knew what I wanted to do with the rest of my life: be an actor. Something about impersonating other characters appealed to me, and only much later did I realize that this draw was part of the biographical impulse: an inherent fascination with the way other lives are put together while one is putting together one's own. The choices people make, the conditions surrounding those choices, the "script" we make of our lives— this was what fascinated me. I loved to hear my father talk about his years as a cop in 1940s Detroit. Ordinarily a taciturn man, he came to life telling me about the Detroit race riots of 1943, when he got knifed in the hand, and then later when he was called to a robbery in progress and had to shoot a man, who took three days to die in the hospital. He even took me to the scene of the shooting and showed me how it had played out. My father was, in short, a romantic figure. My mother thought he bore a resemblance to Clark Gable. If so, it was very slight, but he was a handsome man and nothing like my friends' mild-mannered fathers. I was afraid of my father, but not because he did anything cruel to me. I can't remember him ever hitting me. But then he did not have to. He was just awesome—a character right out of a film noir. He would sit eating dinner, often not uttering a word, reading (usually) a copy of U.S. *News and World Report.* He never finished high school, but he was brilliant. He was also self-defeating—no follow-through, you might say. When he died of cancer at 51, I felt I was on my own. No one else could possibly take my father's place—although my drama teacher, James Allen Jones, a charismatic black man who had played Othello on the British stage—came very close. My mother could not have been more supportive, but she served mainly as a prop that her self-centered son took for granted while he pursued his pell mell course to stardom. But of course I did not become a star. Summer stock: check. Community theater: check. College and some television performances: check. I think I was a contender, but I lacked the nerve to go for broke—the nerve that Dana Andrews ... but I am getting ahead of my story.

In 2010, I became consulting editor for the Hollywood Legends series published by the University Press of Mississippi. The job entails reading proposals and manuscripts, as well as soliciting proposals for biographies of movie stars and others in Hollywood (producers, directors, and so on) who might fairly be considered legends. (Email me if you have a subject in mind). Not too long after I assumed this position, the director of the press, Leila Salisbury, forwarded an email from Susan Andrews, Dana Andrews's youngest child. Susan has an older sister, Katharine, and a brother, Stephen. Dana also had another son by a first marriage that ended tragically with his young wife's death. Susan was looking for a biographer. Did Leila know of anyone who might be interested? She forwarded the query to me.

In this case, I did not have to consider who would be interested. I was—especially when it became clear that Dana had kept a diary, was a wonderful letter writer, and kept all sorts of documents that biographers crave. Even though I was committed to writing a biography of Amy Lowell, I simply could not resist. Other than my powerful attraction to *Laura*, I did not know much about Dana Andrews, to be honest. I reacted with my gut. Although this biography would be written with the full cooperation of his family, I decided to do it mainly because the project seemed not merely right for me, but (again based on very little evidence) something I *must* do.

I knew, for one thing, that Dana and my father were of the same generation and that, on screen, in *Laura*, at any rate, he behaved like my father, one of the walking wounded. (Dana's character, Mark McPherson, carries around a leg full of lead collected during a shoot-out with criminals.) Then I learned that like my father, Dana was one of thirteen children. He had grown up in Texas, the son of a Baptist preacher who railed against movies and drinking—both of which Dana took up the first chance he got. Essentially, Dana ran away from home and hitchhiked to California. My father, who also became an alcoholic, ran away at fifteen and, lying about his age, enlisted in the navy. Both ended up in California in the 1930s, pumping gas. Many people would have predicted that both men would never amount to much, even though both had considerable charisma. At this point, I'm going to leave my father out of it simply because, although the autobiographical impulse may get me started owing to identification with a biographical subject, the subject soon takes over. To be honest, as a biographer I cannot use biography simply as some sort of therapy, even though I find the process of writing biography an analeptic adventure. I'm also going to refrain from telling you how Dana made the transition from pumping gas to appearing on the silver screen. It took nearly ten years (1931–1939) before he signed his first movie contract, but to read the details you're just going to have to read my book.

Since I never made it to the big screen, watching Dana act on film is a vicarious experience for me. But the experience is also a biographer's dream. As Mark McPherson, Dana listens to various Manhattanites describe Laura's career-girl progress through the world of fashion. She comes to New York, as I did, to make a success of herself. Laura's mentor, Waldo Lydecker (Clifton Webb), denigrates Mark as a lowlife type incapable of appreciating a lady like Laura, but our hero is alternately fascinated and repelled by the high-performance, deceitful world of literary and cafe society. I side with Mark, never having liked this milieu, even if my subjects have often been drawn from it. To my surprise, Dana felt the same way about Hollywood. It was mostly phony to him, even though he made his living there. Just how out of it I am was best expressed in super agent Andrew Wylie's reaction to the announcement that my wife and I were writing a biography of Susan Sontag: "Who are these people?" he asked. "I've never heard of them." We were the detectives deemed unworthy since we were not a part of the inner circle—like Mark, the biographer, an outsider having to figure out who murdered Laura. Not only does he interview those close to her, as any respectable biographer/detective would, he gazes at her portrait again and again, reads her letters, rummages through her lingerie drawer, opens a bottle of her perfume and smells it—just as I smelled one of Amy Lowell's cigars, which I found deposited at the Brown University library. Mark's immersion in Laura's things reminds me of a conversation with a Brooklyn neighbor (when I was living in Brooklyn) who knew the man who cleaned Sontag's apartment. I wanted to speak with that man for all the same reasons I had spoken with Rebecca West's hairdresser. Alas, I never did get to that Sontag cleaner-upper. He felt it would be wrong to tattle. I was the criminal, after all—at least that's how some people seem to think of biographers. Now, if Sontag had committed a crime, that would be a different story.

At any rate, Mark makes himself at home in Laura's apartment, thus provoking my envy. He drinks her whisky and falls asleep, only to be startled by her entrance. (In fact, another woman mistaken for Laura was the murder victim). Laura is not dead! Mark rubs his eyes and shakes his head, but the apparition of Laura, the ravishing beauty Gene Tierney, does not disappear. I've had such experiences, but only in dreams, such as when a charming Susan Sontag appeared to me and engaged in friendly chatter— as she did in reality the one time I met her, in Warsaw, Poland.

Even though by this point Mark has fallen in love with Laura, this ideal woman who remains unspoiled despite her success in Manhattan, he cross-examines her, suspecting that he will find a flaw in this too perfect, lovely fantasy of a woman. He takes her down to the police station and shines a bright light on her face, but her beauty does not fade, her innocence remains intact. The murderer is ... well, I won't spoil it for you if you haven't seen the picture. The point is that Laura has not disappointed Mark, her biographer, as the subject of his imaginings.

The movie is profoundly satisfying because Laura falls in love with her biographer (at least that is what Mark has become for me). He has read private correspondence of hers that she never meant anyone to see, and yet, as offended as she is by his prying, she also realizes that he is the first man ever to truly understand and accept her as she is. And that, of course is what biographers are supposed to do. In the end, we must love our subjects (not in the romantic sense) as individuals who have become completely and intrinsically important to us. There are no small parts, only small actors. The same is true for biography: no small subjects, only small biographers.

12

Amy Lowell, the Silent Woman and the Biographical Deficit

This is not another chapter about Sylvia Plath, or about Janet Malcolm. The woman in question is Ada Russell, a.k.a. Ada Dwyer, Amy Lowell's companionate muse. No one knows exactly what to call this actress who gave up the stage to live with the "singer of Lesbos"—to use the epithet applied to the poet by her first derisive biographer, Clement Wood. He published his short, malicious book in 1926, less than a year after Lowell died at the age of fifty-one. His reference to Lowell's lesbianism went unremarked in subsequent biographies. Neither S. Foster Damon in his authorized adulatory book, published in 1935, nor Horace Gregory in his derogatory portrait, which appeared in 1958, comments on Wood's treatment of Lowell's sexuality, which was, quite literally, off the record. Not until the 1970s, after the success of Nancy Milford's biography of Zelda Fitzgerald made the nature of women's lives a burning issue, did Jean Gould bring up the subject of Lowell's sexuality in *Amy Lowell and the Imagist Movement* (1975).

This biographical deficit—not just with regard to Amy Lowell, but also concerning the capacity of the genre to deal honestly and directly with a whole biographical subject—rankled me, contributing to my decision to write about Lowell. I first became interested in her in 2000 while working on an encyclopedia of twentieth-century literature. While checking other reference books, I note that two articles about Lowell—both written by women—deplored her biographies and called for a new one. Approaching a sabbatical year in 2007, I decided to write about Amy Lowell. Then I did something unusual for me. Instead of writing a book proposal I simply sent an email to Ivan R. Dee, a Chicago publisher who had published three of my other books: *Reading Susan Sontag, A Higher Form of Cannibalism? Adventures in the Art and Politics of Biography*, and *Biography: A User's Guide*. Here is what I wrote on April 2, 2007:

Dear Ivan,

Would you be interested in publishing a biography of Amy Lowell? The last biography appeared nearly forty years ago. The only really important one came out in 1935. Needless to say, so much has changed in cultural terms that issues like her lesbianism and its relationship to her poetry need re-evaluation (indeed none of the biographies deal with the issue forthrightly). Several feminist scholars are doing that, but I'm conceiving, of course, of a biography that will be read by a broader audience than academics. I will have access to new archival material and a cooperative estate that will give me any permissions I need to quote from material still in copyright.

Lowell's papers are freely accessible at the Houghton Library. But I'll also be coming to Chicago to look through Harriet Monroe's papers. The archivists have already told me there is plenty of stuff. And Lowell knew everyone in the literary world, so there will be plenty of interesting scenes with Sandburg, Edgar Lee Masters, H.D., and English writers like Thomas Hardy and D. H. Lawrence, both of whom regarded her highly.

I also have the support of several enthusiastic Lowell scholars who have wanted someone to do the biography. I'm applying for an NEH fellowship (deadline May 1) and then for an ACLS fellowship and a Guggenheim in the fall.

This book will be a labor of love, and I don't want to try to persuade some big trade book publisher to give me a sizeable advance (probably hopeless anyway). I want a generous deadline (say five years) and a modest advance carved up any way you like.

I want to write a biography short enough (say 300 printed pages) and readable enough to attract a generation of new readers to Lowell's best work.

Lowell was colorful, smoking cigars and tending to her seven sheepdogs. She was a dynamic platform speaker and the tales of her run-ins with Ezra Pound and others are legendary. Her first biographer, Clement Wood, conducted a sort of vendetta against her similar to what Rufus Griswold conducted against Poe. I don't plan to try to do justice to everything Lowell wrote, but rather I will present a Lowell for contemporaries. My model is Jeffrey Meyers's short biography of Edgar Allen Poe. Meyers focused on what he considered Poe's very best work and wrote a fast-paced narrative.

I would like to say in my NEH application that you have expressed an interest in the book—that is, if you have any interest. I'm not averse to going much further and signing a contract if that appeals to you.

Lowell's poetry is making its way back into the canon. Honor Moore just did an edition of Lowell's poems for Library of America.

There is also Lowell's biography of John Keats, an important work that has been unjustly neglected, although hailed as a masterpiece when it appeared in 1925.

Lowell was obese (five feet tall and 240 pounds), but no one seems to know exactly why. She was not a huge eater, although she certainly liked her food. Even her best biographer can only refer vaguely to a "glandular disorder." I'm going to try to get a better diagnosis.

If none of this appeals to you, let me know if you can think of another publisher who might want my Lowell biography.

Best,

Carl

Ivan was indeed interested, and in short order I had a contract to write a biography of Amy Lowell. I had never sold a book that quickly, and never expect to do so again. Ivan was his own boss and so he could make that decision. And he knew my work well.

After Gould's biography, several scholars, nearly all women, tried to restore the role of the woman Lowell could not live without, who the poet took with her everywhere, and whose absence even for brief periods (to visit her children and grandchildren) drove Lowell to distraction and sometimes even to despair. In the course of a day, when the two women were together at home in Brookline, Massachusetts, Lowell sometimes panicked when she did not know exactly where to find her beloved Ada, a woman she worshipped, a lover who made the fretful poet—often unhappy with herself—feel complete.

I spent four years reading through Lowell's massive archive in the Houghton Library at Harvard. It was a long haul, since Lowell kept copies of her own letters as well as those written to her, together with other documents, diaries, and assorted papers. I perused files in black boxes that contain everything except what I most wanted to know: what it was like for Amy and Ada, what they said to one another, and how they loved one another. Their correspondence was destroyed—by Ada following Lowell's instructions. Ada was Amy's literary executor, and she would have followed Lowell's directive to the letter. Clearly, neither women wanted posterity to pry into their relationship. But with the intrusiveness that befits a biographer, I have decided that Lowell did herself a disservice—not realizing, perhaps, how much the world would change, how much her life with Ada might mean to later generations, and how greatly her biographers' obtuse handling of her private life would damage her own humanity. Or perhaps Lowell believed she *had* told us in her poetry, a point I will address momentarily.

Wood did not deign to mention Ada. Damon recites her theater resume. This is as close as he comes to describing the couple's intimacy after Ada decided in 1914 to live with Amy: "At last Miss Lowell had found the friend who understood her thoroughly and whom she could trust utterly." Gregory repeats Damon's information, adding that Ada was "as much at home in a library or at a literary cocktail party as on the stage, and as securely at ease. She had an air of sparkling gently as she talked, as she inclined her head to listen to someone speaking to her, or as she raised a glass of water to her lips. Her easy alertness had the art of putting others, particularly the restless and unnerved, at perfect ease." Ada, he adds, "gave her warm appreciation, but could and often did express intelligent, forceful adverse criticism of how poetry should be read." And he concludes that Ada and Amy's was a "friendship that was sustained to the end of Amy Lowell's life."

Friendship, ah, friendship. Is that what it was? For God's sake! In the midst of this male reticence, Jean Gould intruded, describing Ada's "generous mouth and long upper lip ... her graceful, rounded arms, and her hands, long and slender, the deep half-moons of her fingernails" that would become, as Gould notes, the "pivotal subject of more than one poem." Indeed. Gould, perhaps wary of all that male precedent, could not quite come out with it, taking refuge instead with a Lowell friend, the publisher John Farrar, who remembered the poet saying there was nothing quite so exciting as a young girl's naked body. As late as 1980, though, C. David Heymann, in a book on the Lowell family, tried to re-attach the veil, saying the Amy/Ada romance was "not necessarily sexual in nature."

Well, what about this:

> My cup is empty to-night.
> Cold and dry are its sides....
> But the cup of the heart is still.
> And cold, and empty.
> When you come it brims
> Red and trembling with blood.
> Heart's blood for your drinking;
> To fill your mouth with love
> And the bitter-sweet taste of a soul.

These were the lines D. H. Lawrence extolled when he expressed his affinity with Lowell, an affinity Lowell herself acknowledged when she quoted back to him his praise for her "insistence on *things*. My things are always, to my mind, more than themselves." Lowell begins with a cup that is always a cup but is also her heart and then her mouth, just as her lover's coming is both a return and a climax; the literal, the sexual, and the symbolic merge.

Who wants to pass off such passionate lines as a testament to a friendship, especially since Lowell admitted to close friends that Ada was the subject of her love poems—in particular the incomparable "Madonna Among the Evening Flowers," which Gould quotes in full and then scurries past, saluting it with a mere word: "lovely." This poem is perhaps as close as Lowell came to outing herself, and a biographer ignores it at her peril. The first three lines express the poet's raw need and her anxiety:

> All day long I have been working.
> Now I am tired.
> I call: "Where are you?"

Lowell would sometimes spend all night in long writing jags, while Ada slept. Depleted after work, the panicky, anxious poet sought her lover, and even in the midst of her great personal wealth, felt desolate:

> But there is only the oak-tree rustling in the wind.
> The house is very quiet,
> The sun shines on your book,
> On your scissors and thimble just put down,
> But you are not there.
> Suddenly I am lonely:
> Where are you?
> I go about searching.

These lines are almost banal, with their expression of an obvious need. And yet, they signify the preciousness of those objects that Ada has just left behind, traces of herself. She cannot have gone far, and yet Lowell feels the urgency of her absence.

Then at the first sight of Ada in the garden—the garden that Lowell wrote about so lovingly in so many poems—the verse itself moves from the mundane to the magisterial:

> Then I see you,
> Standing under a spire of pale blue larkspur,
> With a basket of roses on your arm.
> You are cool, like silver,
> And you smile.
> I think the Canterbury bells are playing little tunes.

These last are flowers too, but they also stand in for a cathedral of love, with their tall pointed flower stalks like spires of a church.

The worshipful Amy (and surely she saw the humor of this) is taken to task by her beloved:

> You tell me that the peonies need spraying,
> That the columbines have overrun all bounds,
> That the pyres japonica should be cut back and rounded.
> You tell me those things.

Carl Sandburg once said that arguing with Amy Lowell was like arguing with a "big blue wave." She was an enormous woman, practically five feet, five inches, weighing as much as 250 pounds in her prime, and yet she had delicate hands and fine features. And she needed someone to tell her a thing or two. As Ada instructs her, though, Amy is adoring:

But I look at you, heart of silver,
White heart-flame of polished silver,
Burning beneath the blue steeples of the larkspur,
And I long to kneel instantly at your feet,
While all about us peal the loud, sweet *Te Deums* of the Canterbury bells.

That mingling of heart and heat and cool silver, the amalgamation of this love-match that Lowell so loved to celebrate is surely a literature and a life worth knowing, worth exploring. The poem is, of course, wonderful without having to know anything about its maker, but isn't it wonderful, too, to know where the poem comes from?

13

Missed Connections

I used to love watching Steve Allen's television series *Meeting of Minds*, in which historical figures from different periods sat at the same table in discussion and debate. In my daydreams I imagine my own program, which would bring together my biographical subjects who never met, or who just missed meeting each other, or met but did not really connect in the way a biographer would want them to.

Sometime in 1950, Johnny Hyde, a powerful William Morris agent, brought a struggling actress with him to the home of Dana Andrews. This actress had been signed by Twentieth Century–Fox in 1946 and then dropped after six months. She had worked another six months at Columbia and was again dropped. Her other small parts seemed to add up to a desultory career. But Hyde had fallen in love with her and with the idea of making her a star. He was able to put her in small, but strategically important parts in *The Asphalt Jungle* and *All About Eve*. I'm referring, of course, to Marilyn Monroe. Dana recalled greeting his visitor, as he later told an interviewer in an oral history I discovered in a Columbia University archive while I was working on *Hollywood Enigma: Dana Andrews* (2012). She made no impression on him.

This sort of encounter was not unusual. Although a few people in Hollywood did perceive Monroe's potential, most did not, simply believing Hyde had become infatuated with a talentless, if beautiful woman. What grieves me here is that it took Marilyn Monroe nearly nine years to become a star—virtually the same amount of time it took Dana to progress from roles in the Van Nuys community theater and at the Pasadena Playhouse, to second leads in B pictures, to small parts in A-list productions, to stardom in *Laura*. Fox studio head Darryl Zanuck initially deemed Monroe unphotogenic! Similarly, after Dana's first screen test, the cameraman told him he photographed "heavy." At best, Dana could expect to have a middling career as a character actor. In short, Dana Andrews and Marilyn Monroe had quite a bit in common. In all likelihood, the shy Monroe would not have opened up to Dana. And Dana was famously reserved among most of his Hollywood confraternity. As mad as he was about becoming a star, he disliked publicity and pageantry and probably dismissed Marilyn as just one of Johnny's show-girls. While revising my *Marilyn Monroe: A Life of the Actress*, my first biography published in 1986, for publication in the spring of 2014, I watched *Bus Stop* again and noticed that as Bo (Don Murray) enters the saloon where Cherie (Marilyn Monroe) sings, the theme music from *Laura* can be heard in the background. It is a subtle, perfect touch, for the music expresses the yearning to connect—a touchstone for the biographer's quest to make sense of lives and stories out of the search for meaning.

Walter Brennan starred in *Scuddo Hoo! Scudda Hay* (1948) when Marilyn Monroe was just starting out. She was one of several starlets cast in scenes that were edited out of the final cut. Did Brennan and Monroe ever exchange a word? I will probably never know, although I have delved as deeply as possible into his life for *A Real American Character: The Life of Walter Brennan*. He also appeared in *Banjo on My Knee*, on which William Faulkner worked. I have yet to discover whether these two men met, and I'd like to know because I am now researching and writing the novelist's life. Faulkner also wrote the screenplay for *To Have and Have Not*, which includes one of Brennan's greatest performances as Humphrey Bogart's rummy sidekick.

Brennan played a variety of roles opposite Gary Cooper, John Wayne, and Jimmy Stewart—not to mention that he was Fritz Lang's choice to act as a Czech professor in *Hangmen Also Die!* Brennan became a huge television star as Grandpa in *The Real McCoys*—and appeared in over two hundred other parts from the silent era to the television age. He could have commiserated with Marilyn, who was already being typed as the dumb blonde. "The greatest bugaboo in Hollywood is being 'typed,'" he said. "And that's exactly what I want to avoid. It's just as easy to be typed in the role of old man as, say, a villain." I watched him in a *Perry Como Show* episode in which he told a joke about Martians who landed in Hollywood. The first thing they said was, "Take us to Marilyn Monroe, then take us to your leader." Somehow the idea of this talent being consigned to the cutting room floor, only to rise again in the imagination of Martians, fulfills my sense of her interplanetary importance—even as I lament that she did not have a mentors like Walter Brennan, who scorned Hollywood ways and would have taken her on her own terms. Dana Andrews was more fortunate, having the benefit of Brennan's advice during the making of two films, *Swamp Water* and *The North Star*.

What all this tells me is that biographers long to make connections that their own subjects fail to forge—or do so only intermittently—but that novelists—God bless them!—can create. What biographer isn't envious of E. L. Doctorow, for example? During an interview about his brilliant novel, *Ragtime*, he was asked whether Emma Goldman and Evelyn Nesbit ever met as they do in his book. Doctorow replied, "They have now."

In Norman Mailer's biography of Marilyn Monroe, you can see him straining to make a connection with her—a connection, by the way, that she did not want, according to Arthur Miller. She told Miller that she had met enough writers. That wasn't true. She kept meeting writers like Carson McCullers and Edith Sitwell, and I have to wonder if Miller was not thwarting a connection that otherwise would have been made. Certainly he did nothing to encourage a meeting between Monroe and Mailer. Miller got jealous when Marilyn danced with poet Norman Rosten. He told me so. No way was Miller going to let Mailer cross his threshold, even though Mailer bugged Miller to invite him over to meet Monroe. Miller never did, and Mailer had to eat his heart out while his friend, Norman Rosten, became close to Marilyn—not so much because he was a friend of Miller as of Sam Shaw, the photographer who was responsible for the iconic photograph of Marilyn with her skirt in the wind, earthbound but on the verge of taking flight. Commercialized as a commodity, she appears in *The Seven Itch* film stills like Amy Lowell's captured goddess, who lays her "rainbow feathers / Aslant on the currents of the air" and is "bargained" for "in silver and gold."

Mailer's biography of Marilyn Monroe was one important reason I decided to write *The Lives of Norman Mailer: A Biography* (1991). I admired the way he opened himself up and explained his desire for Monroe—a physical desire that became, after her death, a desire to understand her life. Mailer had an authorized biographer, and though Mailer considered meeting me, decided against doing so out of loyalty, I believe, to his chosen one. Years later, however, I was gratified to learn that Mailer had said my article about his biography of Marilyn, first published in 1978 in the journal *Biography*, was the best thing written about the book. I don't know why Mailer liked my article, but I imagine he did because I understood that like Monroe, Mailer had multiple identities. She had been a self-described orphanage "mouse," unable to assert herself, and he had been a nice Jewish boy from Brooklyn and a physical coward. Like her, he transformed himself in a powerful embodiment of Napoleonic ambition. Monroe and Mailer wanted the same thing: to project themselves on the world and to transform the consciousness of their times. I dreamed about Mailer frequently while writing his biography, and the dream was always the same. We were alone in conversation, and I was beginning to feel he was about to take me into his confidence, and then I woke up—foiled once again. He experienced the same yearning with regard to Marilyn Monroe. Such is the biographer's plight in a world of missed connections.

There is always something abortive in a biographer's effort to understand the life of another, which is the subject of a piece I wrote for a collection of essays, *AfterWord: Conjuring the Literary Dead* (2011), edited by Dale Salwak. My contribution, "As I Lay Dreaming," was about my dream-like encounter with William Faulkner. Years earlier I had published a piece about Faulkner, his wife Estelle, and his mistress, Meta Carpenter, who I interviewed for the article. Faulkner eluded me, as I tried to fathom why he arranged a dinner in which he had his wife and mistress meet. In the dream, I pressed him about why he would risk such an encounter, and, of course, he was his usual laconic self, although he seemed to yearn for an explanation almost as much as I did! The point about "As I Lay Dreaming" is, in part, to suggest that the conventional rap against biographers— that they cannot possibly fathom another person's life—is true of the biographical subject, too. Even so, I'm not through with William Faulkner. I operate under the illusion that for all the biographies of Faulkner already published, a part of him remains unexplained and elusive. I want to explore the reasons for an elusiveness reminiscent of *Absalom, Absalom!*, his own fable about the quest to understand another's life. In a way, Faulkner's reticence is a rebuke to biography, one that his biographers have not understood. Stephen Oates, for example, even claims in his Faulkner biography that he felt his subject talking to him—decidedly not something Faulkner would do, on either side of the grave.

I had my first dream about Sylvia Plath the day after I started writing this essay. It was the first dream about her since I completed *American Isis: The Life and Art of Sylvia Plath.* The dream was very odd. I was traveling somewhere with a colleague of mine, Susan Locke, of the Baruch College psychology department. We have taught courses together, twice concerning biography. Anyway, in my dream she was introducing me to some friends of hers who knew Sylvia. They showed me some journals. I'm not sure who the journals belonged to, and in one journal there was an account of a group of women who were reading Sylvia Plath. This group included another of my subjects, Jill Craigie. And in one of the journals Susan Sontag's phone number was recorded. That's all I remember. Not much of a connection is made with my subjects in any of my dreams, a deficiency I take to be an allegory about the biographer's inability to plumb a subject's life as deeply as he would wish. This is the kind of oblique dream I usually have about my subjects. I never quite make contact, although I did know Jill Craigie and met Susan Sontag. Biography is a solitary enterprise, no matter how many people you interview, and rare is the moment when the biographer is not alone with his subject. So I dream on about encounters between my subjects, hosting their debates, their sharing of confidences that would make my job more rewarding by making my subjects confront aspects of themselves that they do not want discussed, especially by those Johnny Come Latelys otherwise known as biographers.

Craigie and Sontag both spent time in the Balkans, Jill in Dubrovnik just before Serbia went to war against Croatia, and Susan in Sarajevo during the merciless pounding the city endured during the breakup of Yugoslavia. In London, while working on my Rebecca West biography, I met Craigie for the first time in the company of her husband. Both Jill and Michael had known West, whose colossal book about the Balkans, *Black Lamb and Grey Falcon*, they much admired. When I told them about the plans my wife, Lisa Paddock, and I had to write *Susan Sontag: The Making of an Icon,* I mentioned that Sontag was in Sarajevo directing a production of *Waiting for Godot.* Craigie was aghast. The last thing people needed during a siege was Beckett's bleak drama, she was sure. I tried to explain that there might be a kind of exhilaration in confronting the worst that could be said about life and the human predicament, but Jill, a staunch old Labourite who believed in the perfectibility of society and in the hope that socialist policies brought the populace, dismissed Sontag as some kind of grandstander. Craigie, I hasten to add, was no philistine. She herself had made a documentary during the Second World War, *Out of Chaos,* which was about the painters and sculptors who continued to work during the Blitz, producing exhibitions and encouraging the art of working class artists. Her presentation of Henry Moore is still the best single bit of film about him. Craigie got movie mogul J. Arthur Rank to fund the film and show it in cinemas, an extraordinary achievement for a women in the 1940s in a male-dominated industry. How I would have relished seeing Craigie confront Sontag, who rarely was challenged, about her pretensions. Sontag was smarter and more daring than most of her interlocutors, but she would have had a hard time with feisty Jill, whose house was demolished by a German bomb on the first day of the Blitz and who spent the war ushering people into London tube shelters.

Craigie had known Rebecca West, who in turn had known Martha Gellhorn, a friend of West's in the early 1980s, by which time Martha had come to revere Rebecca, forgetting or not wanting to acknowledge that for decades she had deplored West's virulent anti-communism. West had outlived most of her critics, and she was having the last word in her weekly book reviews in the London Sunday *Telegraph*. She had also attracted the young women of Virago Press (who would also publish Gellhorn) and some members of the older generation like Jill Craigie, who were lobbying the literary world to give Dame Rebecca her due. Gellhorn reveled in the notion of a latter day doyen and cultivated her own gaggle of young "chaps"—reporters and novelists who could perpetuate the legend of the intrepid Gellhorn, who had covered major wars from Spain in the thirties to Vietnam in the sixties. How I would have like to host a party during which I could have caused a ruckus, asking Gellhorn (in front of Rebecca) how she could justify having turned a blind eye to the machinations of the communists in Spain, reporting the Spanish Civil War as though it were simply a matter of a noble nation suffering at the hands of abominable fascists.

Sontag and Gellhorn were opposed to the very idea of biography, which they deemed second-rate and irrelevant to understanding a writer's work—unlike my touchstone, Rebecca West, who wrote and reviewed biographies. West left in her will instructions for two biographers: one to write a short, brisk life, and the other to pen a comprehensive treatment. Yet she was just as touchy as Sontag and Gellhorn about certain subjects. No one during West's lifetime could bring up her ten-year liaison with H. G. Wells with impunity, and when her son Anthony did so in a novel, *Heritage*, he was disinherited—and disconnected (at least in her mind) from her biography.

All this is by way of remarking that sooner or later, the biographer has to deal with the unspeakable. Hence my longing for someone else— preferably my subject—to say it so that I am free to say it again and, I hope, with a narrative and analysis that amounts to "good value," as the Scots say. No wonder historical and biographical novels are appealing. Biographers need a license before they can operate their vehicles; novelists just get into their conveyances and drive, making whatever connections comport with their imaginations.

In the summer of 1952, Sylvia Plath went to see a production of *The Glass Menagerie*, starring Dana Andrews as Tom, Mary Todd (Dana's wife) as Laura, June Walker as Amanda, and Walter Matthau as the Gentleman Caller. And that's all I know! This is just one of those missed connections that bedevil a biographer. Did Plath like the play, the performances? Did she single out Dana? These gnawing questions will never be answered unless a letter or journal fragment turns up to tell us more. Two of my

biographical subjects were in close proximity to one another with no discernible consequences, an event that almost drives me to write fiction,
since I want them to meet and perform for me. I want to know what Plath
made of the play, which concerns, among other things, the irrefutable
nature of family ties, a subject that both Dana Andrews and Sylvia Plath
brooded over.

In the autumn of 1923, Rebecca West and Amy Lowell met for the
first and only time during West's first visit to the United States. West
attended an event sponsored by the Lucy Stone League. There she got a
dressing down from Ruth Hale, the wife of writer Heywood Broun. Hale
was a vehement feminist, outraged that West should have formed an
attachment to the philandering H. G. Wells. But what interests me more
is that Amy Lowell, no feminist, but a diva poet with a sensibility not so
different from West's was present. The two evidently had a conversation
about a well-known book collector (West mentions as much in a letter to
a third party), but I have no idea what West thought of Lowell or vice
versa. Even though my book, *Amy Lowell Anew: A Biography* has been
published, I'm still hoping for a letter or some other document to turn up
that will reveal what these two women said at their only encounter, and
even how they approached one another. In the meantime, I'm stuck with
two more of my biographical subjects circling in the same orbit, but I cannot gauge the degree of consanguinity—or, perhaps, collision. What especially interests me is that just as Eleonora Duse inspired Lowell, Sarah
Bernhardt commanded West's affection. Duse, famed for her understated
performances, appealed to an imagist poet like Lowell, who wanted to
strip poetry of excessive ornamentation, just as the more flamboyant Bernhardt attracted a critic and novelist like West, who created some of the
most brilliantly discursive prose of the twentieth century.

Invited to give a dinner party for West and Lowell, I promise I would
not try to turn the tables on them and go rogue, as I am tempted to do
with Gellhorn and Sontag. Quite the contrary, what I envision is truly a
meeting of minds. Here's how I would goad them into dialogue: "Both of
you are anti–Bolshevik, and yet both of you are firm supporters of the
French Revolution." This seems an especially odd position for Amy Lowell,
who called herself the "last of the barons." As a child, she wrote an essay
opposed to public strikes. She was a staunch Republican of the William
Howard Taft variety. She said she did not believe in progressive causes
such as votes for women, which West positively identified with. Amy was,
after all, a Lowell, a descendant of cotton merchants and industrialists,
and a shrewd businesswoman herself, as she was proud of proclaiming.

And yet, I can see West, who was also good with money, nodding approval, as Lowell tells me that Europe needed shaking up, that freedom and equality would not have emerged without a violent upheaval, and that England, in the late eighteenth century, was a retrograde power just like Germany during World War I. Lowell had read William Godwin's *Caleb Williams,* one of West's favorite novels, which exposes the reactionary English government's assault on civil liberties during the French Revolutionary period. But dinner is just getting started. After inviting their riff on revolution, I would ask, "Why do you both dislike T. S. Eliot and Ezra Pound so much?" Rebecca once had a disagreeable dinner with T. S. Eliot in Barbados, and of course Ezra Pound had dispatched Amy Lowell in their quarrel about Imagism, calling her work "Amygism." But there is far more to it than personal animus. The very question is explosive, and I'm not sure Rebecca would wait for me to quote these lines about Eliot and Pound from Lowell's *A Critical Fable*:

> Each man feels himself so little complete
> That he dreads the least commerce with the man in the street.
> Each imagines the world to be leagued in a dim pact
> To destroy his immaculate taste by its impact.

Contrary to Pound's assertion, Lowell did not want to dumb down poetry for the masses. She did not think poetry would ever appeal to the public at large. She did not even want to educate the common reader in the sense of getting him to appreciate poetry, for she knew plenty of intelligent people who had no interest in poetry and no aptitude for valuing it. If you don't like poetry, she said, leave it alone. But she did believe in readers whose understanding of poetry could be enlarged and enhanced. This was her audience, and this audience was, in her view, far larger than the one admitted of in the Eliot/Pound axis, a malign brotherhood that had virtually made a religion of poetry, requiring adepts and critics patrolling the precincts of the literary world to rid it of anyone like Lowell who attempted to reach that larger, if still not large, audience of readers who ought to be encouraged— and, yes, even entertained as her beloved eighteenth-century novelists amused their readership. Which is where Rebecca, like Lowell, a brilliant platform performer, breaks into the conversation. Eliot's influence, she would add, is as dire in the field of criticism. The very thing he is praised for—a command of history and tradition—she attacks. Just imagine what she would say about Eliot's impersonality theory, the detachment of literature from the lives of those who create it. Biography was in her bones. She could not analyze a traitor like William Joyce without describing the way he walked. She had to attach ideas and thoughts to flesh. Literature had bodies, not just images and metaphors. One could tell a lot about a man's style by the way he employed his walking stick, Lowell might add, reciting lines from "Astigmatism," her poem about Pound:

> With much friendship and admiration and some differences of opinion
> The Poet took his walking-stick
> Of fine and polished ebony.
> Set in the close-grained wood
> Were quaint devices;
> Patterns in ambers,
> And in the clouded green of jades.
> The top was of smooth, yellow ivory,
> And a tassel of tarnished gold
> Hung by a faded cord from a hole
> Pierced in the hard wood,
> Circled with silver.
> For years the Poet had wrought upon this cane.
> His wealth had gone to enrich it,
> His experiences to pattern it,
> His labour to fashion and burnish it.
> To him it was perfect,
> A work of art and a weapon,
> A delight and a defence.
> The Poet took his walking-stick
> And walked abroad.
>
> Peace be with you, Brother.
> The Poet came to a meadow.
> Sifted through the grass were daisies,
> Open-mouthed, wondering, they gazed at the sun.
> The Poet struck them with his cane.
> The little heads flew off, and they lay
> Dying, open-mouthed and wondering,
> On the hard ground.
> "They are useless. They are not roses," said the Poet.

At this point, with Lowell and West in full cry, I would be ready to introduce a tetchy point. It would take all evening for me to work up to this question: "Why is it that both of you are still undervalued?" Neither of these writers has a place in the canon such as that Virginia Woolf enjoys, for example. Both Lowell and West were powerful figures in their time. Lowell received unprecedented coverage in newspapers, not just the big ones, but regional and local rags that quoted and commented on her all the time. West published best-selling novels in the 1950s and 1960s, not to mention her prominent role in Anglo-American literature and journalism from before World War I to the 1980s. Lowell's collection of poetry, *What's O'Clock*, won the Pulitzer Prize in 1926, the year after she died, and for some time her work appeared in influential anthologies. But for both writers those days are long gone. Why?

No single explanation suffices, but while I have them in the room, I am going to propose to them a necessary, if not sufficient, reason for the diminution of their influence and place in Anglo-American culture. Both were Modernists of a very special kind. Even though both were well schooled in French, traveled widely, and wrote about many different societies and historical periods, in the end they were what I call patriotic modernists. They did not want to live in Paris or become any sort of expatriate. They had none of the Modernist's sneering contempt for American culture and institutions that runs right through Eliot and Pound and settles very comfortably in Susan Sontag. And they were on terms with power, with the modern security state, that so many intellectuals despise even as they do not understand its purpose or necessity. West saw no contradiction between dining with Paul Robeson and then with Allen Dulles, any more than Lowell troubled herself about dining with Robert Grosvenor Valentine, Taft's commissioner of Indian Affairs, and then with a scruffy poet and man of letters like Maxwell Bodenheim.

There is a reason Melissa Bradshaw and Adrienne Munich title their collection of criticism *Amy Lowell: American Modern* and conclude, "Lowell encouraged literary patriotism and the development of a uniquely American brand of modern letters." And they quote approvingly from one of her lectures: "The New Poetry is blazing a trail toward Nationality far more subtle and intense than any settlement houses and waving the American flag in schools can ever achieve." In a more political vein, Rebecca West did the same. I can imagine, at this point, West pounding the table and saying once again that the British Left injured itself irreparably when it spent too much time extolling the Russian Revolution and failing to turn Fabianism into a genuine national movement. Never divorcing her politics from personalities, West would have excoriated Sidney and Beatrice Webb for Bolshevizing the British Left and pandering to the Soviets.

In my constellation of missed connections, I regret that Sylvia Plath and Susan Sontag occupied orbits that never brought them into conjunction with Amy Lowell and Rebecca West. Plath did read Lowell, and I do not see how the bold voice of "Daddy" would be heard without Lowell's trailblazing dramatic monologue, "Patterns," with its grief-stricken but brazen ending: "Christ, what are patterns for?" Those words seem to have their natural and inevitable outcome in "Daddy, I'm through." In fact, Plath wrote a college paper about "Patterns." And yet the references to Lowell in Plath's journals are few, and Lowell did not mean what I wish she had meant to a Plath fixated on Yeats and even (sorry, Amy, sorry, Rebecca) T. S. Eliot. Plath actually watched West testify at the D. H. Lawrence obscenity trial, but Plath's reference to West is clearly that of someone who did not know West's work or realize that in *Black Lamb and Grey Falcon*, West had written precisely the kind of female epic that Plath aspired to finesse in her own unfinished novel. The widely read Sontag made no reference at all to West, so far as I have been able to determine. And what a pity, because West could have saved Sontag no end of silly political posturing during the period when she reluctantly came to the conclusion that the fulminations of her leftist comrades were so much bunk.

If I dwell on this failure to connect, it is because the result of these missed opportunities results in the terrible isolation of Lowell and West in their exile from the main currents of modernism, which they can still, if we pay attention, do much to modify and ameliorate.

So many of my biographical subjects occupy a sort of ghetto—as I do, by continuing to write biographies that have virtually no impact on the way literature is taught or read. Owing to New Criticism to Structuralism to Deconstruction to Culture Studies to whatever is the latest trend in academe, I can remain assured that biography will occupy only an outpost—even if it is called something else, like the Levy Center for Biography at the City University of New York. Like my biographical subjects, I have looked to a world elsewhere, to, simply, readers of biography. I can't say this state of affairs makes me unhappy, even if I can relate to West's belief that the literary-academic complex had neglected her. She didn't have much use for such attention, anyway, and she did not want to waste her time courting the canonizers. How she would have felt about being bound up in the two and now three biographies we have of her is hard to say. Speaking for myself, I can only hope I would survive her review. She was always good for starting an argument and blowing up literary classifications and canons. And she continues to bug the hell out of certain people, which is perhaps why she herself will never quite make it to literary sainthood. She performed enough miracles, I think, but she would not leave it at that, would she? For Rebecca West, there is always that last nagging question: "Is that all?" Which is to say, there are more connections to be made even as we are missing others.

Postscript

The night after completing a draft of this essay I had a dream about walking down a Manhattan Street with Yoko Ono. We were headed toward the Dakota, where both Ono and Lauren Bacall lived, and all I could think about, in the dream, was how I could ask Ono if she would introduce me to Bacall, so that I could interview the actress about working with Walter Brennan in *To Have and Have Not.* Although I wrote to Bacall several times she did not answer my letters. She was ailing and died some months before my Walter Brennan biography was published.

Grace Note 1

Of course the biographer's work is not all frustration and wistfulness. While working on Sylvia Plath, I became friends with Peter Steinberg, one of the world's authorities on Plath and an archivist at the Massachusetts Historical Society. He kindly read over my Plath biography before publication and saved me from making some embarrassing errors. In the course of our conversation I told him about my work on Amy Lowell and how I wanted to present her as a romantic woman unlike the pathetic figure depicted by earlier biographers unable to consummate her sexual desires. I thought her poetry showed just the opposite: a woman who had enjoyed the physical act of love and a deep and abiding passion for her companion Ada Russell. Imagine my gratification when Peter emailed me to say that an archivist had discovered in the papers of one of Lowell's friends the poet's romantic relationship with a woman that occurred before she met Ada Russell. These letters at the Massachusetts Historical Society are unique. Nothing like them exists in Lowell's huge archive in Harvard's Houghton Library. With these letters in hand, I was able to rewrite the narrative of Lowell's life, putting an end to several generations of biographies that suggested her passions were all vicarious.

Grace Note 2

During a talk about Amy Lowell at the Philadelphia Atheneum I mentioned that my next project was a biography of Walter Brennan. I joked that this book would complete my New England trilogy begun with Sylvia Plath and continued with Amy Lowell. Brennan, in fact, was schooled just a short walking distance from the Harvard campus where Lowell often visited her brother, then the university's president. An Atheneum audience member approached me after my talk and mentioned that he had a friend in Joseph, Oregon, where Walter Brennan had owned a 12,000-acre ranch. For some time, I had been trying to contact the Brennans who still lived in Joseph, but I had received no reply. Through this audience member, I was put in touch with his friend in Joseph who knew the Brennans quite well. This chain of events led to my visiting Joseph and not only interviewing Walter Brennan's family but also collecting the testimony of several other community members he had befriended and who had done business with him. As a result, I was able to write a much more intimate biography of the actor than I had supposed possible. Even better, like Rebecca West's family, the Brennans allowed me the freedom to explore every issue, every detail, of my subject's life without hindering me in any way. If biography often results in broken connections, and unbridgeable gaps, it can also fill in voids that no other kind of research and writing can achieve.

14

Work in Progress: William Faulkner

After completing my biography of Jill Craigie in 2003, I thought my work as a writer of biographies might be done, but new opportunities arose when I became editor of the Hollywood Legends series for University Press of Mississippi, and my weekly work for *The New York Sun* and bibliobuffet.com came to an end. By 2007, with my work on *A Private Life of Michael Foot* completed and with no prospective publisher, I turned to revising three of my earlier biographies of Lillian Hellman, Norman Mailer, and Rebecca West, as well as writing about biography in several books, including *Reading Biography, Essays in Biography, Female Icons: Marilyn Monroe to Susan Sontag, A Higher Form of Cannibalism? Adventures in the Art and Politics of Biography*, and *Biography: A User's Guide*. In retrospect, I see that these books represented a gathering force, a newfound energy that propelled me into my work on Amy Lowell, Dana Andrews, and Sylvia Plath.

Approaching the time for another sabbatical, I thought in terms of producing one more grand biography, which represented coming full circle to William Faulkner, the subject of my Ph.D. dissertation, then revised as my first book. I felt I could make a compelling case for a new biography, and I thought my reputation would surely enhance the appeal of my proposed biography. My agent was enthusiastic and certain that a trade house would want to buy this substantial 150,000-word narrative, based on new sources and a new interpretation. Here was my pitch, prefaced by a passage from one of Faulkner's letters to Robert Haas, dated April 30, 1940:

> Every so often, in spite of judgment and all else, I take these fits of sort of raging and impotent exasperation at this really quite alarming paradox, which my life reveals: Beginning at the age of thirty I, an artist, a sincere one and of the first class, who should be free even of his own economic responsibilities and with no moral conscience at all, began to

227

become the sole, principal and partial support—food, shelter, heat, clothes, medicine, kotex, school fees, toilet paper and picture show—of my mother ... brother and his wife and two sons, another brother's widow and child, a wife of my own and two step children, my own child; I inherited my father's debts and his dependents white and black without inheriting yet from anyone one inch of land or one stick of furniture or one cent of money.... I am 42 years old and I have already paid for four funerals and will certainly pay for one more and in all likelihood two more beside that, provided none of the people in mine or my wife's family my superior in age outlive me, before I ever come to my own.

No American writer has possessed a stronger sense of home and family. No American writer has ever felt so alone, an outsider at home and abroad. No American writer with so little formal education absorbed more simply living on college campuses, making them the setting for *Absalom, Absalom!*, an American masterpiece. Steeped not only in Southern history, but also in a sense of history as the defining way to explore human character and culture, Faulkner revealed the tenor of his epoch to project a vision of the future that continues to inform the way America and the world contend with matters of race, environment, and sexuality. This protean figure approached life as a story to be told and retold, with each iteration revealing yet another aspect of reality. No biography of William Faulkner has been able to portray the astonishing paradoxes in the man and his work, or to make them—like his fiction—into a tale that has to be retold so as to subsume discordant voices and perspectives in order to illuminate the man and his work.

My own writing about Faulkner began in the 1970s, a response to his profound exploration of Southern history as a fulcrum for understanding the modern world. More recently I have been taken with Faulkner's pivotal position in American culture, as he bridged the worlds of Hollywood and New York via his home in Oxford, Mississippi. Like one of my other subjects, Sylvia Plath, Faulkner deserves to be re-read as not just a literary figure, but as a force still relevant to the contemporary world and to ongoing issues of race, sexuality, and equality. I want to investigate how it is that this artist, drenched in the culture of the Deep South, committed to his family but also to his art, composed a body of work that included screenplays, pot boilers for the *Saturday Evening Post*, and works of enduring, ubiquitous literary significance. His was a life that deserves to be explored in a dramatic narrative that breaks the bounds of the traditional literary biography. I propose to write this narrative, a biography inspired by Faulkner's own methods.

And yet, no biographer should write in Faulkner's style or adopt the structure of his novels, which would mean forsaking a chronological, cause-and-effective narrative. The most recent biography, *Becoming Faulkner* (2009), by Philip Weinstein, reveals the perils of forsaking the biographer's primary strength: a developmental exploration of the life and work. Weinstein divides Faulkner by topics and shifts back and forth in time, and while the biographer does make astute comments on his subject's life and work, he also fragments and dislodges Faulkner from his time and place. Thus Weinstein's back-and-forth treatment of Faulkner and race is disjunctive, detaching the writer who sensitively dramatized the dilemmas of race-consciousness from the man who claimed he would side with the South against any Northern effort to enforce integration and equality. Only a chronological, historically-based narrative of Faulkner's evolving and seemingly contradictory statements and treatments of race can hope to align the man and his art.

In fact, historian Joel Williamson attempted just such an approach in *William Faulkner and Southern History* (1993), investigating the roots of the Faulkner family's involvement in slavery and miscegenation, an approach that resulted in a true breakthrough in Faulkner biography. Even so, Williamson's inattention to the form of Faulkner's work—and to the way the contending forces in his life impinged on his stories and novels— results in a work that is more history than biography. For example, Williamson has very perceptive comments to make on Faulkner's mistress, Meta Carpenter, and yet those comments remain isolated from the work Faulkner was writing during the most intense phase of his affair with Carpenter. What is missing in Williamson is an account of how Faulkner brought to bear upon *Absalom, Absalom!,* for example, his daily life writing for a Hollywood studio, his involvement with Carpenter, his memories of his World War I experiences in Canada, his own experiences on college campuses, his longing to return home to Mississippi, and his worry that surrendering his talent to commercial and familial considerations might well mean the destruction of the design he had for his Yoknapatawpha fiction.

The paradox of a renegade artist who is also a family man—which so alarmed Faulkner that he could not stop writing about it in letters to his friends and publishers—is at the heart of his psyche and his oeuvre. And yet, too often in previous biographies Faulkner has seemed, by turns, only one or the other: aloof writer or exasperated paterfamilias. The paradoxical Faulkner early on set a course that made it impossible for him to live very long anywhere that was not his native home. Mississippi was his material. But he could not create a cosmos of his own without having a sense of counterpull, of being in two places at once, like the characters in the counterpointed chapters of his novel *The Wild Palms*, in which one male character (the convict) desperately seeks to avoid the attachments of love, while the other (Harry Wilbourne) just as desperately seeks to affirm his love even when it is lost.

Judith L. Sensibar's *Faulkner and Love: The Women Who Shaped His Art, a Biography* (2010) advances the work of understanding this great novelist in terms of the familial rootedness of his life and art, for the first time presenting Faulkner's mother, Maud Butler, his black mother surrogate, Callie Barr, and his wife, Estelle, as three-dimensional figures, But like Weinstein, Sensibar is excessively academic in her quest to analyze rather than narrate Faulkner's own story. What is more, Sensibar ignores the crucial turning point in Faulkner's career, when he met Meta Carpenter in Hollywood and began a fifteen-year on-and-off affair that would define much of the way he was to conduct his art and his role as family man and artist.

Jay Parini's Faulkner biography, *One Matchless Time* (2005), draws on the best Faulkner criticism, but as I point out in "The Historians of Yoknapatawpha," a review essay published in *The New York Sun* (November 10, 2004), Parini engages in excessive speculation and overstatement. He declined to make use of certain important Faulkner archives, especially those of biographers Joseph Blotner and Fred Karl, even though these writers discovered much new primary source material that is not fully exploited in their biographies. No reputable scholar credits much of *William Faulkner: Man and Artist* (1988), by Stephen B. Oates, because so much of the book reads like nineteenth-century romantic fiction— although Oates does manage to capture some of Faulkner's world and writerly sensibility. And a new biography of Faulkner needs to be more selective than Fred Karl's thousand-page *William Faulkner: American Writer* (1989), and draw on the newer material in archives that were not available to Richard Gray for his dependable *The Life of William Faulkner: A Critical Biography* (1996).

The recent books by Weinstein and Sensibar recognize that what is not needed is a detailed, point-by-point, novel by novel—almost moment by moment—narrative of the kind Joseph Blotner masterfully assembled first in his two-volume biography, and then revisited ten years later in a one-volume condensation. Blotner's books are the bedrock of Faulkner biography, but his documentary approach of necessity means a loss of interpretive power. Even when he incorporated new material in the second edition of the biography, Blotner could not weave the many threads of

Faulkner's life and work into an analytical framework. To focus on a theme, to concentrate on the seeming inconsistencies and anomalies of Faulkner's behavior, is beyond Blotner's approach. What a new biography of Faulkner must accomplish is a revelation of the man and his work by exploring *Collected Stories, Sartoris, The Sound and the Fury, Absalom, Absalom!, The Wild Palms, Go Down Moses, Intruder in the Dust*, the Snopes trilogy, and his final much misunderstood work, *The Reivers*. This new biography will attend to these works as they interact with Faulkner's saturation in the literature of the Civil War and World War I, his marriage and long-standing affair with Meta Carpenter, and his surprising emergence as a public man even as he deplored the loss of his privacy and that of his fellow Americans.

Faulkner biographies have foundered on efforts to come to terms with the man and his work during the years that followed World War II, when his writing took a turn that was more hortatory than before and seemed a departure from his earlier grim, if darkly humorous, modernism. A case in point is Fred Karl's treatment of *The Reivers* as nostalgic. In the mellow tones of a grandfather, Lucius Priest, the narrator, tells his grandchildren about the Mississippi of 1905, focusing in the main on a seemingly simpler era, when an automobile was a work of wonder, and when a trip from Jefferson (Faulkner's version of Oxford, Mississippi, his home town) to Memphis could seem like an epic adventure. Yoknapatawpha history suffuses the first chapters of the novel, in which descriptions of the Sutpens, the Compsons, the McCaslins, and all the county's important families impinge on Lucius's consciousness. What he does, in other words, will be measured against what his forebears and predecessors have done. In effect, Lucius's decision to lie, to run away from home by stealing his grandfather's Wynton Flyer, is a declaration of independence, but it is also another act in the drama of his community's history. In effect, Lucius as "grandfather" is telling his grandchildren their history, showing how the individual has to understand his past in order to come to terms with himself. Karl regards the narrator's relaxed tone as a sign of the author's more indulgent and less complex art, as well as Faulkner's shying away from racial issues that bedeviled him in his last decade. The biographer's assumption, however, ignores the circumstances of the telling: a grandfather addressing his grandchildren. The narration is all about the child's discovery of the adult world as told by an adult to his own kin, who will, in turn, discover the world in their way. To confuse Faulkner with his narrator— no matter how many similarities between them can be assembled—is to wreck the fiction and to deny the independent existence of his characters.

Certainly the darker events of Faulkner's earlier novels—the suicide of Quentin Compson, the castration of Joe Christmas, and revelations about the evils of slavery—are not explored in *The Reivers*. But their consequences are—especially in the figure of Ned McCaslin, Boss Priest's coachman, whom Lucius refers to as "our family skeleton." Ned is a black man, born in 1860, who claims that his mother "had been the natural daughter of old Lucius Quintus Carothers himself," the original progenitor of the clan. In other words, Ned claims direct descent from a founding father, whereas Lucius's line consists of "mere diminishing connections and hangers-on." To readers of Faulkner's other novels—especially *Go Down, Moses*, which explores the McCaslin genealogy and the white family's inextricable connections with the lives of the McCaslin slaves—Ned's pride and self-assurance are all the more appreciated.

The postwar Faulkner began to emerge in *Intruder in the Dust*, a novel that in effect acknowledged his authority as a writer by engaging directly with political arguments about desegregation. At first, Faulkner reluctantly cooperated with filmmakers who came to Oxford to adapt his work for the screen. Biographers treat this episode as an intrusion in their subject's life, rather than as a turning point. Faulkner, however fitfully, not only became to emerge as a spokesman for the South, but also as a family man conceding to his family's fiercely held conviction that it was time for their patriarch to take his rightful place in the public square, even as they resisted his support for integration. This profound moment has only recently come into focus in the late Dean Faulkner Wells's *Every Day by the Sun: A Memoir of the Faulkners of Mississippi*, published in 2010, which is the first insider account of the family to approach the work of understanding William Faulkner's alarming paradoxes.

Until now, no Faulkner biographer has had the advantage of drawing on Wells's vivid portrayal of her uncle. The daughter of his beloved younger brother Dean—who died in an air crash that Faulkner never got over, since it was he who had encouraged Dean to make flying his career—Wells reveals just how intimately Faulkner was involved in the lives of his family and how his role as father figure has gone unappreciated, despite the wealth of detail available in Blotner's volumes. Wells waited decades to reveal the full scope of her family's racism, for example, which went well beyond simply the disapproval that Blotner and other biographers record. Her testimony, coupled with my interviews with her husband Larry Wells, new material in the Meta Carpenter Wilde papers at the University of Mississippi and in the collections at the Center for Faulkner Studies at Southeast Missouri State University, make the need for a new Faulkner biography imperative.

With my pitch in place, I did a bullet list—an essential tool for trade house editors attempting to coalesce support behind a book they have to sell to their colleagues and to the publisher:

What's New in the Faulkner Archive

- The Meta Carpenter Papers at the University of Mississippi include several audiocassettes that have not been used by earlier Faulkner biographers. These tapes deal with the making of her memoir and contain material that will contribute importantly to the narrative of Faulkner's periods in Hollywood and to their fifteen-year affair. I know about the value of the recordings because I interviewed Carpenter while working on my biography of Lillian Hellman. Carpenter also included in her Mississippi collection several photographs, many of which have never been published. http://www.olemiss.edu/depts/general_library/archives/finding_aids/MUM01773.html
- Material in private hands relating to the late Dean Faulkner's Wells's memoir about the Faulkner family. I will be working closely with her husband, Larry Wells, beginning with my visit to Oxford this June. I will also be interviewing other people in the community that Larry has mentioned in our interviews.
- The Joseph Blotner Papers at the Center for Faulkner Studies at the University of Southwest Missouri. Neither Jay Parini nor Philip Weinstein, the two most recent Faulkner biographers, worked with these papers. A few Faulkner scholars who have seen Blotner's collection tell me they are amazed at material Blotner did not use, including many Faulkner letters. Parini, Weinstein, and Williamson all rely on Blotner as though he were a primary source. And yet in conversation with Carvel Collins, I realized that Blotner perpetuated certain errors by relying too much on Faulkner's own testimony. By going to Blotner's papers, I can trace the origins of certain stories that subsequent biographers repeat without checking primary sources. http://www.semo.edu/cfs/
- The Center for Faulkner Studies also includes the papers of Joseph Daniel Brodsky, one of the most important collectors of Faulkner material.
- The Frederick Karl Papers at the University of South Carolina. Karl worked closely with the Faulkner family and left behind a record of his experiences and other materials related to the production of his Faulkner biography. The late Frederick Karl was a friend of mine, and I had extensive conversations with him about his work and the archive he was putting together. This is another resource that previous Faulkner biographers ignored or did not have access to. http://library.sc.edu/spcoll/amlit/karl.html
- The Carvel Collins Papers at the University of Texas at Austin. Collins

began working on a Faulkner biography in the late 1940s but never was able to complete his work. He collected valuable testimony from Faulkner's friends and associates. Parini makes minimal use of this important archive, which includes other materials acquired from Meta Carpenter and Dean Faulkner Wells. http://norman.hrc. utexas.edu/fasearch/findingAid.cfm?kw=Carvel+Collins&x=38&y= 10&eadid=00608

- The University of Virginia has made available the recordings of Faulkner's sessions with students that were edited and published as *Faulkner in the University*. I will be the first biographer to have access to the unedited, the raw Faulkner, so to speak, which will reveal more of his humor and irony than was apparent in the abridged transcripts. http://faulkner.lib.virginia.edu

I followed up this list with a detailed chapter outline, a reprise of my career, and a sample chapter exploring the biographical background of his greatest novel, *Absalom, Absalom!*

Here is a sampling of two trade editor responses to my agent Colleen Mohyde:

Colleen, I respect the considerable amount of work Carl Rollyson has put into this proposal for a new biography of William Faulkner, and he does seem to have located caches of material that might alter certain local aspects of the life narrative of the squire of Oxford. But Faulkner biographies and life studies, let's call them, are so thick on the ground that it would require a true stop-the-presses revelation or discovery to alter the generally accepted story of Faulkner's life in a way that would generate attention and, you know, sales. It will be a good book for sure, but not one I think Doubleday should take on. Thanks for trying, though, and good luck with other houses.

Thank you and Carl for thinking of me for this. But since RH publish Blotner and there have been other bios since his, I don't think we're the right list for this. Best of luck with it, and do think of me again soon for something else of yours.

I had worked with the first editor and the second had sent me a note praising the Plath biography. These early rejections were not too disheartening. In fact, my proposed Plath biography had met with much the same response early on. But soon the responses began to sound like a Greek chorus:

I'm grateful to have had the honor of considering the proposal for Carl Rollyson's new book, and sorry to be telling you that L, B won't be making an offer for it. We do very few literary biographies, and others thought that the Parini and Weinstein were too recent to merit another life of Faulkner, however superior. I hope to have news of the future publisher for The Alarming Paradox soon—it will be a book I'll want to read.

Thank you very much for sending Carl Rollyson's THIS ALARMING PARADOX. Rollyson's command of the Faulkner biographical landscape, and his new finds, especially the ones relating to Faulkner and his family, are all impressive. But I am in the end slightly intimidated, in marketplace terms, by the number of still-recent Faulkner biographies. And I am finding that women's lives tend to be the ones I commit to these days, as editor and reader.

Again, thanks for giving me a chance with this fine scholar/writer, and best of luck with THIS ALARMING PARADOX.

I'm sorry to decline Carl Rollyson's project on William Faulkner. It's well-written and full of engaging personal details. But I just don't see an audience for this kind of popular biography on Faulkner.

Another trade editor summed up what many had already told my agent: "As you know, literary biography is difficult to sell, particularly in paperback." Another editor at Algonquin confessed she had no feel for Faulkner and had to pass on my book. Louis D. Rubin, a Southern literature scholar who had founded Algonquin, would have been shocked at her admission of ignorance.

There was no trade house we did not try without getting more or less the same response—until THIS:

I liked what I read very much and Carl is a pro. So, the plan now is finish up my review early next week, and then discuss it with colleagues midweek. So, by end of next week I should know which way the wind is blowing—would that be ok?

Of course it was okay, but in the end the editor could not convince his firm they could make money on my book. So perforce we turned to university presses, which initially seemed receptive to my agent's submissions:

I am a lifelong Faulkner fan so I am very happy to take a look. I'll get back to you soon.

But in the end this editor at Yale University Press and another at a similar prestigious house turned the book down because it was not scholarly enough. What that meant was that I had not treated *Absalom, Absalom!* in enough depth that would appeal to the scholars who wrote reports for academic publishers. I had not "done my homework," as the editor at Harvard University Press put it, which meant I had not included detailed attention to recent Faulkner scholarship.

To do so, however, mean forsaking trade houses. At this point, that is exactly what I did, since there were no other trade houses to try. I spent a solid six months surveying all of the recent scholarly work on *Absalom, Absalom!* and adding two substantial sections to my sample chapter and increasing the estimated word length of the biography to 200,000 words.

The Harvard University Press editor actually allowed us to re-submit the proposal, but then sent it to a reader who lauded the scholarly discussion of the novel but deplored what the reader considered to be my too facile connections between Faulkner and his characters. I felt the editor could have headed off this kind of criticism by re-submitting the proposal to one of the previous readers who wanted to see more scholarship. It is all too easy for a book proposal to be rejected unless the editor who wants the book takes a strong hand—not telling scholarly readers what to write but making sure that at least, in principle, the reader is sympathetic to the book proposal's approach.

I had one connection with a university press that was about to publish one of my books, and the editor had expressed an interest in the Faulkner biography. But I had not pursued his query when he made it clear he could not offer much of an advance. Now I asked my agent to submit the book anyway. The editor was enthusiastic and promised a quick decision. But after a few days he wrote to say that a 200,000-word biography was more than his press could afford to publish.

Then an editor at University of Chicago Press, who said my proposed biography was not right for his list, provided us with suggestions of other presses to try. At this point, we found an editor at University of Virginia Press who not only wanted the book but also wanted to get outside readers who were disposed to my approach. This may sound like rigging the process, but no reader would risk his or her credibility just to please an editor. In other words, the reader had to be assured that I had actually fulfilled the promise that the editor had seen in my proposal. In fact, this editor, by accident, contacted a reader who had filed a report on my proposal with Harvard, a report that endorsed my approach but also pointed out its scholarly limitations. The University of Virginia Press editor accepted that report and solicited another one, which extolled my work. The editor then asked me to write a two-page response to both readers' reports. He needed my response to explain to the editorial board why he was accepting a reader's response which had been done for another press. The editor was also giving me the opportunity to put both reports into context, showing what I had learned from the submission process. What I wrote also makes even clearer the kind of biography I wanted to write:

Reader's Report 1 (For Harvard University Press)
I agree, of course, that the timing for a new Faulkner biography "would seem to be propitious." I agree with the reader's assessment of previous biographies, and I would add that the most recent biographical work has been selective—exploring aspects of Faulkner's career and life,

without essaying a comprehensive re-interpretation in light of the most recent scholarship. Jay Parini's biography is a decade old, and if you examine its notes, you will see he has drawn only sparingly on primary sources without giving much attention to recent scholarship.

I also agree that my work in Hollywood and my grounding in film history may be my "most distinctive contribution." In fact, Faulkner scholarship over the last decade has been moving toward my approach: seeing him as much more attuned to popular culture, not quite the aloof, literary figure earlier biographers and scholars made him out to be. And, of course, here is where the interest of general readers who might think of Faulkner as a difficult and inaccessible figure can be captured by my account of his Hollywood years. Faulkner's scripts and friendships in Hollywood have been slighted, I believe. Faulkner wrote a considerably greater number of treatments and screenplays than did Fitzgerald or any other writer in Faulkner's class—and because of his own sometimes dismissive stories about his work for the studios, some of this work is of higher quality than has been generally recognized. Here is where the Meta Carpenter material is most instructive, since I treat it as an integral part of Faulkner's life and creativity, not simply as an episode in his biography.

I especially like the reader's emphasis on the narrative continuity of my sample chapter. I worked very hard to incorporate my understanding of Faulkner's work into the story of his life—always a daunting challenge for a literary biographer. The reader is quite right, though, that my sample chapter did not deal with *Absalom, Absalom!* as a text. Originally I had planned to do so in a subsequent chapter, but I neglected to make my plan clear in my chapter outline. I was therefore dismayed when I realized I may have left the impression that I did not take Faulkner's greatest novel quite seriously enough. If you examine the last two sections of the revised sample chapter, you will see that I do precisely what this reader requires: taking up "issues like New World colonialism, American slavery and racism." So now my chapter does not conclude with treating the novel just as "an allegory of Faulkner's romantic life." I believe I have done "greater justice to the many other formal and thematic achievements that gave the novel such magnitude as an imaginative work." I also believe my narrative, having hooked readers of all kinds, will carry them into the chapter's final two sections, which take into account the extraordinarily rich scholarship that has continued to accrue in the last twenty years. I propose to follow the same kind of structure in addressing other major works, such as *The Sound and the Fury, As I Lay Dying,* and *Light in August*—and also for *The Wild Palms* (to use the first published title), since Faulkner's love for Meta Carpenter informs this work, infusing it with intensity.

Reader's Report

I'm pleased that the reader sees the significance of Carvel Collins's work. Not only is Collins the first Faulkner biographer to conduct extraordinary interviews and collect important primary evidence about

the author, Collins's biographical work presages the kind Richard Ellmann later perfected. Collins was interested in all aspects of his subject's
life, a curiosity that led, for example, to his interviews with the staff at
the Algonquin Hotel. Journalists were doing this sort of work, but no
scholars I know of were so enterprising. As a result, Collins's material
retains an extraordinary immediacy.

I'm gratified the reader recognizes that the women in Faulkner's life
will be treated with a depth and empathy not always apparent in earlier
Faulkner biographies. I am especially interested in his very close relationship with his mother. He wrote part of *Absalom, Absalom!* on her
dining room table—in the home of a woman who was an unrecon-
structed racist, as Dean Faulkner Wells relates in her memoir. Many
biographies acknowledge Maud Faulkner's influence on her son, but
imagine what it was like for him to see her (sometimes every day) and
cope with her racial attitudes and those of other family members.

I'm heartened by this reader's understanding of how I want to link
Faulkner's exploration of power—both in his homeland and in
Hollywood—into a reading that "will bring Faulkner and his works back
into the national imagination." I certainly plan to reach out to readers in
just the way this reader suggests. Through contacts I've developed over
several decades of working on biographies, I believe I can bring the kind
of attention to this book that the reader anticipates. As the reader notes,
the important thing is always to assimilate scholarship into narrative.
The availability of audible versions of Faulkner's classroom sessions at
Virginia is an incalculable asset to my biography, one that will help me
render his own voice—in new and fresh ways—to create a nuanced and
dramatic account of his life.

It took almost two years to find the right publisher for my book. Most agents
would not have stuck with my proposal over such a long period, but
Colleen Mohyde had believed in it from the beginning and, like me, she
refused to give up.

Besides my own story here, I think there is a foreboding aspect for
all literary biographers. "Literary biographies don't sell," my agent was
told again and again. Even university presses are now reluctant to take on
long narratives no matter how engaging. University of Virginia Press
requested that I trim the biography to 180,000 words because anything
longer would result in a noncompetitive retail price. It all feels like my
last hurrah, but like other writers, I doubt I'll ever lose hope so long as I
can believe there is an editor out there who will buy my book. After all,
it only takes one.

Index